Writing Research Papers

A COMPLETE GUIDE · FOURTH EDITION

Writing Research Papers
A COMPLETE GUIDE · FOURTH EDITION

James D. Lester
Austin Peay State University

Scott, Foresman and Company

Glenview, Illinois

Dallas, Tex.   Oakland, N.J.   Palo Alto, Cal.   Tucker, Ga.   London

Cover: Learning Resource Center of Oakton Community College
1600 E. Golf Road, Des Plaines, IL 60016.

Also available:

Instructor's Manual

Study Guide for *Writing Research Papers, Fourth Edition*

These may be obtained through a local Scott, Foresman representative or by writing
to English Editor, College Division, Scott, Foresman and Company,
1900 E. Lake Avenue, Glenview, IL 60025.

Library of Congress Cataloging in Publication Data.

Lester, James D.
  Writing research papers.

  Bibliography: p.
  Includes index.
  1. Report writing. I. Title.
LB2369.L4 1984   808'.02   83–14038
ISBN 0–673–15899–3

  2 3 4 5 6–KPF–87 86 85 84 83

ACKNOWLEDGMENTS   From Table of Contents and "Galaxies" index excerpt in *The Universe*, Revised Third Edition, by Isaac Asimov. Copyright © 1980 by Isaac Asimov. Reprinted by permission of Walker and Company. "Flight, history of" from *The New Encyclopaedia Britannica, Micropaedia,* Volume IV, 1982. Copyright © 1982 by Encyclopaedia Britannica, Inc. Reprinted by permission. From "Aerial Sports" from *The New Encyclopaedia Britannica, Macropaedia,* Volume 1, 1982. Copyright © 1982 by Encyclopaedia Britannica, Inc. Reprinted by permission. Reproduced from Edition 18, *Dewey Decimal Classification and Relative Index* (1971), by permission of Forest Press Division, Lake Placid Education Foundation, owner of copyright. Material from *Readers' Guide to Periodical Literature,* August 1982, Volume 82, p. 498. Copyright © 1982 by The H. W.

Acknowledgments continued on page 298, which constitutes a legal extension of the copyright page.

Preface

The primary goal of the first three editions of *Writing Research Papers* was to make the guidelines of the *MLA Style Sheet* as comprehensible as possible for college and university students inexperienced in research paper writing. A secondary goal was to have the book serve as a reference source for graduate students who wanted ready answers to questions on correct documentation.

This fourth edition of *Writing Research Papers* continues to meet its original goals by presenting the most current guidelines in the MLA style and format. In addition, the book has been expanded to offer increased coverage of the new APA style and format, and to include a more detailed discussion of investigative techniques and the rationale behind research writing. In attempting to meet the needs of today's students, then, the fourth edition is the most extensive revision in the book's history.

MLA Style and Format

The most significant change in *Writing Research Papers,* Fourth Edition, is in regard to the new style of documentation put forth by the MLA Committee on Documentation Style, such as, *PMLA* 97 (1982): 318–24. Journals can no longer afford the cost of typesetting and layout design for both footnotes and a bibliography. Therefore, the latest MLA style omits documentation footnotes in favor of parenthetical citations within the text itself. Accordingly, this edition omits the chapter on footnotes and endnotes and expands the writing chapter to explain the handling of in-text citations and content endnotes. The fundamental changes in MLA style, then, are these:

- Omission of documentation footnotes and the use of parenthetical documentation within the text.
- Arabic numerals are now used for everything except titles (Elizabeth II) or preliminary pages of a text traditionally numbered with Roman numerals (i, ii, v, etc.)
- Omission of "p." or "pp." for page numbers.
- Omission of "l." or "ll." in favor of "lines" until lineation is established in the paper.
- Omission of the comma after journal titles and a new form of entry for volume, year, and page, for example, *PMLA* 98 (1983): 345–52. This new form with spaces between journal number, year, and page numbers will be used in *PMLA* beginning with the January, 1984, issue.
- Use of the colon to separate volume and page (4: 155).

- Limiting the bibliography to a "Works Cited" list.

In effect, the new MLA style moves in the direction of the APA style. However, the philosophy for MLA in-text citations differs from APA. While APA stresses date, MLA prefers to focus on the work's author, title, and page number. Thus, APA style urges "(1978)" or "(1978, p. 16)" while the new MLA style uses "(22–23)" or "(*Masks* 22–23)."

APA Style and Format

Chapter 7, *Form and Styles for Other Disciplines,* has grown from eight pages to twenty to serve the new emphasis on cross-disciplinary writing. By using the guidelines from the new third edition of the Publication Manual of the APA (1983), this chapter represents the latest thinking in APA documentation format. Also included in this chapter are clear format examples for documentation in sociology, business and economics, applied sciences, and many others.

Other New Features

- Expanded focus on the writing process at early stages with new sections on discovery of purpose, asking research questions, determining audience, using invention, and restricting the topic.
- New sections on using the computer for library database searches, writing from computer-generated research materials, and writing with word processors.
- Tabbed pages for quick reference to much-used topics such as "Bibliography Form," "Name and Year Style," and "Plagiarism."
- Expanded material on openings, closings, and handling source materials in in-text citations.
- A new student research paper entitled "Child Abuse: A View of the Victims."

Study Guide

As a special aid to students we have a new *Study Guide to Writing Research Papers, Fourth Edition.* This study guide helps students in three important ways. First, and perhaps most significant, it guides student research by encouraging use of the library. The guide helps students focus their own ideas for a research topic and directs them through the process of researching and writing their paper. Second, it tests student comprehension of the material in the text itself. Third, it gives students practice in using the proper forms for note-taking, documentation, and so on. Answers to most of the questions are provided in the study guide itself so that the instructor need not spend time grading or correcting the students' work; indeed, many of the answers give students further insights into their own ideas and understanding of the questions. However, the pages of the study guide are perforated to be handed in if the instructor wishes.

Instructor's Manual

An Instructor's Manual is available to accompany this fourth edition of *Writing Research Papers*. As always, it features research questions and exercises specifically geared to the book's organization. This manual enables instructors to test student progress at nearly every stage of the research project. Most importantly, the manual contains an alternate sample student research paper. This paper is written on a literary topic for those instructors who prefer to teach a literary paper. It is also organized according to the former MLA style of footnotes and bibliography for those instructors who may prefer to teach that style. The footnotes are organized into endnotes, as well, as yet another alternative for the instructor.

Acknowledgments

Finally, thanks must go to all those persons who down through the years have contributed directly and indirectly to this undertaking. I cannot name them all; I only hope they comprehend my deep gratitude. In particular, I wish to thank those instructors around the country who contributed ideas and thoughts for this new edition: Beverly Beem, Walla Walla College; Duncan Carter, Boston University; Tom Chandler, DeKalb Community College; Joseph Comprone, University of Louisville; Valerie Davis, Golden West College; Richard Gebhardt, Findlay College; J. Robert Hill, Elizabethtown Community College; Christine Hult, Texas Tech University; and Nancy Waring, Boston University. I applaud Amanda Clark and Andrea Coens of the Scott, Foresman staff for their dedication and expertise with this edition. My gratitude goes to Jo Walker, one of my best students, for her help with the sample research paper. My appreciation goes to my son Jim who participated as research assistant for this edition and did a yeoman's task of bringing up to date the list of reference works and journals. Then, of course, I must honor my wife Martha for her support and thank, too, my son Mark.

James D. Lester

Contents

2 Using the Library 28

3 Taking Notes 70

4 Writing Your Paper 100

5   A Format for Your Paper   147

6 Works Cited   194

7 Form and Style for Other Disciplines   220

Appendix
A List of General Reference Books and Journals   246

INTRODUCTION

RATIONALE FOR RESEARCH WRITING

As you begin the task of writing a research paper, you may feel inadequate dealing with such an assignment—ten typewritten pages with all sorts of documentation rules! This writing manual will help you. It takes you step-by-step through the research-writing process—from selecting a significant topic all the way down to typing the final draft. Approach the assignment a step at a time, and you will gain a sense of self-reliance by moving from one stage of the paper to the next, gaining momentum, and, finally, building a longer and better research paper. Self-reliance lets you form judgments and write essays that do more than merely repeat lecture notes or paragraphs from books and articles. You will learn to generate ideas and defend them with the weight of your arguments and the strength of the evidence you have gathered. In particular, you will learn to distinguish your ideas from those of your sources.

You will become adept at the following:

1. Narrowing your focus of an issue to a manageable topic that addresses the problem for your audience
2. Locating source materials and taking notes
3. Analyzing, evaluating, and interpreting materials
4. Arranging and classifying materials
5. Writing the paper with a sense of purpose as well as with clarity and accuracy
6. Handling problems of quoting and properly documenting your sources according to MLA (Modern Language Association) style

This text will carry you through all these stages beginning with the first step in Chapter 1—finding a suitable topic that has merit as a scholarly issue or research question. Take your time selecting a topic because a poor one will cause untold anguish for weeks and weeks while a good one will pave the way to significant research and quality writing.

Chapters 2 and 3 carry you into library research and gathering note cards. Included with that is a section about plagiarism, which is not a disease but a curse that afflicts many students who think proper scholarly credit is unnecessary, or who become confused about proper placement of references.

Chapter 4 will train you to handle quoted and paraphrased material while examining your research question at the same time. Following that in Chapter 5 are matters of format and the technicalities of numbers, margins, spacing, and so on. This text offers answers and models for all your questions—from design of the title page to the minor issues of where to put commas and dates and under-lining.

Chapter 6 introduces you to the role, scope, and design of bibliography entries. This chapter explains the form of entries for your list of references that fully documents the sources used in developing your paper. Short, parenthetical notes in the text itself will point forward to this list of "Works Cited."

Chapter 7 of this text introduces the APA (American Psychological Association) style along with styles for other disciplines. The chapter correlates the similarities of the MLA style with that used in other disciplines such as psychology, biology, or geology. That is, your training in the MLA style of this text is not dissimilar to the APA style or the CBE (Council of Biological Editors) style. If you learn the format rules of one discipline correctly, you should be able to adapt easily to another.

Finally, the appendix contains an exhaustive list of reference works and journals (by subject) to be consulted as you begin research in a particular discipline, be it psychology, home economics, or drama. These reference works will trigger your exploration of issues in numerous fields of study.

1
Finding a Topic

DISCOVERING YOUR PURPOSE

The first step in writing a research paper is to determine the purpose of your research study in a specific field. At this point your instructor may assign a specific topic and relieve you of worries about topic discovery, but most instructors expect you to participate in the search for a narrowed and worthy topic. Only you can determine, with the instructor's input, that your topic of study will interpret a piece of literature or analyze a sociological issue or generate by computer a technical or statistical report. In general, research studies fall into three major categories: argumentative, analytical, and explanatory. Examine the following guidelines to determine your purpose according to your instructor's assignment.

An Argumentative Purpose

The argumentative, or critical paper interprets and argues an issue. That is, you must arrive at judgments about your topic based upon research findings in primary and secondary source materials; your purpose extends beyond investigation to making judgments about the issue at hand. For example, reciting information about child abuse is inadequate; instead, reach beyond a mere collection of evidence in order to argue for strict social guidelines to prevent child abuse. Similarly, a study of female characters in Charles Dickens' novel *Hard Times* would argue about or interpret the view of women as expressed by this Victorian novelist.

The critical purpose requires your utmost care in step-by-step procedures that permit you to express reasoned judgments and guarded opinions, as supported by your reference materials. These critical papers are controversial to some degree and therefore require responsible, impartial findings. Bias has no place in the critical research paper, which requires careful assimilation and presentation of evidence to prevent any possible appearance of prejudice or rash generalization. As a consequence, be especially cautious in your assessment of findings about controversial topics such as abortion, gun control, and the death penalty.

An Analytical Purpose

Many times, instructors require papers that ask you to draw general conclusions from facts and basic evidence. Your purpose in this case becomes one of analysis: you must separate the issues, comment on each one, and arrive, finally, at a synthesis. For example, you might classify and examine the stages of hypnosis as a treatment for curing a bad habit, such as smoking or nail biting.

In brief, your purpose becomes an analysis of component parts so that you arrive at meanings, causes, or consequences. Thus, your analysis of incidents of child abuse during times of high unemployment could lead to conclusions about the unfortunate effects of an economic depression upon children. In a like manner, you might examine the vocabulary of native speakers in one isolated geographical area in order to arrive at general conclusions about dialects or speech patterns.

An Explanatory Purpose

On occasion, instructors will require an informative paper. Your purpose in this case will be to gather and summarize facts; you will be concerned with functions and processes and factual results. This sort of study usually includes graphs, charts, tables, listings, and other statistical data popular in fields such as economics, sociology, business, and political science. Four types of informative writing are applied research, market research, technical reports, and computer-generated studies.

The purpose of *applied research* is the discovery of new uses or new applications of a product or idea; an applied researcher starts with somebody else's discovery and applies it to a new area. For example, the isolation of a germ cell may be useless until somebody connects that germ cell with cancer growth. The purpose of *market research* is the information that will bring better products and services to consumers. For example, market research has produced such a vast array of consumer soap products—from bar soap to soap flakes to liquid soap—that today numerous types of soaps exist, not to mention many brands of each. Market research depends heavily upon the use of questionnaires, sampling, testing, and observation. *Technical research* uses findings or discoveries to serve as the basis for decisions by industrialists or people in business. For example, technical studies might affect production, personnel needs, or space requirements. In particular, your economics professor might ask you to study the traffic patterns at a particular intersection to determine its feasibility as the location for a certain type of business, perhaps a fast food outlet. In short, many vital decisions depend upon the quality of written research studies. The purpose of a *computer-generated research paper* is to control data. The computer lets you store, sort, and retrieve vast amounts of data. In truth, computer studies are now commonplace. Your ability to handle such an assignment will position you in the forefront of contemporary research techniques because most businesses and industries today depend heavily upon both their computers and the personnel who generate the technical data and research reports.

ASKING RESEARCH QUESTIONS

Asking questions about your subject throughout the entire process of research should become a standard activity. Research questions help you confront matters of uncertainty or enable you to isolate an area of dispute so that you can examine it with a critical eye. After all, one of the primary purposes of any research paper is to answer a question or examine and analyze a disputed issue.

Moreover, probing an issue by questioning inevitably narrows your subject and refines it to a manageable topic. Let's suppose that your subject area is shoplifting. Your immediate reaction might be "Who cares? What effect does it have on me?" That might seem a petty, nonscholarly beginning, but it leads to another more profound question: "What are the effects of shoplifting upon the average American shopper?" Now you can sink your teeth into a solid area of the subject by reading reports and statistics in books and journals as well as by conducting personal interviews with shop owners who endure thefts from their shelves and counters. In effect, you are well on your way to a manageable topic.

In brief, asking research questions of all types should become a way of life for several weeks during the preparatory stages and early writing stages of your project. The term *research question* (or *question*) will appear regularly throughout the following sections of this text, from determining your audience, to matters of inventing and narrowing the topic, and to forming a preliminary thesis. Then *questioning* appears again as an important tool for gathering data in the library, for planning your outline, for writing the final thesis statement, or for writing the rough draft.

In addition, make it a practice to write notes every time you ask and then answer any research question. These answers could form the basis of your paper, provide key ideas and thoughts, and help you flesh out your rough draft. Every research question deserves an answer, even if it requires that you spend library time reading an article or book. Every answer deserves a note card because it provides fuel for the final paper. Therefore, asking questions becomes a way of life for the typical researcher.

DETERMINING YOUR AUDIENCE

On one level you write a research paper for your instructor, since he or she serves as your primary audience. However, your instructor expects you to think about a general audience of intelligent, critical readers who expect a certain depth of perception from your writing. Think of your readers as concerned students and serious scholars who are familiar with the subject but wish to know more about it. The readers' involvement with your paper will be sustained by your observations and speculations.

A sense of audience is interdependent with your consideration of your topic. The two develop almost simultaneously. For instance, the nature of your paper—argumentative, analytical, informative—determines whether your readers expect discussion of issues, argument, or information. You develop a feel for readers' interests, concerns, and informational needs. Ask yourself a few questions: Are my readers specialists or nonspecialists? What are my readers' levels of knowledge? What expectations will my readers have about this topic? What sort of conclusions should I work toward?

For example, readers of a paper on social issues such as child abuse or the death penalty expect cause and effect discussions that point to possible answers. In another case, readers of a literary research paper on a poem or a novel expect interpretive analysis of the novel's symbolism, narrative structure, or characterization.

Therefore, establish your strategies of topic development on the basis of your purpose and your assumed audience. This will give you a better feel for who your readers are. You will know that they want a discussion of issues with a child abuse topic, that they expect interpretation, not plot summary, with a novel as your literary topic, and that they demand accurate findings and data with a technical study. A sense of your audience, then, helps you frame a thesis sentence to control the direction of your writing and helps you develop evidence that leads to perceptive conclusions.

INVENTION

Choosing a narrowed topic worthy of your time and effort and then planning your writing strategy require invention—that element of personal ingenuity that enables you to search out significant matters and discard the trivial, the outdated, or the irrelevant. Your inventive capacities might be improved by cultivating three basic attitudes toward your subject: personal experience and observation, perceptive and critical reading, and intellectual speculation. These three general attitudes will sharpen your thinking for the important step of topic restriction.

Personal Experience

Invention depends upon your ability to ask questions about yourself as well as the topic. Depending upon your topic, you should draw upon your own ability as an observer of behavior, of nature, or of social issues. If you are open to ideas and issues, you become involved in experiments, projects, activities, data processing, and so on. If you combine your invention of a topic to areas of personal interest you will have, if nothing else, a topic you can live with for several weeks.

Let's assume, for instance, that three students all have the same subject—crime. Invention now plays a key role as each student searches his or her personal interests to develop an interesting and stimulating topic:

Student 1: Crime and Women's Rights
        Broad subject area: Women in Prison
Later, reading and speculation might produce this narrowed topic:
        Work Release Programs for Women: The Door to Rehabilitation
Student 2: Crime and Computers
        Broad subject area: Theft Control by the Banking Industry
Later, reading and speculation might produce this narrowed topic:
        Computer Control: Safeguards Against Computer Theft in the
        Banking Industry
Student 3: Crime and Fiction
        Broad subject area: William Faulkner's Short Stories
Later, reading and speculation might produce this narrowed topic:
        Crime as Black Humor: Faulkner's Short Fiction

Invention requires extending yourself personally when selecting a topic.

Perceptive and Critical Reading

The invention of topic and your approach to research depends on your ability to read both perceptively and critically. In effect, you reach beyond your personal experience into the knowledge of others, whether you read a novel, a reference book, or a journal article. How you perceive and absorb that knowledge contributes greatly to your control of the research paper. The unconcerned researcher will read until he or she finds something good, and then something else, and so on until he or she can string together a series of quotations and paraphrases that really haven't been absorbed at all. Like personal experience, reading requires involvement. Your instructor wants you to avoid the tendency to read and take notes and then merely summarize and retell what your sources have offered on the topic.

The literature about your topic—let's say child abuse—includes not merely the primary evidence that you gather, such as court reports, case studies, and interviews, but also secondary evidence, such as the essays written about the topic by all sorts of experts from the fields of sociology, psychology, and criminology. Part of your task will be to read and evaluate the abundance of written material on your topic. The earlier you dip into this literature the sooner your invention of topic and approach will be narrowed and controlled (see samples immediately above, page 7). Along the way, you will pick up valuable terminology of the field.

Let's look at it this way. A Steven Spielberg movie such as *E.T., (The Extra Terrestrial)*, does not exist anymore as a mere movie; it exists in unison with all those essays and reviews written about it and about its director. Perhaps you consider it unfair to place such scholastic burdens on a movie, yet you cannot ignore the written materials anymore than you can evaluate *E.T.* objectively. You know it was a smash hit; that knowledge colors your interpretation. Therefore, you must sift through all the evidence to see if you can add a new thought, find a new approach, or discover a new interpretation. That exercise becomes invention.

Intellectual Speculation

The words "intellectual speculation" might seem a somewhat weighty way to refer to the use of your imagination. It asks that you exercise your mind, that you extend yourself slightly more than normal into an issue or idea. Your invention of topic should provide opportunities for investigating issues, for discovering something new, different, or original. Your topic should require judgments and, certainly, should demand much more than a study of one or two encyclopedias. Your instructor expects an examination, for example, of union-management relations in the automobile industry or the significance of Walt Whitman's position on ecology as expressed in his poetry.

Research writing, therefore, requires the invention of a topic and approach that has intellectual depth or that speculates on issues. For example, "Fishing for Trout" or "The American Hot Dog" fail the test, but "Clean Water Standards in Minnesota" and "Junk Food Habits of Today's Consumers" pass. A paper entitled "Pacman Mania" could have significance (despite its catchy title) if it examines in depth the social, psychological, or physiological ramifications of video games.

Speculation about a subject requires you to make new connections, to separate and synthesize items, to draw conclusions. Asking research questions opens areas of the topic for your scrutiny as you systematically begin a process of logical analysis that probes an issue and narrows your area of concern. For example, if your subject area is Ernest Hemingway's *The Old Man and the Sea*, you might begin by asking a question: "Why does Hemingway depict Santiago as a long-suffering man?" Such a question will prompt you toward several others: "Is Santiago like the biblical Job?" "Is he depicted as a Christ figure?" "Does he fit Hemingway's code of the hero?" Answers to such questions, based upon your speculation and ideas gleaned from library readings, will eventually help narrow your perspective and give you a narrowed topic.

In other words, ask questions of yourself, of your instructor, of your source materials. Then speculate on the answers. The result will be a fascinating phase of invention of topic and approach to research writing. You will draw tentative conclusions about your subject that you will want to explore in depth. You will connect one idea with another idea for exploration, such as connecting high unemployment with an increase in child abuse. You will also come to understand the workings of individual parts or aspects of an issue, and that will help you reconstruct the whole or, at the very least, formulate a few conclusions about it.

Now for one final word of advice about invention: keep notes on your ideas. You may want to use note cards alone, or, in addition to note cards, you may want to keep a research journal (the same type of personal journal that you keep in a literature or composition class). These invention notes in a journal or on note cards should reflect and define your thoughts and ideas as you grapple with your subject. Your ideas are invaluable both now, while you search out a suitable topic, and later, when you face the blank sheet of paper in the typewriter. Remember—ultimately you must produce a ten-page composition for others to read.

RESTRICTING THE TOPIC

Invention will have started your mind going in a particular direction; now restriction will enable you to locate materials and refine even further. You should not be too ambitious in what you attempt to cover. Research writing requires you to probe deeply and to present accurately facts and ideas that demonstrate the validity of your contentions. Your various judgments and opinions will be effective only if supported by specific detail. Vague, indefinite statements about a too extensive, too generalized subject won't lead to the type of paper you want.

Another reason you should limit your subject to a specific problem or question is that the research paper is a relatively short work, often no more than about ten typewritten pages, excluding title page, outline, endnotes, and bibliography. The subject, accordingly, should be one that can be handled within these limitations, not one that requires twenty or thirty pages for adequate presentation. For example, you could not deal satisfactorily with "Edgar Allan Poe: His Poetic Genius," but you should get along well with "The Role of the Narrator in 'The Raven.' "

If you need specific devices for narrowing a subject, consider the following techniques:

Using Library Sources to Narrow the Topic

SEARCH A TABLE OF CONTENTS

Look first at this book's table of contents; it should itemize the many subject areas of the course. Then look at the table of contents on the following page.

Table of Contents:

CHAPTER 1 — *The Earth*

CHAPTER 2 — *The Solar System*

CHAPTER 3 — *The Stars*

CHAPTER 4 — *The Galaxy*

As shown here, major areas stand out boldly with subtopics ready for your scrutiny. Select an area of interest and read portions of the text, searching always for a narrowed topic that you can manage in ten or so pages.

For example, you might scan down the list above and pause at the phrase, "Herschel's Lens." Investigation of the text on page 46 could excite your curiosity about Sir William Herschel (1738–1822) who, it turns out, was a founder of star astronomy. He developed a lens that enabled him to discover the planet Uranus. Herschel became a pioneer in developing ideas about the stellar system. The point is this: focusing on some aspect of Herschel and his career would be one method of narrowing the scope of your research study.

EXAMINE A BOOK'S INDEX

The index of your textbooks or library books will contain an alphabetical listing that might excite your investigative imagination. Note the following:

Galaxies
    antimatter and, 257
    classes of, 176-178
    clusters of, 194-195, 284, 300-301
    colliding, 288
    continuous formation of, 224-225
    distances of, 188, 201-203
    electric charge on, 224
    expanding Universe and, 193
    exploding, 288-293
    gravitation and, 193-194
    microwave energies of, 288-298
    number of, 93, 198-199
    peculiar, 290
    radio, 288-298
    recession of, 185-188, 209, 224-229
    red shift of, 185-188
    spectral class of, 178-179
    structure of, 93-94
    x-ray, 250

Fig. 2: Index from *The Universe* by Isaac Asimov

A logical follow-up to scanning the index would be to read the designated pages in order to refine your subject. Remember too that your entire focus may shift during this stage of research. For example, your investigation of the "microwave energies" or "x-ray" in the list above might cause you to change your paper from galaxies and astronomy to more conventional issues or topics about microwave and x-ray technology in our homes and factories rather than in outer space. Remember: shift your focus tighter and tighter until you have something manageable as well as interesting.

SCAN AN ENCYCLOPEDIA ARTICLE

An encyclopedia article will often point the way to a specific topic because it lists numerous details of the subject in summary fashion. The ten minutes or so spent reading the encyclopedia article might easily produce two or three possible topics. Note the following:

Fig. 3: Entry from the *Micropaedia* of *Encyclopaedia Britannica*

flight, history of 7:380. Transportation above the Earth's surface in any form of craft, though first realized by 18th-century balloonists, has had its entire main development in the form of powered, heavier-than-air machines, in the 20th century.

The text article is divided into seven sections: (1) flight in man's imagination; (2) the development of balloons, airships, gliders, models, and kites through the 19th century; (3) the momentous developments from 1900 to 1914: the introduction of the gasoline engine; the contributions of the Wright brothers and others; and helicopter, balloon, airship, and parachute developments; (4) the rapid advances brought by World War I; (5) developments from 1918 to 1930; (6) developments from 1930 to 1945, including those in commercial aviation; private flying and air racing; military aviation; and research; (7) developments since 1945: commercial aviation including development of jet propulsion; general aviation, including private and special uses; military aviation; flight research; and the forseeable future.

REFERENCES in other text articles:
·aerial sport development and form **1**:123h
·aeronautical engineering development **1**:129e
·aerospace industry history **1**:132g
·aircraft design and aerodynamics **1**:370d
·air transport history and development **18**:633a
·Antarctic explorations **1**:962h
·automatic pilot invention **8**:525e
·aviation and space medicine origins **1**:144h
·Goddard's space flight experiments **8**:222g
·hurricane structure and flight patterns **9**:64a
·jet plane development and engine
    design **10**:156b
·life-support system development **10**:918d
·Lindbergh nonstop New York–Paris
    flight **10**:991g
·military aircraft technical development **1**:383b
·military engineering history **6**:864f
·modern aircraft development
    influences **18**:657b
·Montgolfier brothers' balloons **12**:409g
·natural prototypes of aircraft ideas **2**:1032g
·navigational methods and
    instruments **12**:903d
·radio installation in aircraft **15**:427a
·Sikorsky's helicopter development **16**:750e
·technological developments in the
    1900s **18**:48h
·warfare and tactical use of aircraft **19**:585e
·Wright brothers' experiments and
    impact **19**:1032b

RELATED ENTRIES in the *Ready Reference and Index*:
aeronautical engineering; aircraft; airship; autogiro; biplane; glider; ornithopter; Spirit of Saint Louis

This entry from the *Micropaedia* of *Encyclopaedia Britannica* suggests numerous subtopics on "flight" with directions about where to find detailed articles in the *Macropaedia,* as shown below.

Aerial Sports

Aerial sports have a fundamental position in aviation and encompass the true origins of aviation. Individuals in the 1800s and early 1900s imagined, contrived, and developed contraptions that would enable them to experience the unique sensation of being airborne. The development of aircraft for commercial and military purposes came much later. Flight was founded in sport, and sport flying still thrives.

The Fédération Aéronautique Internationale was founded in Paris in 1905 to encourage the progress of world aeronautics. It has long exercised general supervision over most phases of aerial sport, certifying world records and sanctioning international competition. It includes national federations from more than 50 countries in its membership.

This article is intended for the general reader who may have no knowledge of the activities described. It deals chiefly with the four most popular varieties of aerial sport—power-plane sports, soaring (or gliding), sport parachuting (skydiving), and sport ballooning—sketching the history and present status of each. For more detailed information on specific activities, the reader should consult the works listed in the bibliography.

BIBLIOGRAPHY. LINN EMRICH, *The Complete Book of Sky Sports* (1970), an instructional text on the fundamentals of flight in five categories: soaring, parachuting, hot-air ballooning, gyrocopters, and power planes; CARL CONWAY, *Joy of Soaring* (1969), a complete modern training manual on sailplane flying; P.M. BOWERS, *Guide to Homebuilts* (1962), a guide to the history, design, construction, testing, costs, and material sources for homebuilt aircraft, *Antique Plane Guide* (1962), a comprehensive study on the identification, restoration, costs, material and data sources for antique planes; DON VORDERMAN, *The Great Air Races* (1969), a fascinating resume of prominent planes, pilots, and air races since 1909; DUANE COLE, *Roll Around a Point* (1965), an instructional text on how to perform aerobatics by a world authority.

Periodicals: Sailplane and Gliding (bimonthly), official organ of the British Gliding Association; *Soaring* (monthly), a publication of the Soaring Society of America; *Parachutist* (monthly), publication of the U.S. Parachute Association; *National Aeronautics* (quarterly), official publication of the U.S. National Aeronautic Association. See also *Popular Rotorcraft Flying* (bimonthly), *Sport Flying* (monthly), *Motorgliding* (monthly), *Antique Airplane News* (monthly), *Sport Aviation* (monthly), and *Ballooning* (quarterly).

(L.E.)

Not only does an article like this one produce narrowed topics but at the end there is a list of additional readings on the subject. You can be off and running with a narrowed topic in no time at all, and you can even start framing several initial bibliography cards (see 38–39).

USE SUBJECT CARDS

The following subject cards, drawn from a typical card catalog, demonstrate another area for topic searching:

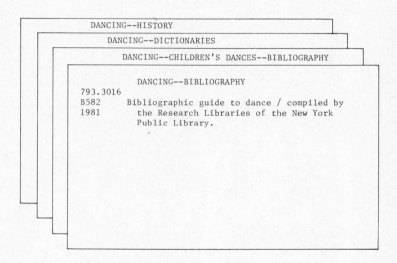

Fig. 5: Subject Cards

DANCING--HISTORY

DANCING--DICTIONARIES

DANCING--CHILDREN'S DANCES--BIBLIOGRAPHY

DANCING--BIBLIOGRAPHY
793.3016
B582   Bibliographic guide to dance / compiled by
1981   the Research Libraries of the New York
             Public Library.

By looking at the top of cards, you will find subtopics on most major subjects. The card catalog, then, serves as another source of topic refinement, especially when you consult the subject cards. Also, while looking through catalog cards or using the computer terminal (see 64), you might begin framing a few bibliography cards (see 38–39) for books of interest.

CHECK THE DEWEY DECIMAL INDEX

If yours is a free-choice topic, the basic 100 divisions of the *Dewey Decimal Classification and Relative Index* will suggest several broad areas for topic selection:

Fig. 6: From the
Dewey Decimal
Classification and
Relative Index

Second Summary *
The 100 Divisions

000	**Generalities**	500	**Pure sciences**	
010	Bibliographies & catalogs	510	Mathematics	
020	Library & information sciences	520	Astronomy & allied sciences	
030	General encyclopedic works	530	Physics	
040		540	Chemistry & allied sciences	
050	General serial publications	550	Sciences of earth & other worlds	
060	General organizations & museology	560	Paleontology	
070	Journalism, publishing, newspapers	570	Life sciences	
080	General collections	580	Botanical sciences	
090	Manuscripts & book rarities	590	Zoological sciences	
100	**Philosophy & related disciplines**	600	**Technology (Applied sciences)**	
110	Metaphysics	610	Medical sciences	
120	Knowledge, cause, purpose, man	620	Engineering & allied operations	
130	Popular & parapsychology, occultism	630	Agriculture & related	
140	Specific philosophical viewpoints	640	Domestic arts & sciences	
150	Psychology	650	Managerial services	
160	Logic	660	Chemical & related technologies	
170	Ethics (Moral philosophy)	670	Manufactures	
180	Ancient, medieval, Oriental	680	Miscellaneous manufactures	
190	Modern Western philosophy	690	Buildings	
200	**Religion**	700	**The arts**	
210	Natural religion	710	Civic & landscape art	
220	Bible	720	Architecture	
230	Christian doctrinal theology	730	Plastic arts Sculpture	
240	Christian moral & devotional	740	Drawing, decorative & minor arts	
250	Local church & religious orders	750	Painting & paintings	
260	Social & ecclesiastical theology	760	Graphic arts Prints	
270	History & geography of church	770	Photography & photographs	
280	Christian denominations & sects	780	Music	
290	Other religions & comparative	790	Recreational & performing arts	
300	**The social sciences**	800	**Literature (Belles-lettres)**	
310	Statistics	810	American literature in English	
320	Political science	820	English & Anglo-Saxon literatures	
330	Economics	830	Literatures of Germanic languages	
340	Law	840	Literatures of Romance languages	
350	Public administration	850	Italian, Romanian, Rhaeto-Romanic	
360	Social pathology & services	860	Spanish & Portuguese literatures	
370	Education	870	Italic languages literatures Latin	
380	Commerce	880	Hellenic languages literatures	
390	Customs & folklore	890	Literatures of other languages	
400	**Language**	900	**General geography & history**	
410	Linguistics	910	General geography Travel	
420	English & Anglo-Saxon languages	920	General biography & genealogy	
430	Germanic languages German	930	General history of ancient world	
440	Romance languages French	940	General history of Europe	
450	Italian, Romanian, Rhaeto-Romanic	950	General history of Asia	
460	Spanish & Portuguese languages	960	General history of Africa	
470	Italic languages Latin	970	General history of North America	
480	Hellenic Classical Greek	980	General history of South America	
490	Other languages	990	General history of other areas	

* Consult schedules for complete and exact headings

If item 500, ''Pure Sciences,'' looks interesting, then look to the ''520'' category on ''Astronomy and allied sciences.''

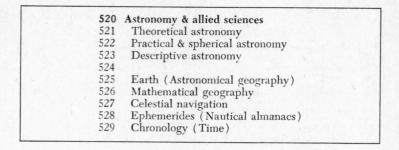

520	Astronomy & allied sciences
521	Theoretical astronomy
522	Practical & spherical astronomy
523	Descriptive astronomy
524	
525	Earth (Astronomical geography)
526	Mathematical geography
527	Celestial navigation
528	Ephemerides (Nautical almanacs)
529	Chronology (Time)

These broad subject areas will require further narrowing toward a topic. You must move to a specific numbered item, such as "523 Descriptive Astronomy":

**Fig. 8: Numbered
Items**

523	**Descriptive astronomy**
	Including quasars, pulsars, zodiac
	Class here comprehensive works on specific celestial bodies, groupings, phenomena
	Use 523.001–523.009 for standard subdivisions, classing planetariums [*formerly* 523.28] in 523.0074
	Class "earth" sciences of other worlds in 550
	For theoretical astronomy, see 521.5–521.8
.01	Astrophysics
	Physics and chemistry of celestial bodies and phenomena
.013	Heat
	Add to 523.013 the numbers following 536 in 536.1–536.7, e.g., heat transfer 523.0132
.015	Visible light and paraphotic phenomena
	Add to 523.015 the numbers following 535 in 535.01–535.89, e.g., ultraviolet radiation 523.015014
[.016–.017]	Radio and radar astronomy
	Class in 522.68
.018	Electricity and magnetism
	Add to 523.018 the numbers following 53 in 537–538, e.g., magnetism 523.0188
.019	Molecular, atomic, nuclear physics
	Add to 523.019 the numbers following 539 in 539.1–539.7, e.g., cosmic rays 523.0197223

As shown before, specifics and details of a broad subject are subdivided for you, and the narrower the topic the more manageable it becomes.

EXAMINE THE LIBRARY OF CONGRESS SYSTEM

Major categories of this system are as follows:

Fig. 9: From the
Library of
Congress System

LIBRARY OF CONGRESS CLASSIFICATION SCHEDULES

For sale by the Cataloging Distribution Service, Library of Congress,
Building 159, Navy Yard Annex, Washington, D.C. 20541,
to which inquiries on current availability and
price should be addressed.

A	General Works
B-BJ	Philosophy. Psychology
BL-BX	Religion
C	Auxiliary Sciences of History
D	History: General and Old World (Eastern Hemisphere)
E-F	History: America (Western Hemisphere)
G	Geography. Maps. Anthropology. Recreation
H	Social Sciences
J	Political Science
K	Law (General)
KD	Law of the United Kingdom and Ireland
KE	Law of Canada
KF	Law of the United States
L	Education
M	Music
N	Fine Arts
P-PA	General Philology and Linguistics. Classical Languages and Literatures
PA Supplement	Byzantine and Modern Greek Literature. Medieval and Modern Latin Literature
PB-PH	Modern European Languages
PG	Russian Literature
PJ-PM	Languages and Literatures of Asia, Africa, Oceania. American Indian Languages. Artifical Languages
P-PM Supplement	Index to Languages and Dialects
PN, PR, PS, PZ	General Literature. English and American Literature. Fiction in English. Juvenile Belles Lettres
PQ Part 1	French Literature
PQ Part 2	Italian, Spanish, and Portuguese Literatures
PT Part 1	German Literature
PT Part 2	Dutch and Scandinavian Literatures
Q	Science
R	Medicine
S	Agriculture
T	Technology
U	Military Science
V	Naval Science
Z	Bibliography. Library Science

These general categories, subdivided into specific areas, provide you with numerous suggestions for topic restriction, as shown here:

**Fig. 10: Specific
Areas**

```
QB                                    Astronomy
            140-237                   Practical and spherical astronomy
            275-343                   Geodesy
            349-421                   Theoretical astronomy and celestial mechanics
                                        Including perturbations, tides
            460-465                   Astrophysics
            468-479                   Non-optical methods of astronomy
            500-991                   Descriptive astronomy
                                        Including stellar spectroscopy, cosmogony
```

Here is a portion of another entry that narrows it even further.

**Fig. 11: Narrowed
Topic**

```
                                                                        QB
                            ASTRONOMY

                    Popular works
        44             Through 1969
          .2           1970-
        45          Elementary textbooks
        46          Juvenile works
                       Cf. QB63, Stargazers' guides
        47          Special aspects of the subject as a whole
        51          Addresses, essays, lectures
          .5        Astronomy as a profession
        52          Miscellany and curiosa
        54          Extraterrestrial life
       (55)         Astronomical myths, legends, and superstitions, see GR625
        61          Study and teaching. Research
        62             Outlines, syllabi
          .5           Problems, exercises, examinations
          .7           Laboratory manuals
        63          Stargazers' guides
        64          Observers' handbooks
                       Cf. TL796.8, Artificial satellites
        65          Atlases and charts
        66          Astronomical globes
                       Cf. GA12, Manual for globes
        67          Miscellaneous models
        68          Pictorial works and atlases
        70          Planetaria
                       Including orreries
                       Subarranged like Q105
                    Observatories
        81             General works
        82             By region or country, A-Z
                          Under each country:
                          .x   General works
                          .x2  Individual observatories. By name, A-Z
                                 Including description, history, annual
                                   reports, etc.
        84             Observatory buildings
                          Including domes, piers, rising floors, chairs
```

Also available is the *Library of Congress: Subject Headings* which categorizes
subjects into subtopics. The following is a portion of the entry for "flight":

Flight   *(Bird flight. QL698; Mechanics of*
                      flight. TL570-578)
   sa Aeronautics
     Animal flight
     Flying-machines
     Stability of airplanes
     Wings
   x Flying
  xx Aeronautics
     Locomotion
     Wings
  — Medical aspects
    See Aviation medicine
  — Physiological aspects   *(RC1075)*
    x Aviation physiology
      Physiological aspects of flight
   xx Aviation medicine
      Aviation toxicology
  — — Age factors
  — Psychological aspects
    See Aeronautics—Psychology
Flight, Unpowered
  See Gliding and soaring
Flight attendants
  See Air lines—Flight attendants

Fig. 12: From the
*Library of
Congress: Subject
Headings*

SEARCH THE HEADINGS IN PERIODICAL INDEXES

Consultation of any index to periodicals, such as *Readers' Guide* or *Bibliography Index* or *Index to the Humanities* will furnish you with a topic list subdivided into numerous categories, thereby suggesting many possible topics:

a portion of *Readers' Guide*

Universe
  An African cosmology. S. S. Nyang. il UNESCO
    Cour 35:26-33 F '82
  Beyond the black horizon [expanding universe
    theory of J. R. Gott] Sci Am 246:92+ My '82
  The big-bubble theory. S. Begley. il Newsweek
    99:83 Je 7 '82
  Cosmic clumps. W. Tucker. il Sci Dig 90:40
    Je '82
  Exploring the naked singularity [excerpt from
    The edge of infinity] P. Davies. il Sci Dig
    90:30-2 My '82
  Phenomena, comment and notes. J. P. Wiley, Jr.
    Smithsonian 13:28+ My '82
  The six cosmic questions of this decade. T. Dick-
    inson. il Pop Mech 157:92-5+ Ap '82
  Was there really a big bang? [steady state uni-
    verse; theory of Sir Fred Hoyle and Jayant
    Narlikar] W. Kaufmann, III. il Sci Dig 90:40
    Mr '82

Fig. 13: From
*Readers' Guide to
Periodical
Literature*

a portion of another index

WOMEN and men
   Communication and helping behavior: the effects
     of information, reinforcement, and sex on help-
     ing responses. R. N. Bostrom and others. bibl
     Comm Q 29:147-55 Summ '81
   How to do things without words: the taken-for-
     granted as speech-action. R. Hopper. bibl
     Comm Q 29:228-36 Summ '81
   Interruption in conversational interaction, and
     its relation to the sex and status of the
     interactants. G. W. Beattie. bibl Linguistics
     19 no 1/2:15-35 '81
   Partnership in marriage and family: problems
     and possibilities. C. Frühauf. Ecum R 32:410-15
     O '80
   Presence and absence: joy and sorrow. Ecum R
     32:427-9 O '80

Subdividing the Topic

You can narrow your topic by dividing the general subject into specific
areas. Restricting your subject requires careful study of all available sources. For
example, let us say you are assigned the general subject area of the U.S. presi-
dency. A first step in restriction could be to limit the topic to one president—
Ronald Reagan. You discover, however, that there is an overwhelming amount
of written data about Reagan. Therefore, you want to limit yourself to one aspect
of Reagan's administration, for example, his efforts to decontrol natural gas or
perhaps his redefinition of America's policies with Israel. At this point, remember the fundamentals of invention: read the related documents, articles, and government reports, and study particularly all material about decontrol of natural gas
or, in the other case, about Reagan's Israeli policies. You might then speculate
that Reagan's proposals were effective or ineffective, positive or negative, innovative or stultifying. Either way, you have invented a manageable topic in "The
Results of President Reagan's Foreign Policy with Israel" or "The Effects of
President Reagan's Decontrol of Natural Gas." You may, of course, select any
policy or proposal of the president, handle it in this restricted fashion, and write
an acceptable political science paper.

Narrowing the Topic to Special Interests

Relate your subject to your own special interest. If your general subject is
poetry and your special interest is ecology, you might join the two by studying
poems about ecology and nature. Similarly, you might join the subject "Crime"
with your interest in detective fiction, or you might connect the subject "The
State Legislature" with legislation affecting your special interest area, such as
state fund allocations to colleges, or state abortion laws, or state licensing policies
for nursing homes.

An *interest list* or *free writing list* may help you refine the subject. With this method, jot down anything and everything that comes to mind as you concentrate on your subject, as shown below:

Flight:
Lindbergh	Phoenix reborn
Spirit of St. Louis	Birds
Airplanes	Eagles
Jets	Ducks
DC-10	Hunting
Crashes	Duck Blind
Tragedy	

Studying this free association list might provoke your investigation of the myth of the Phoenix or motivate you to search the literature about the Spirit of St. Louis.

Restricting Investigative and Discovery Topics

First, let's go back again to the research question to see how discovery topics develop. "Are football jocks really dumb?" may serve as the beginning of an investigative search of academic records to uncover any misrepresentations of such stereotyping. Put another way, it's not the subject but your treatment of the subject that determines the topic's merit. On the surface, a title such as "Cookbooks" appears unworthy of scholarly study, but your careful focus on copyright infringements in cookbook publishing could develop into an interesting investigation. Your instructor expects you to spend time in the library on investigative matters; therefore, explore the options and select a topic that permits innovative investigation.

Remember too that investigative research may produce interesting findings with regard to contemporary topics such as junk food, video games, outlandish dress codes, and so on. However, your research paper should have the appearance, format, and language of a scholarly paper, including proper documentation. Avoid the temptation to write in conversational street language about a contemporary subject. That is, maintain your intellectual level.

Narrowing and Focusing Comparison Topics

Historians automatically think of comparing Lee and Grant or Hamilton and Jefferson. Political science researchers lean toward presidential comparison. In literature, writers compare one Elizabethan sonneteer with another; in fact, comparative literature is a major area of scholarship. Any two works, any two authors, any two characters may constitute a comparative study.

Psychology papers compare theories. Sociology papers compare social reform programs. Biologists compare water samples. And you, as a researcher, may compare to your heart's content. Yet you must structure the topic for comparison carefully so that your structure or outline will look like this sample:

Hamilton and Jefferson: The Fiscal Policies

   I. Introduction
  II. National Bank
     A. Hamilton
     B. Jefferson
 III. Currency
     A. Hamilton
     B. Jefferson
 IV. Tariffs
     A. Hamilton
     B. Jefferson
  V. Conclusion

and not like this:

   I. Introduction
  II. Hamilton and Jefferson: Fiscal Control
 III. Hamilton
     A. National Bank
     B. Currency
     C. Tariffs
 IV. Jefferson
     A. National Bank
     B. Currency
     C. Tariffs
  V. Conclusion

Under each major category, you must discuss both historical figures. Avoid arranging your comparative topic to discuss one side and then the other.

Narrowing and Focusing Argumentative Topics

Generally, the research paper will contain certain value judgments about the topic. Occasionally, a topic will require a persuasive voice. In this case, you will pick one side of a controversial issue and defend it vigorously; you carry your investigation one step beyond analysis of the issues. You now argue that:

> Alexander Hamilton's theories have proved disastrous for conducting the affairs of the Treasury Department today.
>
> A tax cut by the federal government does not pay for itself but plunges the government into greater deficit spending.
>
> Fresh water legislation by the state government will destroy rather than preserve the recreational value of rivers and streams.

Obviously, you need accurate documentation for such argumentative topics. The burden of proof lies with you, and you'd better have it. Such papers are subject to scrutiny of even minor details because, should your readers find even a small error, they may view the entire argument as suspect.

Controlling Topics for Computer-Generated Papers

Data processing and computer use grow in popularity every year. Your instructor may accept a computer-generated paper if you demonstrate competence in the management of both computers and the software programming that achieves specific results. However, your paper should be one that truly demands the complex functions of a computer; a word processor may serve your typing needs better than a computer. Use the computer when you must examine test results, analyze a survey, tabulate statistical materials, or process other kinds of data. Your reasons for using a computer should be valid in terms of complex materials that require random input and then controlled retrieval.

Restricting and Narrowing Literary Topics

When focusing upon a work of literature, you will usually search out a topic that explores one or more of the following analytical categories of literary research:

Language
Figurative Language (Imagery and Symbolism)
Theme
Character
History
Autobiography
Biography
Psychology (both Freudian and Archetypal)
Setting
Narration
Structure

Using this list and your specific piece of literature, you should narrow your invention of topic to a manageable size by correlating your subject with an analytical approach. For example, Dickens' *Hard Times* may be reduced to a character study of the female figures in the novel. The poetry of Gerard Manley Hopkins may be narrowed to figurative language in "Wreck of the Deutschland," especially the crucifixion imagery.

In addition, you may correlate your literary topic with other disciplines, such as sociology or political science. That is, a psychology major might focus on sibling rivalry in Jane Austen's novel *Emma,* or a history student might correlate events of the Civil War in relation to Stephen Crane's portrayal of the war in *The Red Badge of Courage.*

Finally, narrowing your topic, whatever your approach, depends upon your invention of topic as determined by your personal ingenuity and intellectual speculation.

DEVELOPING A PRELIMINARY THESIS

A preliminary thesis right now will guide and control your research. A final thesis sentence later on will control the writing of your paper and serve as a guide to your reader. The two differ slightly because the preliminary thesis helps you explore issues for discussion while the final thesis sentence informs your audience of the particular issue being discussed. Both are important, but for now the next major influence upon the success of your work is the development of a *preliminary thesis,* a distinctive investigative approach to the topic that limits the scope of research and points toward a final thesis sentence. As you progress more and more toward the invention of your research subject, you will need the unity of a central purpose. You may frame a sentence that begins "The purpose of this paper is . . ."; but you may not want to phrase the beginning that way in the formal paper. Determining your approach clears the path of investigation, while your early focus enables you to gather pertinent data and pass quickly over nonessential matters. Rather than search through a book, you may turn immediately to the book's index for the page number of specific data. Likewise, your perusal of indexes will go faster because you can search out specifics, as shown here:

> Galaxies
>   antimatter and, 257
>   classes of, 176-178
>   clusters of, 194-195, 284, 300-301
>   colliding, 288
>   continuous formation of, 224-225
>   distances of, 188, 201-203
>   electric charge on, 224
>   expanding Universe and, 193

exploding, 288-293
gravitation and, 193-194
microwave energies of, 288-298
number of, 93, 198-199
peculiar, 290
radio, 288-298
recession of, 185-188, 209, 224-229
red shift of, 185-188
spectral class of, 178-179
structure of, 93-94
x-ray, 250

If your approach were galaxies and gravitation, then your search of sources would move rapidly to pages 193–194 of this particular book.

Let us look at three possibilities. If your general topic is "Demand for Energy Production in the U.S." and your preliminary questions of invention have restricted it to the effects of the energy crisis upon the environment, then your purpose is to examine the critical issues in this push-pull debate. Further research questions will surface. Does the energy crisis require that we sacrifice the environment? Should we allow utility companies to pollute air and water in order to heat our homes? Can we have a safe, clean environment and also drive our automobiles at will? Asking such questions during preliminary reading will refine your approach to the topic: The Effects of Energy Demands Upon Pollution Controls. Ultimately, this approach may lead to your final thesis statement, for example: "The demands for energy production in the United States will increase environmental pollution and delay, perhaps forever, our chances for clean air and water."

If, on the other hand, your general topic is Robert Frost's poetry and you have narrowed it to a study of his imagery, then you might ask such research questions as, "Is there an image or image cluster that appears often? Is it a significant image in several important poems?" Such questions may suggest a note-taking approach: the mystery of snow in Robert Frost's poetry. At a later point you would frame the final thesis sentence: "As an image, 'snow' is suggestive of mystery in Robert Frost's poetry."

If your general topic is the role of the pediatric nurse, you might ask, "Whom does the pediatric nurse serve—the child, the family, or the medical community? How does he or she serve? What functions are important?" Your approach may then narrow toward the relationship of the nurse to the child, to the medical community, to the child's family, or to all three. Later, your thesis might read: "The pediatric nurse satisfies several needs of the community—the health needs of the child, the personnel demands of the medical community, and the medical education of the family."

For now, the research questions, a narrowed topic, and an investigative approach to the issues will serve for note-taking purposes. During note-taking and before you start writing your first draft, you must arrive at a final thesis sentence that will control the flow of your paper. The final thesis sentence should unite your various findings, serve as the nerve center for all your paragraphs, and lead toward your demonstrable conclusions at the end of the paper.

The earlier you can formulate a thesis sentence, the earlier you can set satisfactory limitations on note-taking. But you should not bind yourself, early in your work, to a thesis you cannot support or do not believe in. In fact, you cannot properly state your final thesis until after you complete note-taking and are ready to begin writing the paper.

Keep your approach and your thesis flexible at this early stage. Researchers may change theses and directions several times during the course of research. You may find that there is not enough information to support your thesis fully. Or you may find too much information, which will require further narrowing of your topic. New or unanticipated information may change the direction of your thinking and your thesis. Be open to this change.

TIME/TASK CHECKLIST

Use the following timetable to determine your progress. Questions are keyed to sections of the text so that you may quickly refer to the textual discussion if you notice a weak area in your preparation.

TOPIC   Topic Approval Date _____

Have you: ☐ determined your primary purpose? (3–4)
             ☐ identified your audience? (5–6)
             ☐ begun reading and speculating? (6–9)
             ☐ restricted the subject to a narrowed topic? (9–24)
             ☐ developed your preliminary thesis sentence? (24–26)

LIBRARY WORK   Working Bibliography Approval Date _____

Have you: ☐ finished preliminary reading? (32–35)
             ☐ gained familiarity with the library arrangement? (29–31)
             ☐ learned basic bibliography form? (35–42)
             ☐ searched the bibliographies and indexes? (42–53)
             ☐ dipped into the microforms and computer databases? (55–63)
             ☐ searched out call numbers at the card catalog? (64–69)
             ☐ finished your set of working bibliography cards? (38–42)

TAKING NOTES   Note Card Approval Date _____

Have you: ☐ framed a preliminary outline? (70–74)
             ☐ evaluated questionable source materials? (74–79)

☐ balanced primary sources with secondary sources? (79–81)
☐ used various methods for note card variety? (82–94)
☐ avoided plagiarism of any source? (94–99)

WRITING   Rough Draft Approval Date _____

Have you:
☐ written your final thesis sentence? (100–101)
☐ selected a title? (101)
☐ developed an outline for writing? (102–110)
☐ reviewed your outline, approach, and note cards? (110–12)
☐ written an effective opening? (117–22)
☐ used the proper tense? (115–17)
☐ handled properly all quotations and paraphrases? (125–29)
☐ punctuated properly? (131–36)
☐ featured a few content endnotes? (141–45)
☐ written an effective conclusion? (122–25)
☐ revised the rough draft carefully and consciously? (145–46)

FORMAT—TYPING THE FINAL DRAFT   Final Draft Due _____

Have you:
☐ typed a correct title page? (147–48)
☐ included your outline in typed form? (148)
☐ handled properly all technicalities of manuscript form, including margins, numbers, capitalization, etc.? (150–69)
☐ provided accurate tables, graphs, or charts, as necessary? (158–62)
☐ studied the sample research paper for details of form and style? (170–93)
☐ included a separate page for content endnotes? (190)
☐ included a "Works Cited" page? (see below)

WORKS CITED

Have you:
☐ included a bibliography entry for every work cited within your text and/or endnotes? (194)
☐ used proper form for book entries? (195–209)
☐ used proper form for periodical entries? (209–214)
☐ used proper form for other miscellaneous sources? (214–19)

Checklist

2
Using the Library

GATHERING DATA

Despite the popularity of the student center, the library remains the heart of any university community. Every college student must acquire working knowledge of the library, not only for finding items of general interest but also for researching specific areas. Your professor expects more than a quick dip into an encyclopedia; he or she demands a search of indexes and the subsequent review of scholarship on a topic.

You are therefore encouraged to learn about catalogs, indexes, and bibliographies as tools of research study. The card catalog, which most students understand and use regularly, has value for finding books, but it offers no help in locating valuable articles in periodicals or important essays in collections and anthologies.

Don't be intimidated by the library. New techniques of research are designed for you, including printed catalogues, citation indexes, retrospective indexes, and databases by computer storage. Also, don't get bewildered! There is one easily accessible source of library information that will always set you straight—the librarian. The staff of librarians works constantly to ease your way into scholarly matters. They are there to serve you. Any time you find yourself confused or uncertain, seek help. For example, if your study centers on Robert Frost's poetry, the librarian can direct you to the *MLA Bibliography, Humanities Index, Essay and General Literature Index,* and *Poetry Explicator*. But if your topic is shoplifting, the librarian will send you to different sources, such as *Social Sciences Index, Sociological Abstracts,* and perhaps *Psychological Abstracts*. Thus the librarian builds a bridge from the context of your study to the library resources.

In this regard, refer to pages 246–85 of this text for an exhaustive list of reference works and journals by discipline. For example, under ''Black Literature,'' 263–64, you will find the major reference works and journals for that area. As a student-scholar you must decide upon a search strategy that determines which resources are appropriate. Your professor and especially your librarians should be willing partners in this venture.

To that end, this text moves from the general to the specific so that you move with the flow of the library, tracing issues from general reference works to specific articles and essays. Your research strategy, if modeled according to plan, will develop step-by-step from the general to the specific, as shown in this chart:

Preliminary reading of:	Development of bibli-ography cards during search of:	Reading and note-taking from:
encyclopedias	reference books	articles
biographies	bibliographies	essays
dictionaries	indexes	books
handbooks	the card catalog	reviews
atlases	computer databases	abstracts
almanacs	other guides to	government documents
	source materials	bulletins
		other materials

Thus your research should progress from preliminary reading for topic restriction, to reference searching for building a set of bibliography cards, to reading and note-taking from books and articles, and then to writing the first draft. Such a plan helps you (1) avoid shallow plot summary, (2) avoid switching your topic every other day, (3) prevent the tendency to work backward rather than forward, and best of all (4) helps to avoid a paper with no focus, no thesis and with too many paraphrases and outright plagiarism from the source materials.

LIBRARY ORGANIZATION

Because of the sheer numbers of books and magazines, plus the vast array of retrieval systems, it will be to your advantage to tour the library and learn its arrangement—from the circulation desk, to the reference room, and on to the stacks. As you use the library, it is important for you to learn and follow the rules of your library.

Circulation Desk

The circulation desk is usually located at the front of the library. The personnel at this desk are there to point you in the right directions and later to check out your books for withdrawal. Many libraries have computerized machines for book checkout and electronic security devices to prevent theft.

Whenever you cannot find a book in the stacks, check with the circulation desk to determine whether it is checked out, on reserve, or lost. If checked out, you may place a hold order on the book, and the librarians will contact you when it returns. The circulation desk also handles most general business, such as renewals, collection of fines, and handling of keys and change for video and photocopying machines.

The Reference Room

The next part of the step-by-step research process is a visit to your library's reference room. Here encyclopedias, biographical dictionaries, and other general works will help you to refine your topic (see "Preliminary Reading," 32–35). After you have restricted your topic, the reference room provides the bibliographies and indexes for your primary search of the sources (see "Searching the Bibliographies," 42–47, and "Searching the Indexes," 47–55). Here in the reference area you should develop a set of bibliography cards that will direct your search for the books and articles for reading and note-taking.

Reserve Desk

Teachers often place books and articles on reserve with short loan periods—two hours or one day—so that large numbers of students will have access to them. This system prevents one student keeping an important, even crucial, book for two weeks while others suffer its absence. Your library may also place on reserve other valuable items that might otherwise be subject to theft, such as recordings, video tapes, statistical information, or unbound pamphlets and papers.

The Card Catalog

Your library places its holdings in the card catalog by call numbers to index and provide the location of all books. Usually in dictionary form, the card catalog lists books by author, title, and subject—all interfiled in one alphabetical catalog.

Today, more and more libraries are updating the card catalog system with microfilm systems or computer terminals. The call number is always essential to locating books quickly. (For detailed information, see "Finding the Call Number," 63–68).

Stacks

The stacks of the library hold the books where, armed with proper call numbers from the card catalog, you locate your desired books and browse for others of interest. However, libraries with closed stacks will not permit you into the stacks at all. Rather, you provide the call number(s) to an attendant who goes into the stacks for you.

Computer Facilities

Over the past decade libraries have increased use of on-line database computer facilities. A new type of librarian now assists the researcher because computerized networks dispatch information nationwide on almost any topic. After initial searching through indexes and bibliographies, some researchers can narrow or broaden the scope of their research with the help of a database search (see "Searching the Computer Databases," 55–63).

Interlibrary Loans

Interlibrary loans are transactions in which one library borrows from another. The interlibrary loan service supplements a library's resources by making materials available from other libraries, as does the database system mentioned above. Understand, however, that receiving a book or article by interlibrary loan may take seven to ten days.

Photocopiers

Photocopying services provide a real convenience, enabling you to carry home articles from journals and reserve books that cannot be withdrawn from the library. However, copyright laws protect authors and place certain restrictions on the library. You may use the copying machines and services for your own individual purposes, but be sure that you credit sources correctly for their quotations and materials (see "Avoiding Plagiarism," 94–99).

Nonprint Materials

Libraries serve as a storehouse for recordings, video tapes, film, microfilm and microfiche, plus other items. These nonprint materials are usually located in a certain section of the libary. Some libraries provide a catalog of nonprint items. Valuable lectures on tape about your topic might be available if you know how to search this overlooked area of scholarly holding in the library.

PRELIMINARY READING IN THE REFERENCE ROOM

Your introductory reading will serve several purposes: it offers an overview of the subject, provides a working bibliography (see 35–37), suggests the availability of sufficient source materials, and begins invention and restriction of the subject. Since you cannot yet be certain of your needs, this preliminary reading requires no note-taking.

As a starting point, you might begin with a book or journal articles recommended by your instructor or librarian. You might also start with a general survey, such as *Literary History of the United States* (see Appendix, 246–48, for a list of general reference works and journals in your field). Or you may also begin with an encyclopedia, a biographical dictionary, or some other general reference work, as listed below:

Encyclopedias

Chambers's Encyclopedia. New rev. ed. 15 vols. Fairview Park, N.Y.: Maxwell Scientific International, 1973.

Encyclopedia Americana. 30 vols. New York: Americana Corporation, 1978.

Encyclopedia of Philosophy. 4 vols. New York: Free Press, 1973.

The New Columbia Encyclopedia. 4th ed. New York: Columbia Univ. Press, 1975.

The Encyclopaedia Britannica. 15th ed. 30 vols. Chicago: Encyclopaedia Britannica, 1980.

Biographical Dictionaries

Universal

Deceased

Chambers's Biographical Dictionary. Rev. ed. London: W & R Chambers, 1974.

Webster's Biographical Dictionary. Rev. ed. Springfield, Mass.: Merriam, 1976.

Living

Current Biography Yearbooks. New York: H. W. Wilson, 1940–date.

Dictionary of International Biography. London: Oxford, 1978; supplements to date by International Biography Center.

A Dictionary of Universal Biography of All Ages and of All People. Ed. Albert M. Hyamson. 3rd ed. N.Y.: Routledge and Kegan, 1976.

Index to Women of the World from Ancient to Modern Times: Biographies and Portraits. Ed. Norma O. Ireland. Westwood, Mass.: Faxon, 1970.

International Who's Who. New York: International Publications Service, 1935–date.

Twentieth Century Authors: A Biographical Dictionary of Modern Literature. Ed. Stanley J. Kunitz and Howard Haycraft. New York: H. W. Wilson, 1942. Supplement 1955.

Webster's Biographical Dictionary. Rev. ed. Springfield, Mass.: Merriam, 1976.

Who's Who in the World. 5th ed. Chicago: Marquis Who's Who, 1980.

American

Deceased

Dictionary of American Biography. 10 vols. New York: Scribner's, 1980.
National Cyclopedia of American Biography. 71 vols. Clifton, N.J.: J. T.
   White, 1978.
Who Was Who in America. 7 vols. Chicago: Marquis Who's Who, 1607–
   date.

Living

*Contemporary Authors: A Bio-Bibliographical Guide to Current Authors and
   Their Works.* Detroit: Gale, 1962–date.
Encyclopedia of American Biography. Ed. John A. Garraty and Jerome L.
   Sternstein. New York: Harper & Row, 1974.
National Cyclopedia of American Biography. 71 vols. Clifton, N.J.: J. T.
   White, 1978.
Webster's American Biographies. Springfield, Mass.: Merriam, 1975.
Who's Who Among Black Americans. 2nd ed. Northbrook, Ill.: Who's Who
   Among Black Americans, Inc., 1978.
Who's Who in America. Chicago: Marquis Who's Who, 1899–date.
Who's Who of American Women. Chicago: Marquis Who's Who, 1958–date.

British

Deceased

Burke's Landed Gentry. 18th ed. 3 vols. Elmsford, N.Y.: British Book Center,
   1965–69.
Dictionary of National Biography. Ed. Leslie Stephen and Sidney Lee. 22 vols.
   1882–1953; rpt. New York: Oxford Univ. Press, 1981. 7 Supplements.
Who Was Who: Companion to Who's Who. 6 vols. New York: St. Martin's,
   1952–62.

Living

Who's Who. London: A & C Black, 1849–date.

Almanacs and Yearbooks

Americana Annual 1982. Danbury, Conn.: Grolier Educational Corp., 1978.
Annual Register of World Events. Ed. I. Macadam and H. V. Hodson. New
   York: St. Martin's, Annually.
Britannica Book of the Year. Ed. James Ertel. Chicago: Encyclopaedia Britan-
   nica, 1938–date.
Facts on File Yearbook. New York: Facts on File, 1941–date.
Information Please Almanac 1982: Atlas & Yearbook. New York: Simon &
   Schuster, 1981.
Kane, Joseph N. *Famous First Facts: A Record of First Happenings, Discov-
   eries and Inventions in the United States.* 4th ed. New York: H. W. Wilson,
   1981.
Kane, Joseph Nathan. *Facts About the Presidents.* 4th ed. New York: H. W.
   Wilson, 1981.
The Negro Almanac: A Reference Work on the Black American. Ed. Harry A.
   Ploski and Warren Marr. New York: Bellwether, 1976.

The Statesman's Year-Book: Statistical and Historical Annual of the States of the World. Ed. John Paxton. 119th ed. New York: St. Martin's, 1982.

The World Almanac and Book of Facts. New York: Newspaper Enterprise Association, 1868–date.

Yearbook of the United Nations. Lake Success, N.Y.: United Nations, 1947–date.

Atlases and Gazetteers

Atlas of American History. Ed. Kenneth T. Jackson. N.Y.: Scribner's, 1978.

The Atlas of the Universe. New York: Rand McNally, 1970.

Atlas of United States History. Maplewood, N.J.: Hammond, n.d.

Atlas of World History. Maplewood, N.J.: Hammond, n.d.

Britannica Atlas: Geography Edition. Ed. William A. Cleveland. Chicago: Encyclopaedia Britannica, 1974.

Commercial Atlas. Rev. ed. New York: American Map, 1978.

Goode's World Atlas. Ed. Edward B. Espenshade, Jr. 15th ed. Chicago: Rand McNally, 1978.

Grosset World Atlas (originally: *Hammond World Atlas*). New York: Grosset and Dunlap, 1973.

National Geographic Atlas of the World. 5th ed. Washington, D.C.: National Geographic Society, 1981.

The New York Times Atlas of the World. Rev. ed. In collaboration with *The Times of London.* New York: Times Books, 1981.

Oxford Economic Atlas of the World. 4th ed. London: Oxford Univ. Press, 1972.

Oxford World Atlas. Ed. Saul B. Cohen, London: Oxford Univ. Press, 1972.

Shepherd, W. R. *Shepherd's Historical Atlas.* 9th ed. 1964; rpt. New York: Barnes & Noble, 1976.

The Times Atlas of the World. Comprehensive ed., produced by *The Times of London.* New York: Times Books, 1980.

Dictionaries

Concise Oxford Dictionary of Current English. Ed. J. B. Sykes. 6th ed. London: Oxford Univ. Press, 1976.

Funk and Wagnalls Standard Dictionary. New updated ed. New York: Funk & Wagnalls, 1980.

Oxford English Dictionary. Ed. James A. H. Murray et al. 13 vols. New York: Oxford Univ. Press, 1933.

Random House College Dictionary. New York: Random House, 1975.

The Shorter Oxford English Dictionary. Ed. William Little et al. 3rd ed. 2 vols. New York: Oxford Univ. Press, 1973.

Webster's New Collegiate Dictionary. Ed. Henry Bosley Woolf. 8th ed. Springfield, Mass.: Merriam, 1981.

Webster's New World Dictionary of the American Language. 2nd concise ed. Cleveland: Collins-World, 1979.

Webster's Third New International Dictionary, Unabridged: The Great Library of the English Language. Springfield, Mass.: Merriam, 1981.

Books of Usage, Synonyms, and Dialect

Americanisms: A Dictionary of Selected Americanisms on Historical Principles. Ed. Mitford M. Mathews. Chicago: Univ. of Chicago Press, 1966.

A Dictionary of American English on Historical Principles. Ed. Sir William Craigie and J. R. Hulbert. 4 vols. Chicago: Univ. of Chicago Press, 1938–44.

Dictionary of American Slang. Ed. Harold Wentworth and Stuart B. Flexner. New York: Crowell, 1975.

Ebbitt, Wilma R., and David R. Ebbitt. *Writer's Guide and Index to English.* 7th ed. Glenview, Ill.: Scott, Foresman, 1982.

Fowler, H. W. *A Dictionary of Modern English Usage.* Rev. Sir Ernest Gowers. 2nd ed. Oxford: Clarendon Press, 1965.

Partridge, Eric. *A Dictionary of Slang and Unconventional English.* 7th ed. New York: Macmillan, 1970.

Roget's Thesaurus of English Words and Phrases. Rev. Robert A. Dutch. New York: St. Martin's, 1965.

This initial reading need not be extensive. You accomplish your purpose in preliminary reading when you understand your material well enough to decide what restricted phase of it you wish to pursue. As soon as your search strategy is formulated, you should begin developing bibliography cards as you scan the resource materials.

THE WORKING BIBLIOGRAPHY

Early in your research you should begin developing a working bibliography—a list of reference sources that you will eventually investigate for information about your subject. Therefore, during your preliminary reading you should begin writing bibliography cards for all references that show promise of giving clues about your topic. Specifically, you need to watch for bibliographies and notes that list new source materials. Most books of critical evaluation will contain extensive bibliographies at the ends of the chapters or at the end of the book. Journal articles usually have footnotes at the bottom of the page and a bibliography at the end. General reference works, such as encyclopedias and biographical dictionaries, normally offer brief bibliographies at the end of each entry.

Suppose your topic concerns some aspect of Benjamin Franklin's political activities. Your preliminary reading of *Encyclopaedia Britannica* will uncover not only a brief biography but also the following bibliography:

Fig. 15: From *The
New Encyclopaedia
Britannica*

MAJOR WORKS

POLITICAL AND ECONOMIC: *A Modest Enquiry into the Nature and Necessity of a Paper Currency* (1729); *Plain Truth; or Serious Considerations on the Present State of the City of Philadelphia* (1747); *Proposals Relating to the Education of Youth in Pensilvania* (1749); *Observations Concerning the Increase of Mankind* (1755); *The Way to Wealth* (1757); *The Interest of Great Britain Considered with Regard to Her Colonies and the Acquisition of Canada and Guadaloupe* (1760); *Positions to be Examined Concerning National Wealth* (1769); *Journal of the Negotiations for Peace* (1782).

RELIGIOUS, PHILOSOPHICAL, AND SCIENTIFIC: *A Dissertation on Liberty and Necessity, Pleasure and Pain* (1725); *Articles of Belief and Acts of Religion* (1728); *Experiments and Observations on Electricity* (1751).

OTHER WORKS: *Poor Richard's* (1732–57), an almanac containing a number of famous maxims; Franklin's *Autobiography* (1771–88); "Information to those who would remove to America" (1784).

BIBLIOGRAPHY. *The Papers of Benjamin Franklin*, 15 vol., ed. by L.W. LABAREE *et al.* (1959–71), with 25 additional volumes expected, will be the definitive collection. *The Writings of Benjamin Franklin*, 10 vol., ed. by A.H. SMYTH (1905–07), has heretofore been the chief collection. The fullest biography is CARL VAN DOREN, *Benjamin Franklin* (1938); the best brief one is VERNER W. CRANE, *Benjamin Franklin and a Rising People* (1954). The most recent life is THOMAS FLEMING, *The Man Who Dared the Lightning: A New Look at Benjamin Franklin* (1971). An interesting specialized study is BRUCE INGHAM GRANGER, *Benjamin Franklin, An American Man of Letters* (1964).

(T.Hor.)

Since several of these sources will appear promising, you will want to begin making bibliography cards, such as:

Fig. 16: Sample
Bibliography Card

Crane, Verner W.

Benjamin Franklin
and a Rising
People, 1954.

Later, at the card catalog, you must insert the proper library call number (see 63–68) and the missing publication information (see Figure 17, 38). Then, when you are ready to study this particular book, your card provides the information for finding it. In addition, your card will have the necessary data for the final bibliography.

As you discover each new reference, you should record the bibliographical data onto *individual,* three-by-five-inch index cards. (But if you have a system that works well for you, by all means use it, provided, of course, that your system is accurate and efficient.) Individual cards have one great advantage over other systems: you can shuffle and arrange them in alphabetical order.

As you record information, check carefully to make certain that each card includes the following:

1. *Author's name,* followed by a period. Arrange the name in inverted order, surname first, for alphabetizing purposes. Provide the name in the fullest form available, for example, "Hart, Thomas P.," not "Hart, T. P."
2. *Title of the work,* followed by a period. Enclose within quotation marks titles of articles, essays, chapters, sections, programs on radio or television, short poems, stories, and songs. Underline titles of books, journals, pamphlets, magazines, newspapers, plays, movies (including television movies), long poems, and operas.
3. *Publication information.* For a book: the place, followed by a colon; the publisher, followed by a comma; the date, followed by a period. For a journal article: the name of the journal, the volume number in Arabic numerals, the date in parentheses, followed by a colon, the page(s), followed by a period. Spell in full titles of periodicals, for example, *Journal of Higher Education,* not *J. of Higher Ed.*
4. *Other items of documentation* as necessary (see Chapter 6, 194–219 for exact information about positioning these items on the card):

   name of the editor or translator

   edition used, whenever it is not the first

   series number

   number of volumes with this particular title

   volume number if one of two or more

5. *Library call number* of a book or magazine, placed in the upper right-hand corner of the card. This item is valuable when you are ready to search out and read your sources.
6. *A personal note,* at the bottom of the card, as to the type of material to be found in this source or any special aspect it presents. Perhaps include the name of the index in which you first found mention of this source, just in case you need to go back and double-check the facts (see Figure 5).

SAMPLE BIBLIOGRAPHY CARDS

In addition to the examples provided below, you may also study the bibliographical entries in Chapter 6.

Fig. 17: Card for an Entire Book

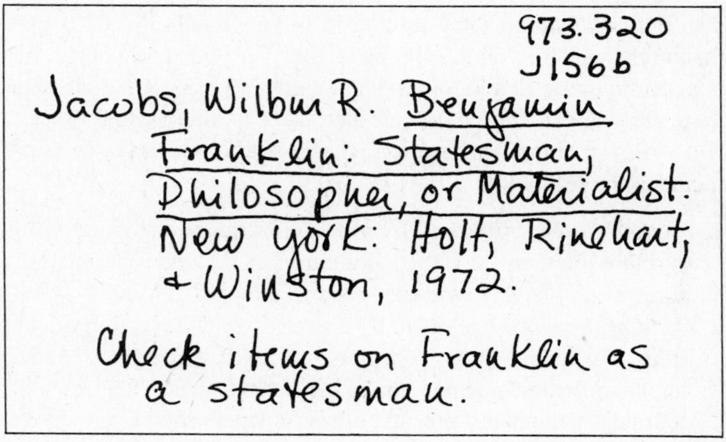

> 973.320
> J156b
>
> Jacobs, Wilbur R. Benjamin Franklin: Statesman, Philosopher, or Materialist. New York: Holt, Rinehart, & Winston, 1972.
>
> Check items on Franklin as a statesman.

Fig. 18: Card for a Journal Article

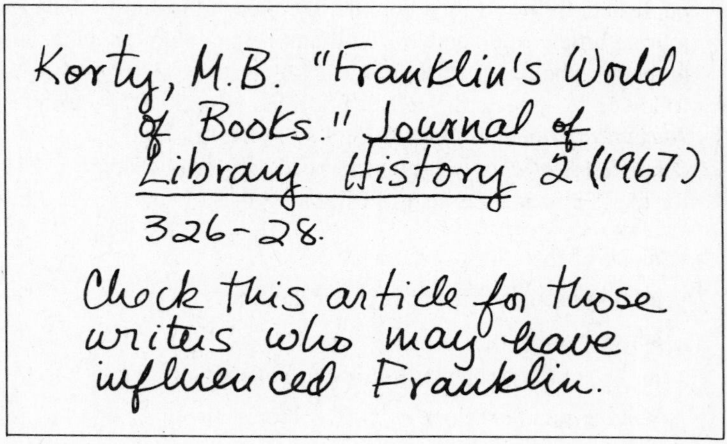

> Korty, M.B. "Franklin's World of Books." Journal of Library History 2 (1967) 326–28.
>
> Check this article for those writers who may have influenced Franklin.

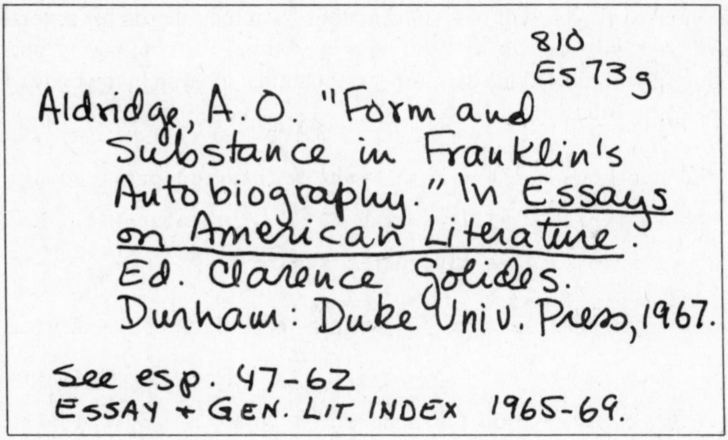

Aldridge, A.O. "Form and Substance in Franklin's Autobiography." In <u>Essays on American Literature</u>. Ed. Clarence Golides. Durham: Duke Univ. Press, 1967.

810
Es73g

See esp. 47-62
ESSAY + GEN. LIT. INDEX 1965-69.

Fig. 19: Card for Entry Found in *Essay and General Literature Index*

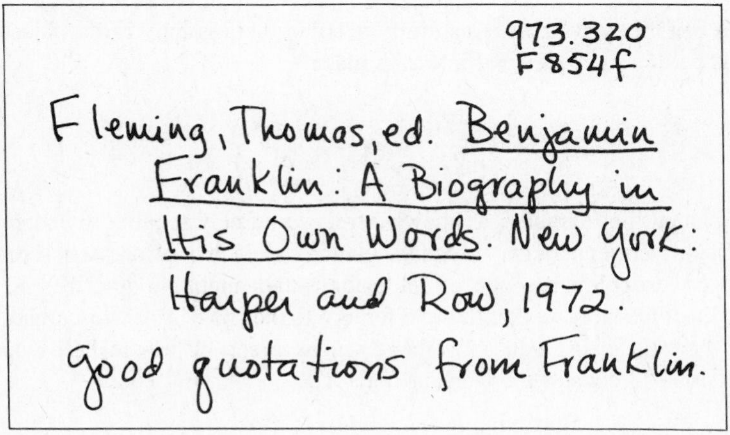

Fleming, Thomas, ed. <u>Benjamin Franklin: A Biography in His Own Words</u>. New York: Harper and Row, 1972.

973.320
F854f

Good quotations from Franklin.

Fig. 20: Card for an Editor

Paul, Sherman, ed. <u>Six Classic American Writers: An Introduction</u>. Minneapolis: University of Minnesota Press, 1970.

810.9
P55s

Study 235-38.

Fig. 21: Card That Refers to a Portion of a Book

Later in your work you will need information from these cards for several purposes. First, you will want to find the book or journal for note-taking purposes. Second, you will refer to the card for correct textual citation in the body of your paper, as in the following:

```
. . . the numerous writers that Franklin studied provided him
with rich rhetorical skills (Korty 327).  The role models he
found in classic writers tipped him toward . . .
```

Third, you will again need the card for writing the bibliography entry, as shown:

```
Korty, M. B.  "Franklin's World of Books."  Journal of
Library History 2 (1967): 326–28.
```

Obviously, it benefits you to write carefully detailed bibliography cards. Also, you should keep them in order and in a safe place.

WRITING THE ANNOTATED BIBLIOGRAPHY

An annotated bibliography, as shown here, is routinely required by some instructors. It adds a brief summary about the contents of each book and article on your list. Placed just below the facts of publication, the annotation describes the essential details of the work so that future reference to the entry by any researcher will provide essential data. You and others will have certain tips to help you determine whether to consult the work or not.

Follow these suggestions:

1. Explain the main purpose of the work.
2. Briefly describe the contents.
3. Indicate the possible audience for the work.
4. Note any special features.
5. Warn of any defect, weakness, or bias.

Provide enough information in about three sentences for a reader to have a fairly clear image of the book's purpose, contents, and special value.

The sample list on the opposite page provides models of short, effective annotations:

Annotated Bibliography

Burhans, Clinton S., Jr. The Would-Be Writer.
     Lexington, Mass.: Xerox, 1971.

          This book helps students in writing courses

          grasp the basic writing process, thereby

          making more meaningful their subsequent

          training in more advanced thinking and

          writing. The book helps one to think

          through a topic with pre-writing, writing,

          and re-writing steps.

Christensen, Francis. Notes Toward a New Rhetoric.
     New York: Harper & Row, 1967.

          The author's purpose is to present six es-

          says on the structure of the sentence and

          paragraph. The major areas are: generative

          rhetoric of the sentence and of the para-

          graph, sentence openers, and restrictive

          and nonrestrictive modifiers.

Gibson, Walker. Tough, Sweet and Stuffy. Blooming-
     ton: Indiana Univ. Press, 1966.

          This essay on modern prose styles describes

          the three extreme styles: tough talk, sweet

          talk, and stuffy talk. Samplers in the

          appendix are especially helpful.

SEARCHING THE BIBLIOGRAPHIES

In the reference room you will find separate bibliographies on a wide range of subjects. Some, like *A Shakespeare Bibliography,* are standard bibliographies that list sources in existence for some time. Others, like *Bibliographic Index,* are current bibliographies that list recent publications and that are kept up-to-date by supplements.

Bibliographies also appear within other works. As noted previously, encyclopedias usually contain brief bibliographies at the ends of most articles. Critical and biographical studies often have bibliographies at the end of the book; for example, Thomas J. Fleming's *Man Who Dared the Lightning* has a four-page bibliography. Most scholarly journals maintain up-to-date bibliographies: for example, history students depend upon *English Historical Review,* literature students look to the *MLA Bibliography,* and biology students consult *Biological Abstracts.*

As a beginning researcher, you need a comprehensive list of major reference materials in your subject field. To that end, the Appendix of this manual contains lists of standard reference works and journals in the following subject areas: applied sciences (247–53), art (253–55), biological sciences (255–57), business (257–59), computer technology (259–60), education (260–62), English language and literature (262–67), foreign languages (267–71), health and physical education (271–72), home economics (272–73), music (273–74), philosophy (274–75), psychology (275–76), religion (277–78), social sciences (278–84), and speech and drama (284–85). A brief glance at these lists will show you that they contain titles of major bibliographies in all these disciplines.

Then, for thorough coverage of your field, examine the following reference sources; each of these books functions as a bibliography that offers a list of other bibliographies:

Bell, Marion V., and Eleanor A. Swidan, eds. *Reference Books: A Brief Guide.* 8th ed. Baltimore: Enoch Pratt, 1978.

Besterman, Theodore. *A World Bibliography of Bibliographies.* 4th ed. 5 vols. Lausanne: Societas Bibliographica, 1965.

Murphey, Robert W. *How and Where to Look It Up: A Guide to Standard Sources of Information.* New York: McGraw-Hill, 1958.

Sheehy, Eugene Paul. *Guide to Reference Books.* 9th ed. Chicago: American Library Association, 1976. Revised, Expanded, & Updated Version of the 8th ed. by C. M. Winchell.

Shores, Louis. *Basic Reference Sources.* Ed. Lee Ash. Library Reference Series. 1954; rpt. Boston: Gregg, 1972.

Walford, Arthur J., ed. *Guide to Reference Material.* 3rd ed. 3 vols. London: Library Association, 1973, 1975, 1977.

Let us assume you wish to proceed with the investigation of Ben Franklin begun earlier in this chapter. You would first examine the listings under "History" (280–82), "Political Science" (282–83), and "American Literature" (262–63) in the Appendix and perhaps one or two of the books listed immediately above. As a result, you find works such as:

American Historical Association. *Guide to Historical Literature*. Ed. George F. Howe and others. New York: MacMillan, 1961.
Beers, Henry P. *Bibliographies in American History*. 1942; rpt. New York: Octagon, 1973.
Northup, Clark S. *A Register of Bibliographies of the English Language and Literature*. New York: Hafner, 1962.

After examining these books and others like them, you then search for special bibliographies of Franklin. In this case, fortunately, there are two bibliographies exclusively concerned with our subject:

Ford, Paul Leicester. *Franklin Bibliography: A List of Books Written by, or Relating to, Benjamin Franklin*. Brooklin: n.p., 1889. Rev. by R. R. Bowker in *Library Journal*, XIV, 425.
"List of Works Relating to Benjamin Franklin Published Since the Franklin Bicentenary." Washington, D.C.: Library of Congress, 1924.

However, if your thorough investigation uncovers the fact that no bibliography devoted solely to your subject exists, you still have plenty of other reference material to work with. Even with the Franklin bibliographies above, you need up-to-date reference sources because new discoveries about historical figures are made regularly. Scholars are constantly reinterpreting such things as Franklin's writings, the circumstances surrounding him during his age, and the effect he had upon others.

Therefore, in addition to such special bibliographies you should also examine the following:

Bibliographic Index: A Cumulative Bibliography of Bibliographies. New York: H. W. Wilson, 1938–date.

Although *Bibliographic Index* originally covered only the years 1937–42, it is kept current by supplements. It is therefore valuable for bringing your investigation of a topic up-to-date. A sample entry from *Bibliographic Index* of 1971 uncovers these sources:

Fig. 22: From
Bibliographic
Index, 1971.
1. Subject heading
2. Entry of a book
that contains a
bibliography on
Franklin 3. Specific
pages on which
bibliography is
located.

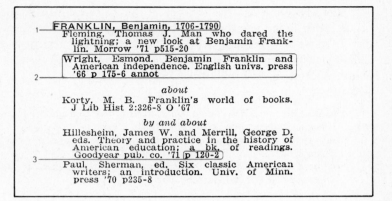

Each entry in *Bibliographic Index* directs you to the specific bibliographic section within a critical study. In other words, by consulting this text, you discover not only five books about Franklin but also five additional bibliographic lists. For example, a bibliography on Franklin is found on pp. 515–20 of Thomas J. Fleming's *Man Who Dared the Lightning* and on pp. 175–76 of Esmond Wright's *Benjamin Franklin and American Independence*. This information should be noted on a bibliography card, as follows:

Fig. 23: Card
Listing a
Bibliographic
Source

Paul, Sherman, ed. <u>Six Classic</u>
<u>American Writers: An</u>
<u>Introduction</u>. Minneapolis:
University of Minnesota
Press, 1970.

Bibliography on pp. 235–38.

Another reference aid of this general nature is *Bulletin of Bibliography and Magazine Notes* (Boston: F. W. Faxon, 1897–date). This first page of each volume contains an index.

Trade Bibliographies

You may also want to use the trade bibliographies, which are works intended primarily for use by booksellers and librarians. As a researcher, you will find them helpful in three ways: to discover sources which may not be listed in other bibliographies or in the card catalog of your library; to locate facts of publication, such as place and date; and, especially, to learn if a book is in print.

Subject Guide to Books in Print (New York: Bowker, 1957–date) supplies a subject index that enables you to discover new sources. *Books in Print* and its companion volume, *Subject Guide to Books in Print* is published annually in October. The 1974 edition contains an extensive listing about Benjamin Franklin. A small portion follows:

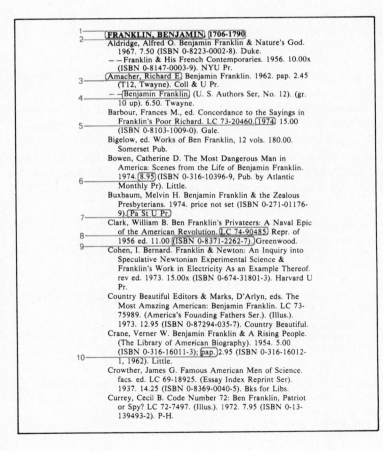

Fig. 24: From Subject Guide to Books in Print
1. Subject 2. Dates of subject's life span 3. Author 4. Title 5. Date of publication 6. Price 7. Publisher 8. Library of Congress Number 9. International Standard Book Number (used when ordering) 10. Paperback book

Many items from this *Subject Guide to Books in Print* will lend themselves to your study. Therefore, bibliography cards should be made for the most promising, as in this sample card:

> Aldridge, Alfred O.
> Benjamin Franklin and
> Nature's God. Durham,
> N.C.: Duke Univ.
> Press, 1967.

In like manner, you should become familiar with *Books in Print* (New York: Bowker, 1948–date). This work provides an author-title index to the *Publishers' Trade List Annual* (New York: Bowker, 1874–date), a list of books currently in print. Also, *Publishers' Weekly* (New York: Bowker, 1872–date) offers current publication data. In short, you cannot overlook the trade bibliographies as a possible source of information. Others are:

Paperbound Books in Print. New York: Bowker, 1955–date.

> Since the publication of paperback books is increasing annually and since important books are occasionally found only in paperback form, you may find this text a necessary tool.

Cumulative Book Index. Minneapolis [later New York]: H. W. Wilson, 1900–date.

> This work lists books by author, subject, editor, and translator. Use it to find complete publication data or to locate *all* material in English on a particular subject.

The National Union Catalog: A Cumulative Author List. Ann Arbor: Edwards, 1953–date.

> Basically, this work is the card catalog in book form; that is, it provides a list representing the Library of Congress printed cards and also titles reported by other libraries. It supplements the *Library of Congress Catalog*.

Library of Congress Catalog: Books: Subjects. Washington, D.C.: Library of Congress, 1950–date.

> This catalog complements *The National Union Catalog* by supplying a subject classification. Separate volumes are available for the years 1950–54, 1955–59, 1960–64, and annually thereafter.

General Catalogue of Printed Books. London: Trustees of the British Museum, 1881–date.

> This British publication serves a corresponding function to *The National Union Catalog*. Such listings are available for most nations.

Union List of Serials in Libraries of the United States and Canada. 3rd ed. New York: H. W. Wilson, 1965. Supplements, *New Serial Titles*, Washington, D.C.: Library of Congress, 1953–date.

> You may consult this work to determine if a nearby library has a magazine that is unavailable in your library.

Ulrich's International Periodicals Directory. Ed. Merle Rohinsky. 15th ed. New York: Bowker, 1973.

> This work is a guide to current periodicals, both domestic and foreign.

SEARCHING THE INDEXES

A general index furnishes the page number(s) of another book or magazine where you will find specific information. Fundamentally, there are three types: indexes to materials in books and collections, indexes to literature in periodicals, and indexes to materials in newspapers.

Indexes to Books and Collections

First, you should recall *Bibliographic Index* (see 49), which refers you to books or collections as well as bibliographies. In addition, you should familiarize yourself with:

Essay and General Literature Index, 1900–1933. New York: H. W. Wilson, 1934. Supplements, 1934–date.
Biography Index: A Quarterly Index to Biographical Material in Books and Magazines. New York: H. W. Wilson, 1946/47–date.

The first index directs you to material within books and collections of both a biographical and a critical nature. Note the following entry from a supplement of *Essay and General Literature Index:*

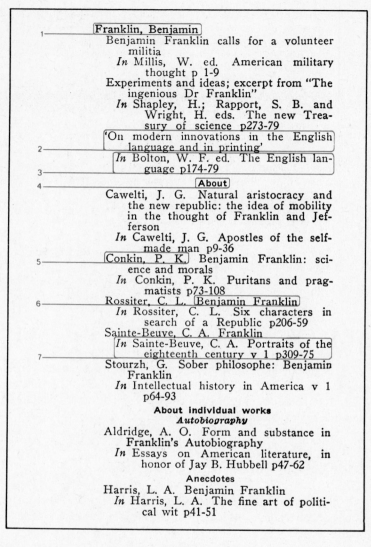

Franklin, Benjamin

Benjamin Franklin calls for a volunteer
   militia
In Millis, W. ed. American military
   thought p 1-9
Experiments and ideas; excerpt from "The
   ingenious Dr Franklin"
In Shapley, H.; Rapport, S. B. and
   Wright, H. eds. The new Treasury of science p273-79
'On modern innovations in the English
   language and in printing'
In Bolton, W. F. ed. The English language p174-79

About

Cawelti, J. G. Natural aristocracy and
   the new republic: the idea of mobility
   in the thought of Franklin and Jef-
   ferson
In Cawelti, J. G. Apostles of the self-
   made man p9-36
Conkin, P. K. Benjamin Franklin: sci-
   ence and morals
In Conkin, P. K. Puritans and prag-
   matists p73-108
Rossiter, C. L. Benjamin Franklin
In Rossiter, C. L. Six characters in
   search of a Republic p206-59
Sainte-Beuve, C. A. Franklin
In Sainte-Beuve, C. A. Portraits of the
   eighteenth century **v** 1 p309-75
Stourzh, G. Sober philosophe: Benjamin
   Franklin
In Intellectual history in America **v** 1
   p64-93
About individual works
Autobiography
Aldridge, A. O. Form and substance in
   Franklin's Autobiography
In Essays on American literature, in
   honor of Jay B. Hubbell p47-62
Anecdotes
Harris, L. A. Benjamin Franklin
In Harris, L. A. The fine art of politi-
   cal wit p41-51

Note that this index sends you to essays *within* books that you might otherwise
overlook; for example, J. G. Cawelti's essay appears in *Apostles of the Self-Made*
Man and P. K. Conkin's essay appears in a book with the deceptive title *Puritans*
and Pragmatists. The publishers and dates for these entries are found in a "List
of Books Indexed" at the end of each volume of *Essay and General Literature*
Index.

   Biography Index is a good starting point if your study involves a famous
person. It gives clues to biographical information for people of all lands. (However, for the years 1900–47 you should see *Essay and General Literature Index*.)
Note the following short excerpt from *Biography Index:*

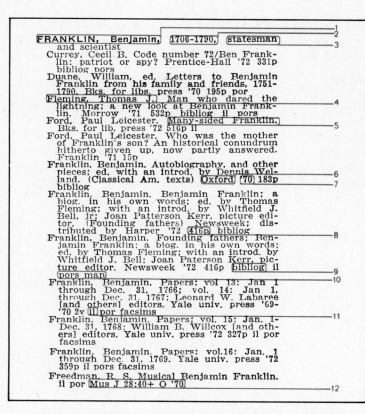

Fig. 27: From Biography Index
1. Subject 2. Dates of subject's birth and death 3. Subject's profession 4. Author of the biography 5. Title of the biography 6. Publisher 7. Date of publication 8. Number of pages 9. Contains a bibliography 10. Contains portraits and a map 11. Illustrated 12. Publication data for a periodical

Most indexes published by the H. W. Wilson Company uses this same code system. Specifically, note the code for journal volumes and page numbers—"23:81–91 D'71." To conform to the suggestions in this manual, you will want to record this data differently on your bibliography card, as follows:

Fig. 28: Sample Bibliography Card

Morris, R.B. "Meet Dr. Franklin." American Heritage 23 (1971): 81-91.

50 Using the Library

When looking for biographical information, you should also consult a good biographical dictionary (see 32–33).

Other important sources are the cumulated subject and author indexes to *Dissertation Abstracts International* (Ann Arbor: Univ. Microfilms, 1970–date; formerly *Microfilm Abstracts,* 1938–51, and *Dissertation Abstracts,* 1952–69). Issue No. 12, Part II, of each volume contains the cumulated subject and author indexes for Issues 1–12 of the volume's two sections—A, Humanities and Social Sciences and B, Sciences and Engineering. (Note that since 1972 the indexes have included authors only.) In addition to these indexes, the *Comprehensive Dissertation Index* lists dissertations from 1861 to date according to subject and author. For example, Volume 29 includes the following entries for Benjamin Franklin:

Fig. 29: From the Comprehensive Dissertation Index 1861–1972

FRANKLIN
AN ANNOTATED CHECKLIST OF THE LETTERS OF
FRANKLIN BENJAMIN SANBORN (1831-1917)—
CLARKSON, JOHN W, JR (PH D 1971 COLUMBIA
UNIVERSITY) X1971, p 222
FRANKLIN AND CREVECOEUR INDIVIDUALISM AND
THE AMERICAN DREAM IN THE EIGHTEENTH
CENTURY— AGEE, WILLIAM HERBERT (PH D 1969
UNIVERSITY OF MINNESOTA) 600p 31/01-A, p 380
70–01830
BENJAMIN FRANKLIN AND HIS BIOGRAPHERS A
CRITICAL STUDY— KUSHEN, BETTY SANDRA (PH D
1969 NEW YORK UNIVERSITY) 317p 30/09-A,
p 3946   70–03081
BENJAMIN FRANKLIN AND THE ZEALOUS
PRESBYTERIANS— BUXBAUM, MELVIN (PH D 1968
UNIVERSITY OF CHICAGO) X1968, p 172
SPIRITUAL AUTOBIOGRAPHY IN SELECTED WRITINGS
OF SEWALL, EDWARDS, BYRD, WOOLMAN, AND
FRANKLIN A COMPARISON OF TECHNIQUE AND
CONTENT— MILLAR, ALBERT EDWARD, JR (PH D
1968 UNIVERSITY OF DELAWARE) 362p 29/06-A,
p 1873   68–15542
BENJAMIN FRANKLIN A STUDY IN SELF-
MYTHOLOGY— WHITE, CHARLES WILLIAM (PH D
1967 HARVARD UNIVERSITY) X1967, p 175
THE GROWTH OF THE BENJAMIN FRANKLIN IMAGE
THE PHILADELPHIA YEARS — SAPPENFIELD, JAMES
ALLEN (PH D 1966 STANFORD UNIVERSITY) 233p
27/10-A, p 3469   67–04426
FRANKLIN'S STYLE IRONY AND THE COMIC— CLASBY,
NANCY TENFELDE (PH D 1966 THE UNIVERSITY OF
WISCONSIN) 273p 28/02-A, p 622   66–09892

An abstract of the eighth entry, "Franklin's Style: Irony and the Comic" by Nancy Tenfelde Clasby, is to be found in Vol. 28, No. 2A, p. 622, of *Dissertation Abstracts International*. A portion of that abstract follows:*

*The dissertation titles and abstracts contained here are published with permission of University Microfilms International, publishers of *Dissertation Abstracts International* (copyright © 1969 by University Microfilms International), and may not be reproduced without their prior permission.

FRANKLIN'S STYLE: IRONY AND THE COMIC. ⎤————1

(Order No. 66-9892)⎤————2

Nancy Tenfelde Clasby, Ph.D.
The University of Wisconsin, 1966⎤————3

Supervisor: Professor Harry Hayden Clark⎤————4

Since Benjamin Franklin's style is the product and essence
of a lifetime of expressive action, an analysis of it should
bring us closer to an understanding of his extremely complex
man. My dissertation is aimed at collating and interpreting
those elements of his style which will help to fill in the outlines of the figure which modern Franklin scholars have only
begun to discover. There are three parts to this dissertation:
the first deals with the expressive character of certain elements of style, the second with Franklin's mind, the source
of expression, and the third, and longest, section presents and
interprets statistics on such features of his style as parallel-
ism, metaphor and tone. The comic and ironic tones which
inform so much of Franklin's best work are treated at length
in the third section.

••• ••• ••• ••• ••• ••• ••• ••• ••• ••• ••• ••• •••

Reservations about the eighteenth-century world and its
values did not, however, dull Franklin's passion for communication. In life, Franklin was an _eiron_, a maskmaker whose
activities were shaped to present various appearances when
seen from various angles. He made sure that people saw only
those aspects of himself that they were capable of recognizing
as parts of some coherent personality. In its myriad delicate
adjustments to varied audiences his prose bears the marks of
the same consuming effort to clarify, to make sense. The
style is concrete and direct, never abstract, seldom merely
decorative. It aims at the attractive statement of certain
limited truths, and its aspect changes as Franklin adopts
various masks. Beneath the multiple surface characteristics
of the style, however, is a radical unity, a gestalt which reflects in miniature the quality and direction of a lifetime of
communicative gestures. The whole effort of this paper, in
its various parts, is directed toward a clarification of the full
outlines of a carefully structured life and style.

273 pages.⎤ 5

**Fig. 30: From
_Dissertation
Abstracts
International_**
1. Title of
dissertation **2.** Order
number if you desire
to buy a copy of the
work **3.** Author,
school, and date
4. Faculty chairman
of the dissertation
committee **5.** Total
number of pages of
the dissertation

An abstract, of course, is only a brief summary of the entire work. If the dissertation is pertinent to your topic or if you plan an exhaustive investigation, you
may wish to order a copy of the complete work from University Microfilms,
Inc.

Indexes to Literature in Periodicals

The use of articles in periodicals is a must. Articles provide the following four types of information better than any other source. They contain: the most recent articles on any subject; obscure, temporary, or extremely new materials; the climate of opinion of a particular period; and supplements to professional literature. Remember, too, that materials often appear as journal articles before their publication in book form.

There are two main types of periodicals: general periodicals (for example, *Time, Ladies' Home Journal, Reader's Digest*) and professional journals (for example, *American Historical Review, Journal of Psychology,* or *National Tax Journal*). You will use both types, of course, but you should depend mainly upon the learned journals whose treatment of topics is more critically detailed.

As an index to articles in periodicals, you should first investigate:

Readers' Guide to Periodical Literature. New York: H. W. Wilson, 1900–date.

A sample entry follows:

Fig. 31: From *Readers' Guide to Periodical Literature*
1. Subject 2. A piece by Franklin himself 3. Designates that the following articles are *about* Franklin 4. Title of article 5. Author 6. Illustrated with portraits 7. Indicates a review: Van Doren's book *Benjamin Franklin* was reviewed in *Commonweal* by J. Cournos 8. Name of periodical and publication data

FRANKLIN, Benjamin —1
Benjamin Franklin meets the press; excerpts from his writings. por facsim Scholastic 67:14-15 Ja 12 '56
Benjamin Franklin on his religious faith; letter to Ezra Stiles. Am Heritage 7:105 D '55 —2
Excerpts from his voluminous writings. por N Y Times Mag p76 Ja 15 '56
Farther experiments and observations in electricity; excerpt from Experiments and observations on electricity. bibliog Science 123:47-50 Ja 13 '56
From Ben's letters. Time 67:90 Ja 30 '56
Mr Franklin, self-revealed. facsim Life 40:74-7+ Ja 9 '56
about —3
Americana page. Hobbies 61:100 Jl '56
Ben Franklin: an affectionate portrait, by N. B. Keyes. Review
Sat R 39:16 Ja 21 '56. W. M. Wallace
Ben Franklin, trail blazer for inventors. P. Lee. il pors map Pop Mech 105:99-102+ Ja '56 —4
Benjamin and the bell. M. Alkus. Ladies Home J 72:180 Ap '55 —5
Benjamin Franklin and the French alliance; adapted from Secret war of independence. H. Augur. il por Am Heritage 7:65-88 Ap '56 —6
Benjamin Franklin, by C. Van Doren. Review
Commonweal 63:497 F 10 '56. J. Cournos —7
Benjamin Franklin in modern life and education. T. Woody. Sch & Soc 84:102-7 S 29 '56
Benjamin Franklin the diplomat. por U S Dept State Bul 34:50-1 Ja 9 '56
Benjamin Franklin's grand design; Albany plan of union. R. B. Morris. il por map Am Heritage 7:4-7+ F '56 —8

Again, you would want to write out bibliography cards for those entries that look promising, as in the following example:

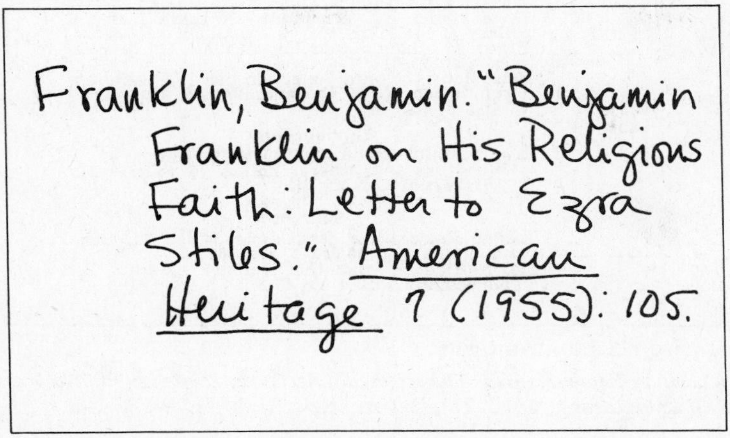

Fig. 32:
Bibliography Card
for Entry Taken
from *Readers'
Guide to Periodical
Literature*

Franklin, Benjamin. "Benjamin Franklin on His Religious Faith: Letter to Ezra Stiles." <u>American Heritage</u> 7 (1955): 105.

In most instances, this index directs you to general periodicals, though since 1953 certain scientific periodicals have been included. If you wish a more in-depth examination of the scholarly journals, such as *New England Quarterly* and *Political Science Quarterly,* you should investigate the following (listed in chronological order):

International Index. Vols. 1–18. New York: H. W. Wilson, 1907–65.
Social Sciences and Humanities Index. Vols. 19–61. New York: H. W. Wilson, 1965–74.
Humanities Index. Vols. 1– . New York: H. W. Wilson, 1974–date.
Social Sciences Index. Vols. 1– . New York: H. W. Wilson, 1974–date.

Both the new *Humanities Index* and the *Social Sciences Index* supersede the *Social Sciences and Humanities Index.* The *Humanities Index* now serves as an index to articles in 260 magazines in the following fields: archaeology, classical studies, area studies, folklore, history, language and literature, literary and political criticism, performing arts, philosophy, religion, and theology. *Social Sciences Index* catalogs articles in 263 magazines in these fields: anthropology, economics, environmental science, geography, law and criminology, medical sciences, political science, psychology, public administration, and sociology.

A sample entry from the 1960–62 issue of the *International Index* lists the following sources on Benjamin Franklin:

Fig. 33: From
International Index
1. Subject **2.** Title of
article **3.** Author
4. Name of journal
and publication data

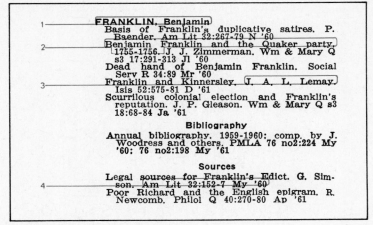

You may also need to investigate:

Nineteenth Century Readers' Guide to Periodical Literature, 1890–1899 [with
supplementary indexing, 1900–22]. 2 vols. New York: H. W. Wilson,
1944.

Poole's Index to Periodical Literature, 1802–1881. Rev. ed. Boston: Houghton
Mifflin, 1891. Supplements cover the years 1882–1906.

With this work you may locate information on materials from 1802–1906.
Note that *Poole's Index* has only a subject classification list. See, however,
Marion V. Bell and Jean C. Bacon, *Poole's Index Date and Volume Key*
(Chicago: Association of College and Reference Libraries, 1957) for an
alphabetical title listing.

Newspaper Indexes

Newspapers are an excellent source of information. Therefore, you should
familiarize yourself with the *New York Times Index* (New York: New York
Times, 1913–date). It not only indexes the *New York Times* but also indirectly
indexes most other newspapers by revealing the date on which the same news was
probably reported in other newspapers. Many libraries have the *New York Times*
on microfilm. A sample entry from the *New York Times Index* follows:

Fig. 34: From *New*
York Times Index
1. Subject **2.** Cross
reference **3.** Date,
section number, and
page number
(November 25,
Section 8, p. 22)

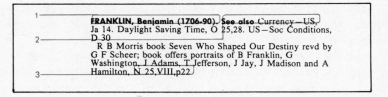

For British newspapers a similar index is the *Official Index* [to *The London
Times*] (London: Times, 1907–date). It is available in most American public and
university libraries.

Pamphlet Indexes

The principal index to most pamphlet material is:

Vertical File Index: A Subject and Title Index to Selected Pamphlet Material.
New York: H. W. Wilson, 1932/35–date.

Your library may not own many of the items listed, but the catalog gives a description of each entry, the price, and the means by which you may order the pamphlet.

Microforms

Your library has a choice when ordering periodicals. It may buy either printed issues and volumes or microfilm versions of the same material. The Cardex file or Periodicals Index at your library will specify how journals and magazines are housed. You may discover, for example, that current year issues of a journal are kept in printed forms but that issues of prior years are on microfilm. Therefore, check the Periodicals Index regularly because you may find a missing issue of a printed volume on microfilm.

Most college libraries now store national newspapers and dissertation abstracts on microfilm. Therefore, consult the following:

The New York Times Index. New York: New York Times Co., annually.
Wall Street Journal Index. New York: Dow Jones, annually.
Bell and Howell's Index to the Christian Science Monitor. Wooster, Ohio:
  Christian Science Publishing Society, annually.
Dissertation Abstracts International. Ann Arbor: Univ. Microfilms, annually.

You should also watch for other indexes or guides to microfilm holdings at your library. These guides will carry such titles as *American Culture 1493–1806: A Guide to the Microfilm Collection* or perhaps *American Periodicals 1800–1850: A Guide to the Microfilm Collection.*

The point is this: every library has its own peculiar holdings of microfilm and microfiche materials. Your obligation as researcher will be to familiarize yourself with these holdings.

SEARCHING THE COMPUTER DATABASES

After your development of bibliography cards from the indexes located in the reference room, you may wish to consult with the library staff in the computer room to review database files. You may wish to order a bibliographic/retrospective search of your topic (especially if you have multifaceted aspects of a subject) since the computer terminal at your library connects into a national network of research files.

Let's suppose that your topic concerns the deregulation of the trucking industry. Your first responsibility will be to examine basic printed indexes and bibliographies under single concept headings, such as "trucking" or "deregulation" or "freight." Such monolithic subjects are examined easier in printed indexes, such as *Readers' Guide to Periodical Literature,* than by computer. If you determine that additional sources may be necessary, you may request a database search. If so, the computer librarian will ask you to complete a "Search Request," which features questions such as those in the following sample:

SEARCH REQUEST

Your name _____ Campus Box No. _____

1. If your paper were finished, what title would best describe its content?

2. List all specific topics, synonyms, closely related phrases, and alternate spellings of your subject, using scientific, technical, and common names:

3. Explain any interrelationship of any terms listed above in item 2.

4. List related topics that you wish to exclude in order to narrow the search.

5. Do you desire any foreign language entries? Which languages?

6. Do you wish to limit citations to a publication year(s)?

7. Which do you prefer: A narrow search of discrete ideas _____
                          A broad search of general topics _____

The purpose of this questionnaire should be fairly obvious: the computer operator needs terminology to feed into the database file.

You will also pay a fee that might range from $5.00 all the way up to $60 or $70. Fee schedules vary from university to university with some libraries absorbing the cost but with others charging you for computer time. You should determine these charges *in advance.*

Next, the computer librarian will interview you to formulate terminology for the computer and to select specific files for searching. A file contains a collection of similar records as created by a database producer, such as ERIC (Education Resources Information Center), which produces two files: *Research in Education* and *Current Index to Journals in Education.* Your library's computer terminal will be connected to a national database vendor. This vendor transmits various files, such as the ERIC files, by telephone hookup to users like your college library. The primary computer might be located in California; you and your library are logged on by means of a local terminal and a telephone module.

Therefore, at the appropriate time your computer librarian will log on to the file via the telephone module. Before that time you must select proper terminology for your topic, let's say a trucking industry article, because the computer will only read the language of the file(s) that you choose to search:

    trucking industry
    deregulation
    rules and regulations
    freight
    transportation
    automotive-freight

These key words, known as descriptors, will be determined in part by a computer dictionary and/or computer thesaurus, such as:

Thesaurus of ERIC Descriptors
Energy Data Base Subject Thesaurus
Medical Subject Headings
Thesaurus of Psychological Index Terms

The key terms will form the duality or triad of a retrospective search, which scans the citation history of these terms. In this instance, the key words of your subject profile are:

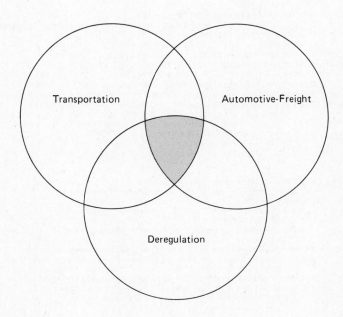

The computer will browse through records to select only those that match the darkened area, that is, all records that feature in title and content the three key terms. Your librarian, having selected File 148: *Trade and Industry Index,* will now dial up by telephone module the appropriate
database ——→
                logs on ——→
                                enters subject profile ——→
                                                begins computer search ——→
until the printout of a report is handed to you, as shown below:

Fig. 35: From *Trade*   Print 99/5/1-5
and Industry Index   DIALOG File148: Trade and Industry Index - 81-83/Apr

            1089910   DATABASE: NNI File 111
            **Piggybacks make inroads on trucking. (piggyback rail-freight
            traffic)**
              Salpukas, Agis
              New York Times   v131   p31(N) pD1(L)   June 16   1982
              CODEN: NYTIA
              col 3   030 col in.
              illustration; photograph; graph
              EDITION: Wed
              SIC CODE: 4210; 40LL
              CAPTIONS: Piggyback freight traffic.
              NAMED PEOPLE: Boyd, David M.-quotations
              DESCRIPTORS: piggyback transportation-economic aspects;
            transportation,   automotive-freight;   railroads-freight;
            freight-cars   on   truck   trailers-economic   aspects;
            Conrail-officials and employees;   transportation   and
            state-rules and regulations
              IDENTIFIERS: deregulation-railroads

            0957807   DATABASE: TI File 148
            **ICC to open hearings regarding trucking licenses for
            Canadian, U.S. carriers.**
              Feedstuffs   v54   p2(2)   April 12   1982
              GEOGRAPHIC LOCATION: United States; Canada
              GEOGRAPHIC CODE: NNUS; NNCN   SIC CODE: 9621; 4210
              DESCRIPTORS: United   States.   Interstate   Commerce
            Commission-investigations; transportation, automotive-freight;
            carriers-international aspects; United States-relations with
            Canada; Canada-relations with the United States; American
            Trucking Associations Inc.-political activity; Motor Carrier
            Act of 1980-interpretation and construction;   industry and
            state-international aspects
              IDENTIFIERS: deregulation-transportation

            0828784   DATABASE: TI File 148
            Export shifts help shape transport needs.
              Marsh, Barb
              Feedstuffs   v54   p1(2)   Feb 8   1982
              SIC CODE: 4000
              NAMED PEOPLE: Fruin, Jerry-addresses, essays, lectures
              DESCRIPTORS: Farmers'   Elevator   Association   of
            Minnesota-meetings;   farm   produce-transportation;   export
            sales-statistics; food supply-economic aspects; transportatio-
            n, automotive-freight; road construction-finance; inland water
            transportation-economic aspects; agriculture and state-econom-
            ic aspects; railroads and state-economic aspects
              IDENTIFIERS: deregulation-railroads

If this list seems limited in scope (and it is), then you and the computer librarian might try another file, such as *Management Contents,* which might produce this:

Print 99/5/1-6
DIALOG File75: Management Contents - 74-83/Mar

Fig. 36: From
Management
Contents

208773   HSM82CO074
The New Movers and Shakers.
Becker, H.G.
Handling & Shipping Management, Vol.23, No.3,March 1982, P. 74-80., Journal.
With the passage of various trucking deregulation legislation and the Household Goods Act of 1980, van lines have begun to offer innovative types of services that had not formerly been possible under the previous regulatory environment. The economic recession forcing many people to become less mobile has also had a dramatic impact on van line marketing strategy. Various major van lines are now offering volume discounts for national account shippers, specialized service for certain commodities, and complete settling-in services for corporate transferees. North American Van Lines is even hauling general freight through one of its commercial divisions. The re-regulation of the moving industry will mean van lines will continue to change their traditional ways for new innovative ones.
Descriptors: Motor Carriers; Household Goods; Trucking Industry; United States; Transportation; Deregulation; 1208; 1619; 0833; 0528; 0274; 0188

205162   HSM82AO026
Stuck With Overcapacity, Truckers Await the Recovery.
Gallagher, P.
Handling & Shipping Management, Vol.23, No.1,Jan. 1982, P. 26-30., Journal.
A weak economy, the regulatory reform of the Motor Carrier Act of 1980 and changes in ERISA have all combined to create overcapacity in the trucking industry. Deregulation has allowed many new carriers to enter the market at the same time tonnage is down. Company mergers and consolidations have become more difficult under a new amendment to ERISA; the Multi-Employer Pension Plan Amendments Act makes a unionized carrier's pension liability so large that it cannot go out of business or merge. Many large companies who would otherwise go bankrupt are forced to continue operations at losing levels just to stay in compliance with ERISA. Independent non-unionized carriers are offering freight discounts which the unionized carriers cannot match or compete with; they have instead countered with better service packages. The trucking industry's outlook in 1982 will be poor. An economic turnaround will be its only recovery, even with expected union wage freezes and work rule changes.
Descriptors: Transportation; Trucking Industry; Outlook; Deregulation; Motor Carriers; Motor Carrier Law; ERISA; United States; 0274; 0833; 0564; 0188; 1208; 1846; 0736; 0528

205017   FBR82AO4I3
Truckers and Shippers.
Brophy, B.
Forbes, Vol.129, No.1, Jan. 4, 1982, P. 193-194., Journal.
Truckers and shippers are charted by profitability ratings. The Interstate Commerce Commission is attempting to slow deregulation on technicalities.
Descriptors: Trucking Industry; Shipping; Ratings; Profitability; Deregulation; ICC; Interstate Commerce Commission; Charts; 0833; 0634; 2460; 0972; 0188; 0927; 0301; 1227

You must now determine if these sources add to your working bibliography. Generally, librarians discourage undergraduate use of computer searches for two reasons. First, a beginning researcher needs traditional training in the basic indexes and bibliographies, and second, the computer is cost-effective on *large* retrospective searches, not on narrow research paper subjects. After all, the database vendors charge the library about $75 per hour when logged on. Your library may pass on to you these entire charges.

Yet the day rapidly approaches when the printed indexes will disappear to be replaced by floppy disks and a computer printout. For instance, rather than search the printed volumes of *Readers' Guide to Literature,* you will in the future sit down at a small computer, enter the floppy disk for a specific period, say 1960–65, and scan the terminal screen for your topic. If the list looks good to you, then you will order a printout on the high speed printer and soon be on your way.

Already, *Biological Abstracts* is available on B-I-T-S, which is a floppy disk system. This new BITTERN software creates files and performs retrospective searches on the small microcomputers. Many more systems like B-I-T-S will become available during this decade.

The following list by disciplines names a few files now available for computer searching. The list is by no means comprehensive, but it should provide you with enough files to begin a retrospective search.

Current Affairs

Biography Master Index

> Information on 2 million people from 600 source publications

Comprehensive Dissertation Index

> About 800,000 abstracts of virtually every American dissertation written

Congressional Record Abstracts

> Provides comprehensive abstracts for each issue of the *Congressional Record,* which is the printed version of Senate and House proceedings

Federal Register Abstracts

> Provides coverage of activities of federal agencies

GPO Monthly Catalog

> Contains Government Printing Office records of federal reports, studies, maps, handbooks, proceedings, etc.

Magazine Index

> Covers the contents of about 400 popular magazines for coverage of current affairs, leisure time, travel, sports, the home, business, etc.

National Newspaper Index

> Indexes *The New York Times, The Wall Street Journal,* and the *Christian Science Monitor*

Newsearch

> A daily index of over 2000 news articles from 1400 newspapers and periodicals; at month's end magazine data is transferred to *Magazine Index* (see above) and newspaper data is transferred to *National Newspaper Index* (see above)

Science

Agricola

> A massive database file of agriculture by the National Agricultural Library

Biosis Previews

> Indexes *Biological Abstracts* and provides coverage of nearly 8,000 journals of biology, botany, zoology, etc.

CA Search

> Indexes *Chemical Abstracts*

Excerpta Medica

> Indexes over 3500 biomedical journals

Geoarchive

> Indexes thousands of geology journals, books, dissertations, and conferences

Georef

> The database of the American Geological Institute

Medline

> Corresponds to printed indexes: *Index Medicus, Index to Dental Literature,* and *International Nursing Index*

Scisearch

> Multidisciplinary index to records published in *Science Citation Index* and *Current Contents*

SPIN (Searchable Physics Information Notices)

> Indexes the physics journals

Applied Science and Technology

Aptic

> Indexes air pollution journals

Aquaculture

> Provides access to information on marine and freshwater organisms

Claims/Uniterm

> Database of chemical patents, 1950–present

Compendex

> Database version of *Engineering Index,* 1970–present

Doe Energy

> Indexes all aspects of energy and related topics

Environmental Bibliography

> A database of ecology, energy, land and water resources, and nutrition

FSTA

> Indexes *Food Science and Technology Abstracts*

International Pharmaceutical Abstracts

> Indexes all important pharmaceutical and medical journals, 1970–present.

ISMEC

> Index of mechanical engineering

TRIS

> Provides transportation information for air, highway, rail, and maritime

Social Sciences and Humanities

ERIC

> A massive index of educational materials

Historical Abstracts

> A database for history and related social sciences

MLA Bibliography

> Indexes articles on language, literature, and linguistics, 1976 with annual updates

NICEM

> Indexes non-print educational materials such as films, filmstrips, recordings, video tapes, etc.

PAIS (Public Affairs Information Service)

> Database to political science, banking, economics, sociology, etc.

PHILOSOPHER'S INDEX

> Provides indexing to over 270 philosophy journals

PSYCINFO (formerly *Psychological Abstracts*)

> Covers the world's literature on psychology and the behavioral sciences, including *Psychological Abstracts*

Social Scisearch

> Indexes about 1000 social science journals as well as social science articles in other journals

Sociological Abstracts

> Database for literature of sociology and related disciplines from about 1200 journals

Business and Economics

Economics Abstracts International

> Database on economic data from about 1800 journals

Labor Statistics

> A database of eight subfiles on labor and price indices

Management Contents

> Indexes areas of accounting, marketing, administration, etc.

PTS F&S Index

> Database on corporate affairs such as acquisitions, mergers, new products, technological developments, etc.

PTS International Time Series

> Contains two subfiles: *Worldcasts Composites* on population, income, employment, etc., by country and *Worldcasts Basebook* on production and consumption by country

Standard & Poor's News

> Indexes information on more than 9000 U.S. companies, especially earnings, dividends, and stock values

FINDING THE CALL NUMBER

Sometime before completing your work in the reference room, you probably will want to begin preliminary investigations of some of the more promising sources you have listed on your bibliography cards. For that purpose you should turn to the card catalog, which specifies the location of all books in the library.

(For periodicals most libraries have a separate, smaller catalog, sometimes called a *cardex*.) With your bibliography cards arranged alphabetically, you can easily find and record the call number for each book. Some libraries now have computerized card catalogs; that is, you must use a computer terminal to call up subject listings, authors and their works, or single titles. You may then either write out your call numbers or order a printout.

For each book you will usually find at least three separate entries in the catalog, filed under: (1) the author's name, printed on the first line (see below); (2) the title of the work, typed in black ink at the top of the card (see 65); and (3) the subject, typed in red ink at the top of the card (see 14). Additional catalog cards are filed for coauthors, translators, editors, illustrators, and for other subject headings.

Main Entry Card

As you go through the card catalog you will quickly discover that there is a main entry card for each book you are seeking, usually filed under the author's name. For example:

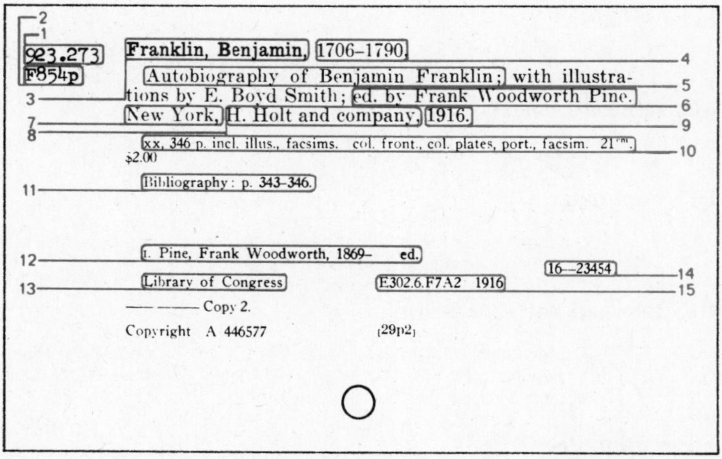

Fig. 37: Main Entry Card (Author Card)
1. Classification number **2.** Author number **3.** Author **4.** Life span of author. **5.** Title **6.** Editor **7.** Place of publication **8.** Publisher **9.** Date of publication **10.** Technical description: size, number of pages, illustrations, etc. **11.** Note on contents of book **12.** Separate card also filed under editor's name **13.** Publisher of this card **14.** Order number-Library of Congress **15.** Library of Congress Call Number and date

```
 ┌─2
 ┌─1
 923.273   Franklin, Benjamin, 1706–1790.                        ─4
 F854p        Autobiography of Benjamin Franklin; with illustra- ─5
 3──────── tions by E. Boyd Smith; ed. by Frank Woodworth Pine.  ─6
 7──────── New York, H. Holt and company, 1916.                  ─9
 8──────
              xx, 346 p. incl. illus., facsims.  col. front., col. plates, port., facsim.  21ᶜᵐ. ─10
              $2.00

 11──────     Bibliography: p. 343–346.


 12──────     I. Pine, Frank Woodworth, 1869–      ed.)
                                                                [16—23454]
 13──────     Library of Congress       E302.6.F7A2  1916        ─14
                                                                ─15
              ──── ──── Copy 2.
              Copyright  A 446577                    [29p2]


                              ◯
```

You may gather several kinds of information from this main entry card. Specifically, you should record the *complete* call number—in this case, $\frac{923.273}{F854p}$. Do not copy the first line only! You must have the full number, usually consisting of two (and sometimes three) lines of symbols. In addition, you should record any bibliographical notations, such as "Bibliography: 343–46." Data of this sort can direct you to additional sources.

Title Card

Another card is always filed alphabetically by the book title:

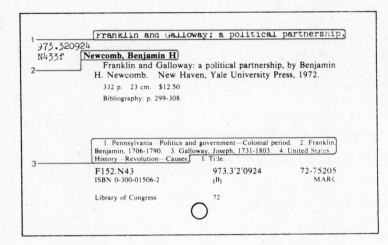

Fig. 38: Title Card
1. Title, usually typed in black ink
2. Main entry card filed under "Newcomb, Benjamin H."
3. Subject headings under which you will find this same card

A third type of card found in the catalog is the subject card—but we will come to that in a moment. (See also Chapter 1, 14, on using subject cards to restrict your topic.)

The Call Number

The library classifies and arranges its books by the call number, which is usually a combination of the Dewey Decimal System and the Cutter Author Number. In a call number such as $\frac{973.320924}{N433f}$, the first line is the Dewey Decimal Number and the second line is the Cutter Author Number. The Dewey system divides all books into ten general classifications:

000–099 General Works
100–199 Philosophy
200–299 Religion
300–399 Social Sciences
400–499 Language
500–599 Pure Science
600–699 Technology (Applied Sciences)
700–799 The Arts
800–899 Literature
900–999 History

The Dewey system then divides each of these ten general classes into ten smaller divisions. For example, the general literature classification (800–899) is broken down into:

800–809 General Works [on Literature]
810–819 American Literature
820–829 English Literature
830–839 German Literature
840–849 French Literature
850–859 Italian Literature
860–869 Spanish Literature
870–879 Latin Literature
880–889 Greek and Classical Literature
890–899 Literature of Other Languages

Next, American Literature (810–819) is divided into the following classifications:

810 American Literature (General)
811 Poetry
812 Drama
813 Fiction
814 Essays
815 Speeches
816 Letters
817 Satire and Humor
818 Miscellany
819 Minor Related Literature

Immediately below the Dewey classification number, most libraries also insert an author number, a set of letters and numerals based on the Cutter Three-Figure Author Table. For example, "N433f" is the author number for Newcomb's *Franklin and Galloway*. The letter "N" is the initial of the author's last name; next the Cutter table stipulates the Arabic numeral "433"; and the lowercase "f" designates the first important letter(s) in the title to distinguish this entry from similar books by Newcomb. Thus, the complete call number for Newcomb's book is $\frac{973.320924}{N433f}$. You must use both items to locate the book.

Some libraries employ the Library of Congress classification system, which features capital letters followed by Arabic numerals to designate the subdivisions. The major divisions of the Library of Congress system follow:

A General Works and Polygraphy
B Philosophy and Religion
C History and Auxiliary Sciences
D History and Topography
  (excluding America)
E-F History: America
 G Geography and Anthropology
 H Social Sciences
  J Political Science
 K Law
 L Education
M Music
 N Fine Arts
 P Language and Literature
 Q Science
 R Medicine
  S Agriculture and Plant and Animal Husbandry
 T Technology
 U Military Science
 V Naval Science
 Z Bibliography and Library Science

An example of this system might be as follows:

 TD Environmental Technology
 833 Air Pollution
.H48 Author Number

This call number for the Library of Congress system directs the researcher to the following book: Howard E. Hesketh, *Understanding and Controlling Air Pollution,* 2nd ed. (Ann Arbor, Michigan: Ann Arbor Science Publishers, 1974). In contrast, the Dewey classification number would be $\frac{628.53}{H461u}$.

Other Catalog Cards

Always be alert for special kinds of catalog cards. Temporary cards are of a different color and usually indicate that a book is not in circulation. However, ask the librarian about the book, for it may be available.

```
923.273
F854lab      Franklin, Benjamin



             The autobiography of Benjamin
        Franklin, edited by Leonard W. Labaree and
        others. New Haven, Yale University Press,
        1964.

        Now on temporary display in the History
        Today book display in the Roberta White
        Reading Room, second floor
```

Cross-reference cards refer you to alternate or related headings. There are two types. The "see" card indicates the correct heading under which material is listed, while the "see also" card directs you to related subjects that contain additional material:

```
        United States--History--Revolution

            see also

        Pennsylvania--Politics and government--
            Colonial period
```

Your best procedure with the card catalog is a combination of practices: you can easily record call numbers while you search for new sources. For example, with your bibliography cards in hand, you should look first under the proper subject heading—"Franklin, Benjamin," in this instance. There you will find index cards for all books *by* Franklin that precede the books *about* him. At the same time, you will learn the call numbers for most of your sources. Also, you may uncover new sources that supplement your working bibliography.

SUPPLEMENTING LIBRARY MATERIALS

Without doubt the library is your best source of information when writing a research paper. But you may also find material in other places. For instance, you could write your U.S. senator or representative for one of the many booklets printed by the Government Printing Office. You will find a list of these materials, many of which are free, in a monthly catalog issued by the Superintendent of Documents, *United States Government Publications Monthly Catalog* (Washington, D.C.: GPO, 1895–date).

Also important are audiovisual materials: films, filmstrips, music, phonograph recordings, slides, and tape recordings. You may find these in the library or in some other location on or off campus.

Other good sources of information are: radio and television programs, lectures, letters, public addresses, personal interviews, and questionnaires.

3
Taking Notes

After preliminary investigations in the library, it's time to take stock of your progress. For example, as you gathered materials for your working bibliography cards, you should also have uncovered and skimmed briefly into some of the more promising books and articles. For these you will have gained an initial familiarity with your general subject. You must now narrow the focus of your future research, as framed by a preliminary thesis sentence and a rough topic outline. You can afford neither the time nor the effort of taking notes on a scattered, hit-or-miss basis. The information in every note should answer a research question or relate to an issue of your topic's preliminary thesis. Careful note-taking will thereby narrow the subject even more.

THE PRELIMINARY OUTLINE

Before you progress very far in your note-taking, you should prepare a preliminary outline (the final outline comes only after note-taking). This early outline is a rough sketch of your major concerns, based upon ideas that you have absorbed while choosing and restricting your subject. It serves the valuable purpose of giving order to your note-taking, thereby enabling you to evaluate and choose quotations and material for paraphrase more wisely.

To develop the preliminary outline, follow two fairly simple steps: (1) jot down your ideas in a rough list and (2) arrange the list into major and minor ideas. Suppose, for example, that your general topic is ''Child Abuse'' and your preliminary thesis sentence states: ''The parents, not just the children, should be a major focus of social concern.'' Your rough list might look something like this:

discipline

the battered child

social workers

parents or the unfit parent

step-parents

sexual abuse

short-term effects

long-term consequences

agencies and organizations

case studies

physical abuse

psychological abuse

neglect

mistreatment

aggression

behavioral patterns

The list might be longer; it could be shorter. Obviously, it needs order, but your major ideas may now be examined for relationships and categories. If you organize the items, grouping main topics and relating subordinate elements to them, you will, in turn, develop a rough outline for your paper. One possible arrangement is shown here:

Rough Outline

The Battered Child
  Discipline
  Physical abuse
  Psychological abuse
Effects
  Physical
  Mental
Public Concern
  Governmental Agencies
  Private Organizations
Spotting Unfit Parents
  Mothers
  Fathers
  Friends
  Step-Parents

The outline above is sketchy, but it guides note-taking because you know the type of material to search out during research reading and note-taking. This early outline might prove wholly inadequate for writing the first draft, but you will have an opportunity to develop a final outline after your basic note-taking. For now, however, you have a fairly good idea of things to search for in books and articles—that is, case studies of abuse, physical and mental effects, information on abusing parents, and material about the agencies that seem active in this social arena.

Question Outline

Another method for bringing order to your note-taking would be the preliminary question outline, as follows:

What is child abuse?

How does it differ from "discipline"?

What causes abuse?

How prevalent is it?

What are short-term consequences?

What are long-term consequences?

What can the average citizen do about it?

Using this question method of outlining before note-taking, you develop clear directions for your reading. Each note card, as it develops, should fit under one of these questions or possibly provoke another question. Keep in mind that each question above could be the basis for an entire paper. Always look for ways to narrow your topic.

Rhetorical Outline

A third method used successfully by some writers features the rhetorical outline. With this method you jot down those modes of development that best suit your topic, as follows:

Definition of abuse

Contrast abuse with discipline

Statistics of incidents (by age, sex, types, etc.)

Examples and case studies of abuse

Causes with focus on parents

Consequences with focus on children

Again, the writer of this preliminary outline has clear guidelines for note-taking. For example, he knows that he needs a good definition, several case studies, plenty of cause-effect material on both parents and children, and statistical evidence to document frequency, age, or sex.

Deductive Outline

Remember that you may arrange your preliminary concepts in the topic outline in one of two structures, either general to particular (deductive order) or particular to general (inductive order). If you arrange your note materials deductively, you must first have a general concept that you want to support with specific details and instances. For example, your paper on child abuse might originate with generalizations about the long-term consequences of child abuse. Your note cards must then cite particulars and specifics to support the generalizations.

> Thesis: Child abuse reaches beyond the formative years into the adult life of the abused child.
>
> Physical impairment
>
> Psychological disorders
>
> Withdrawal from society
>
> Marital strife
>
> Abuse of his/her own children

This rough outline indicates the specific areas you have to research in order to defend your opening generalization. Note that the deductive procedure may be used in other kinds of research papers: stating the theme of a novel and then searching out details from the work to prove it, presenting the conclusions of an experiment and then uncovering the particulars of the methods and testing, or declaring the ruthlessness of a political dictator and then surveying the evidence.

Inductive Outline

In other papers, however, you may wish to explore the particulars inductively before arriving at your conclusions. In this preliminary topic outline plan, you first consider the specifics of your argument and then work carefully toward a general conclusion. For example, the person writing about child abuse might examine and take notes on several case studies before arriving at any generalizations. Before offering any answers, this researcher would examine:

> Case study A
>
> Case study B
>
> Case study C
>
> Compare the three cases
>
> Focus on causal elements (that is, parents in each case, perhaps, have been abused themselves)

This writer is less certain about the thesis, but the nature of the research procedure assures an orderly search for conclusions

Altering the Preliminary Outline

Brief as they are, rough outlines, whether on paper or in your head, help you locate and record the important, necessary data and omit information that may look valuable but that contributes little to the overall plan. The preliminary outline is almost always ragged and incomplete, but only you will see it. Such outlines represent the best you can do before your note-taking is very far along.

Always be prepared to alter the outline as your focus on the literature sharpens your thinking, especially as you discover ways to narrow the topic. In that regard, evaluate your role in three specific areas, as demonstrated below:

My role as researcher: To examine the literature about child abuse and to comment on one specific aspect of it.

My preliminary thesis: Parents of abused children may be victims themselves—of their marriage, their backgrounds, their economic condition.

My audience: Concerned, intelligent readers who want discussion of substantive issues, not quick-fix solutions.

As shown above, you may decide to examine the parent or guardian more than the abused child, or you may decide to limit the study to sexual abuse. In either case, you should periodically adjust your outline accordingly. The rough outline is not a binding contract. Instead, let it develop and grow: add new topics and discard others, rearrange your order, evaluate topics, and subordinate minor elements. In short, as your ideas materialize, you should allow your outline to expand or tighten accordingly. (For additional tips about writing your final outline, see Chapter 4, 102–109).

EVALUATING YOUR SOURCE MATERIALS

Relevance to Your Topic

Limitations established by your rough outline will help you determine the value a book or article has for your research. Learn to skim articles and sections of books to determine their relevance to your specific needs. When you discover something pertinent, you can then write accurate, detailed notes, recording only that material which will aid in the development and clarification of the thesis and outline.

With magazine and journal articles you might read the opening and closing for relevance, turning to the body of the article only if it appears promising. With a book you face a larger task. When you pull a book from the shelf, look at the following:

1. The *title and subtitle* determine relevance. *Children and Parents* may look ideal for a child abuse topic until you read the subtitle: *Children and Parents: Growing Up in New Guinea*. Literary titles, more so than scientific ones, cause confusion; for example, *The Crying Children* might look promising until you note the subtitle: *The Crying Children: Poems of Nostalgia*. Check subtitles whenever possible at the card catalog. Better sources would be: a book entitled *Physical and Sexual Abuse of Children: Cause and Treatment* or a journal article, ''The Incidence of Child Abuse in the United States.''

2. The *index* of the book lists specific concepts, events, and names with page numbers where they are mentioned within the text. The index will tell you whether the book discusses your subject at all. Professional researchers turn almost automatically to the back of a book and begin their examination of it with the index. For example, the student researching child abuse should look in a book's index under ''child abuse,'' ''abuse,'' and ''children'' to determine the book's value to his or her study. If the entire text is devoted to child abuse, then you may look for specific issues, such as ''sexual abuse'' or ''alcoholic parents.''

3. The *table of contents* helps you discover the chapters that deal directly or indirectly with your topic. You may find, for example, that only one chapter is potentially useful for your study.

4. The *preface or introduction* might serve as a critical overview of the entire book, pinpointing the primary subject of the text and approaches taken toward it.

5. The *appendix* offers additional materials of a supplementary nature not pertinent to the primary text but perhaps important to your study. Charts and graphs are often placed in an appendix.

6. The *glossary* lists and defines complex terminology within the subject area. On this note, you would do well to continually jot down words and phrases related to your topic so that later, when writing your rough draft, you may draw appropriate terminology from the list.

7. The *bibliography and footnotes* suggest new sources for later investigation. Some of your best sources will be added to your own bibliography during the note-taking phase of research. When the same names keep appearing time and again in the citations, then you have a clue to the best authorities.

Recent Sources

Be sure to use the most recent, reliable sources of information. You may find a book that treats your topic extensively, but if the copyright date is 1938, then the content becomes suspect. Time and new developments have passed beyond the 1938 text, unless, of course, the writer has updated it with new editions (in which case you should search out the newest version) or unless the work is a classic in its field.

Knowledge now doubles every few years. Topics in scientific and technical fields require up-to-date research to the point that recent copyright dates may become mandatory for your study. Scientific textbooks are often out of date in some sections almost as soon as they are printed. Therefore, you must learn to depend upon the monthly and quarterly journals more than books.

One additional advantage of a recent publication will be its reviews of previous works in the field. A 1983 overview of prior works enables you to expand your working bibliography cards with recognized sources.

Quote the Best Scholars

The most influential authorities on your topic are usually mentioned again and again in the sources you uncover. Whatever the field, the names of certain key authors come up often, and it would pay to look at their work(s). For example, in black studies there is Martin Luther King, Jr.; in early space rocketry there is Wernher von Braun; in James Joyce studies there is Richard Ellmann; in recent American history there is Arthur Schlesinger; and the list goes on.

There are several methods of discovering the key people in your area: (1) ask your instructor; (2) watch for certain names that keep reappearing in scholarly materials; (3) if available, check the credentials of an author. Has the individual written several books? Has the individual been quoted in articles and listed in footnotes and bibliographies? Has he or she had wide experience in this field? Is the individual a chairperson of a national committee on this subject? Has the individual held an elected or appointed position in this field?

Reliable Sources

Beware of biased reporting. In general, scholarly journals offer more reliable evidence than magazines. Journal writers document their sources and publish through university presses and other responsible organizations. Magazine writers, working under pressure of time, seldom document their sources or

authenticate their findings. In other words, a journal article about child abuse as found in *Child Development* or in *Journal of Studies in Alcohol* should be reliable source material. A magazine article about the topic in a Sunday newspaper supplement or in a popular magazine is suspect and should be examined for bias or exaggeration by a writer attempting to create newsworthy effects. The best source of a brief biography on a contemporary writer is *Contemporary Authors;* consult this if you have any doubts about the source of your article.

You should learn quickly that certain organizations publish slanted, biased articles to promote their views. The *New Republic* tends toward a liberal view of society while the *National Review* remains staunchly conservative. A report on health care may seem reasonable on the surface, but if the publication has been sponsored by a health care insurance company, you must exercise caution. Therefore, look carefully at the name of the publisher in every instance if you plan to quote from a pamphlet, report, newspaper, newspaper supplement, or a newsstand magazine. Common sense should warn you that an explosive topic such as child abuse lends itself easily to sensationalism and headline grabbing distortions.

Examine the Book Reviews

Whenever one book serves as a cornerstone for your work, you might wish to test its validity and critical reputation. Certain publications devote themselves to reviewing books.

For example, writers about women's liberation refer often to Kate Millett, a pivotal figure in the movement. If women's liberation is your general subject area, you certainly must look at Millett's *Sexual Politics*.

The *Book Review Digest* (New York: H. W. Wilson, 1905–date) serves as a reliable source for checking the critical reception of a book. Here is a portion of the 1970 edition which demonstrates several entries that summarize the reviews for Kate Millett's *Sexual Politics:*

Fig. 41: From *Book*
Review Digest
1. Author, title, and
facts of publication
2. Call number,
subject entry for
card catalog, and
Library of Congress
number
3. Description of the
book **4.** Reviewer's
evaluation of the
book **5.** A review
that the *Book*
Review Digest has
not summarized.
6. Facts of
publication of the
review—*Christian*
Science Monitor
(September 10,
1970), p. 15, 850
words

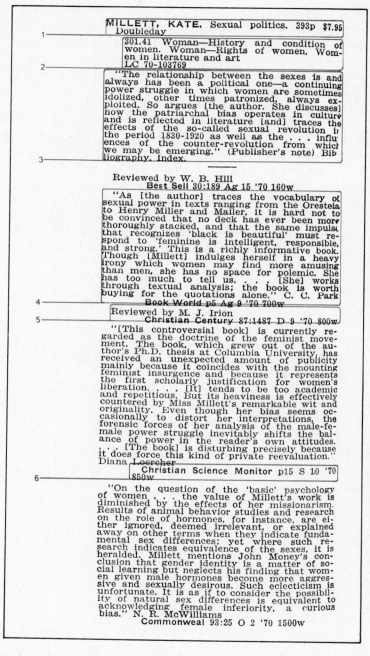

Arranged alphabetically by author, the *Book Review Digest* provides an evaluation of several thousand books each year. You might also examine these two
works:

Index to Book Reviews in the Humanities
Index to Book Reviews in the Social Sciences

Although these two works do not contain summaries of reviews or capsule evaluations as in *Book Review Digest,* they nevertheless provide additional reference information on current book reviews.

In addition, you will find evaluation of source material in any of the following:

The Booklist. Chicago: American Library Assn., 1905–date.

> This work offers a selective list of new books that will meet the needs of the average public library. Annotations make it valuable for student use.

The Reader's Adviser. 12th ed. New York: Bowker, 1974.

> This work provides a systematic treatment of many books, as indicated by its subtitle: "A guide to the best in print in literature, biographies, dictionaries, encyclopedias, bibles, classics, drama, poetry, fiction, science, philosophy, travel, history."

United States Quarterly Book List. New Brunswick, N. J.: Rutgers Univ. Press, 1945–56.

> Critical annotations and biographies of the authors make this a valuable reference. However, you will not find recent material because it has ceased publication.

Finally, it will pay for you to be curious and somewhat skeptical during research. Curiosity will keep you searching and tracking down facts from the library and other sources. Skepticism will prevent you from accepting the printed word as absolute. Analyze the printed page just as you analyze the spoken words of instructors and friends. Verify and document your facts and findings. Your critical perception will enable you to interpret and report your findings in an interesting as well as a reliable manner.

Primary and Secondary Sources

Whenever possible, you should make use of primary sources—that is, original findings or the actual words of a person directly involved. Primary sources include such things as novels, speeches, eyewitness accounts (diaries, journals), and market research. At the same time, you should also make extensive use of secondary sources—books and articles about a poem, a document, or a scientific finding. When the President addresses the nation, his speech becomes a *primary* source of information. The instant analysis of his speech by news reporters serves as *secondary* source material. As researcher, you usually need a mixture of both.

For example, the study of child abuse would produce these primary sources: case studies, reports from social workers, and evidence from surveys and questionnaires. Secondary sources on child abuse would include magazine and journal articles, books on the subject, and any commentary or evaluation of primary evidence by experts such as doctors and social workers. Again, a well-balanced paper has a mixture of both primary and secondary materials.

The subject area of your research paper determines in part the nature of the source materials. Use the following chart as a guide:

	Primary Sources	**Secondary Sources**
Literary topics	novels, poems, plays, short stories, letters, diaries, manuscripts, autobiographies	journal articles, reviews, biographies, critical books about writers and their works
Government Political science History	speeches, writings by presidents & others, the *Congressional Record,* reports of agencies and departments, documents written by historic figures (for example, Ben Franklin)	newspaper reports, newsmagazines, political journals and newsletters, journal articles, and history books
Social Sciences	case studies, findings from surveys and from questionnaires, reports of social workers, psychiatrists, and lab technicians	commentary and evaluations in reports, documents, journal articles, and books
Sciences	tools and methods, experiments, findings from tests and experiments, observations, discoveries, and test patterns	interpretations and discussions of test data as found in journals and books (note that scientific books, which are quickly dated, are less valuable than up-to-date journals)
Fine Arts	films, paintings, music, sculptures as well as reproductions and synopses of these for research purposes	evaluations in journal articles, critical reviews, biographies, and critical books about the artists and their works
Business	market research and testing, technical studies and investigations, drawings, designs, models, memoranda and letters, computer data	discussion of the business world in newspapers, business magazines, and journals, government documents, and books

| Education | pilot studies, term projects, sampling results, tests and test data, surveys, interviews, observations, statistics, and computer data | analysis and evaluation of educational experimentation in journals, reports, pamphlets, and books |

In reading any of the above-named sources, even primary sources, you must judge carefully the difference between fact and opinion or bias. Even test results often prove to be biased because of bias built into the test questions. Just because a book prints a statement does not prove its validity. You must learn to rely primarily on facts, and then base your own interpretations and opinions upon these.

TECHNIQUE OF NOTE CARDS

As with the bibliography cards, you should be exact in recording note card information. The following tips may help:

1. **Use ink.** Write your notes legibly in ink because penciled notes become blurred after repeated shuffling of the cards.
2. **Use index cards.** In general, use either four-by-six or three-by-five-inch index cards for taking notes. Unlike large sheets of paper, cards are easily shuffled and rearranged to fit the outline. Some researchers prefer the larger cards to avoid getting them mixed up with the three-by-five bibliography cards; others prefer the four-by-six card because it provides more space for notes.
3. **One item per card.** If you place only one item of information on each card, you may then shuffle and rearrange the cards during all stages of organization.
4. **Write on one side of card.** Since material on the back of a card may be overlooked, write only on one side of the card. However, if material should run a few lines beyond the one side, staple a second card to the first or write "OVER" conspicuously on the face of the first card and finish on the back.
5. **List source.** Even before writing the note, indicate in an abbreviated form the exact source of the information, for example, "Thornton 341." Give both author and specific page(s). Keep it brief because full information on the reference will be recorded on your bibliography card. If you have not already done so, make a bibliography card before writing the note. Avoid fancy, elaborate systems, such as a key number system, because you need author and page number for your textual citation, not a key number.
6. **Label each card.** Use the major headings of your outline as headings for individual cards. This label at the top of each card will speed arrangement of notes in accordance with the outline.

7. **Write a full note.** While the information is before you, now is the time to write out full, well-developed sentences. Try to create your own wording now in order to speed the writing of your first draft later on. Especially avoid the temptation to photocopy everything in hopes it will fall in place later.
8. **Keep everything.** Try to save every card, sheet, or scraps and notes because at some point you will probably need to authenticate a date, page number, or full name of the author or book.

METHODS OF NOTE-TAKING

Personal Note Cards

How often have you developed a good thought only to lose it before writing it down? This happens to many researchers; the best way to avoid it is to learn the practice of writing notes to yourself during research reading. After all, when you start writing the rough draft, the contents should be your thoughts and ideas interspersed with and supported by your sources. If you have no personal notes, then your writing will develop slowly.

Let's look at two hypothetical instances. In the first one, the student sits down with his outline and note cards drawn entirely from the sources. He faces a major hurdle: how to write his own paper while avoiding the temptation to string together an endless cycle of quotations and paraphrases. In the second instance, the student uses her personal note cards in combination with the source cards in order to write out her argument as supported by the sources. The difference is monumental.

Two samples of the personal note card follow:

Preventing abuse   mine

I'm concerned that most of the time the agencies try makeshift remedies after the fact. Maybe the answer lies in preventing abuse. Or am I being too naive?

> **Parents as victims**   **mine**
>
> Are the parents victims? The more I read, The more it seems that parents are depressed, not deranged. What causes it? I think maybe a mother who reaches a breaking point just takes it out on The kids. She doesn't hate them; she's just striking out because things are coming down hard on her.

Eventually, these notes became a part of page three of the child abuse paper (the entire sample paper appears on 170–93). The second note became significant because it formed the basis of the thesis statement, as shown here:

This example, however, prompts this thought: If people like the Jane Neilsons of our society could be identified and given help in a timely fashion, then perhaps children would not be victimized. Perhaps an answer lies in preventing abuse, not in makeshift remedies after the fact. Parents who abuse their children should be treated as victims, not criminals. Child abuse is a symptom of the parent's condition. Reaching out to the parent before a child appears in the emergency room may prove difficult, but our solving the causes of abuse may be the only way to stop this escalating maltreatment of America's precious children.

The lesson ought to be clear: the more personal notes you write, the more you write the paper itself.

Summary Cards

Many times you will want to write a brief sketch of your material without great concern for style or expression. Your primary need is to put summary notes onto your card, quickly and concisely—there is no concern here for careful wording or exact paraphrase. In other words, the source material may not be well written, may be statistical, or may be borderline in terms of possible usage in your paper. A summary note card serves your purposes in this instance. Later, if you need the source material for your paper, you may write a note in a clear, appropriate prose style.

Your chief purpose with the summary card is to extract the significant facts. Narrow your focus to the essentials; if you merely copy entire paragraphs verbatim, you will still have to summarize the material. Save some time: select the key information, summarize it, and get on with other matters. Remember, however, that you must document the source of summarized material; therefore, always list the author and page number on your note card.

A sample summary note card from the child abuse paper follows:

> statistics   from Cohen + Sussman 433
> Nobody seems to know for certain,
> but the Education Commission
> of the states reports 60,000 cases
> of abuse every year. Others
> suggest 75,000 and one
> argues that figure should be
> 120,000.

Another summary note card by the same writer contains this information:

statistics   from Chase 104
This source says boys outnumber girls in being abused
until they are teenagers. Parents
argue more with girls who date
and fight less with older boys
who might fight back.

Eventually, these summary notes were incorporated into the final draft of the child abuse paper, as follows:

> Even worse, severe abuse is on the rise. Each year more and more children suffer the trauma of physical and emotional abuse. Although the exact number remains un-known, the Education Commission of the States reports that some 60,000 cases occur annually (Cohen and Sussman 433). Boys suffer more abuse than girls until the teen years, when girls then suffer more (Chase 104). The death rate

As demonstrated above, summary notes are valuable for giving you a rough sketch of material you may need, but can express more fluently, when you write your first draft.

Plot Summary Note Cards

Another type of summary card is one that briefly summarizes the plot of a drama or story that serves as your primary source. In truth, it should be called a précis (see below), but "plot summary" is a standard term that most people employ. You will have occasion to use this note whenever you write about a novel, short story, drama, or similar literary work. The following note demonstrates the plot summary card:

> plot   Hansberry's Raisin in the Sun
>
> The drama portrays a black family's determination to move from the ghetto. Mama younger dominates the family members. However, each member rebels in his or her own way, especially Walter, who squanders the family's inheritance and brings them to a crisis that threatens their survival as a family unit.

Such a plot summary should be brief, offering only enough information to clarify the plot for your reader. Avoid writing a plot summary that extends beyond one paragraph.

Précis Note Cards

The précis, a very brief summary in your own words, differs from the rough summary in that the précis is more polished in style. It differs from the paraphrase in being far more concise. The plot summary, as noted above, is a précis because it condenses into a few words the entire plot of a drama or story. Write the précis note in a polished form with complete sentences in formal English. (Only rough summary notes allow abbreviations and sentence fragments.) You will have success with the précis if you:

1. Condense the original with precision and directness. Reduce a long paragraph into a sentence, tighten an article into a brief paragraph, and summarize a longer work, such as a biography or critical study, into a page or two.
2. Preserve the tone of the original. If the original is humorous, suggest that tone in your précis. In the same way, retain moods of satire, exaggeration, doubt, irony, and so on.
3. Limit the use of key words or phrases from the original by writing the précis in your own language. However, retain exceptional words or phrases from the original, enclosing them in quotation marks.

4. Provide documentation locating the source of your material. A sample
   précis note card follows:

> Loss of jobs + abuse   from Steinberg + others
>
> This article explores the abuse of
> children in relation to economic con-
> ditions. These experts are quick to
> note a correlation of unemployment
> in a town or nation with increased
> danger to children, their well being,
> and even their lives. Thus loss of
> jobs may endanger the children.
>
> Good conclusion about this on p. 982

In only a few sentences, the student has summarized the essential elements of the
entire article. Transitions to bridge across omitted information are necessary, as
shown with: "This article explores" or "These experts" and "Thus." The manner in which she used the précis and the quotation mentioned at the bottom of the
card is shown here:

increase in child abuse all across the nation. The year

1982 was also one of extremely high unemployment. Experts

are quick to note the correlation that unemployment in a

town or a nation may endanger the well-being of the chil-

dren as well as their very lives (Steinberg, Catalano, and

Dooley 975). These three authorities reach rather distress-

ing conclusions:

>   Declines in the work force are significantly
>
>   related to reported child abuse in two metropoli-
>
>   tan communities. This finding is consistent with

the hypothesis that undesirable economic change

causes family stress, resulting subsequently in

child abuse.   (982)

On an individual basis the family scenario might go like

this: the father loses his job so the mother enters the job

. A similar summarization is demonstrated in the following excerpt from the sample research paper:

Depression also causes a parent to beat his child, but

E. Milling Kinard suggests that treating the parent for de-

pression without removing the social problems of economic

poverty and emotional stress will probably have only limited

success (403–06). The causal chain leading. . . .

Note the student's citation to pages 403–06, indicating that she has condensed several pages of the original into her one sentence précis. Accordingly, you will have success with the précis note card if you can say in a sentence or two the very essence of a longer work.

Paraphrase Note Cards

You should write most of your notes in the form of paraphrase, restating in your own style the thought or meaning expressed by someone else. In other words, you borrow an idea, opinion, interpretation, or statement and rewrite it in your own language. Later, when you are writing your paper, you will find it easier to maintain an even stylistic flow and to avoid jumping from one language level to another as different experts speak in their own particular jargon.

Write paraphrase notes in about the same number of words as the original (hence the distinction between paraphrase and précis, the latter being a very *brief* condensation). Some researchers keep accurate, exhaustive note cards of quoted materials and then paraphrase later during the writing phase. Generally, it is wiser to paraphrase material during note-taking rather than to fill card after card with directly quoted matter; you will need material in your own words and style.

Writing goes quickly when many items are paraphrased. Also, plagiarism is one danger of relying primarily on carelessly documented quoted materials (see "Avoiding Plagiarism" 94–99). Of course, you are saved from plagiarism when paraphrasing only if you credit the thoughts you have borrowed. The point of view and the presentation may be yours, but you must always remember that the idea belongs to the original author and, therefore, requires proper documentation.

You will have success with paraphrasing if you:

1. Rewrite the original in your own style in about the same number of words.
2. Preserve the tone of the original by maintaining moods of satire, anger, humor, doubt, and so on.
3. Retain exceptional words and phrasing from the original and enclose them within quotation marks. You must double-check your paraphrase with your note card to be certain that your paraphrase is an adequate rewriting of the original and that any terminology of the original is placed within quotation marks.
4. Provide documentation indicating the source of your material. For example, an original article on child abuse states:

> There are many abusive parents for whom groups may be the only answer, not only because of the quality of services offered, or the potential benefits they promise, but chiefly for the fact that a group of this type is the only service that some abusive parents will attend and participate in.
> —From: Marlin Blizinsky, "Parents Anonymous and the Private Agency: Administrative Cooperation," *Child Welfare* 61 (1982): 305–11.

The student's paraphrased note card, based on this source, is shown:

group therapy   from Blizinsky 311

This critic reports that group sessions may be the only answer for some folks because group sessions might be the only thing a person will participate in whether he is the abuser or the abused.

Eventually, this note appeared in the final paper, slightly altered for the better, as shown on the next page:

~~~~~~

First, the idea of group therapy and self-help sessions

for adults seems sound. Marlin Blizinsky reports that group

sessions may be the only answer for some persons because a

group session might be the only program in which an abusive

person will participate (311).

~~~~~~

In another instance, the student discovered this source material that appeared
promising:

> A child who witnesses parental attempts to solve family problems or release frus-
> trations through aggressive behavior is likely to incorporate this into his or her own
> behavior patterns. If being abused as a child does in fact lead to aggressive behav-
> ior, the seeds of this cycle may be manifested early in life in relationships with peers
> and/or siblings, and, when greater strength is gained, in confrontations with parents
> or caretakers.
> —From: Peter C. Kratcoski, ''Child Abuse and Violence Against the Family.''
> *Child Welfare* 61 (1982): 437.

The language and wording of this piece differ rather markedly from a student's
language level; therefore, the student rewrote the material as a paraphrase:

> learning how to abuse from Kratcoski 437
> This critic reaches an obvious con-
> clusion, that children who experi-
> ence violence as kids tend to use
> that behavior in their own adult
> patterns for handling stress. He
> also argues that abusing
> parents had better get ready for
> the children to turn on them
> and beat their parents.

Eventually, this paraphrased note, incorporated into the finished paper, read like
this:

Kratcoski reaches a rather obvious conclusion, saying that children who experience violence as children tend to incorporate such behavior into their own patterns for handling stress, but this authority also argues that abusing parents should be prepared for their children to turn on them and become parent abusers (437).

To repeat, you will have success with paraphrasing your source material if you keep the length of it about the same as the original but convert the original into your language and style.

Quotation Note Cards

Students frequently overuse direct quotation in taking notes, and, as a result, they overuse quotations in the final paper. In the worst cases, they rush to the photo copier and do some wholesale copying of page after page only to discover that the writing still remains to be done. Probably only ten to twenty percent of your final manuscript should appear as directly quoted matter. Therefore, you can save time by limiting the amount of exact transcribing of source materials while taking notes. Writing a research paper is a continuing process that cannot be accomplished in one sitting. Phrasing material into your words and style should concern you both early in your note-taking and later during writing and revision stages. The overuse of quotations indicates either that you did not have a clear focus for your argument and are jotting down verbatim just about everything you find related to your subject or that you have inadequate development of your topic and are using numerous quotations only as padding. Specific cases for using direct quotation of secondary sources are these:

1. To display excellence in ideas and expression by the source.
2. To explain complex material.
3. To set up a statement of your own, especially if it spins off, adds to, or takes exception to the source as quoted.

Originality in research writing requires your personal presentation of material that you have thoroughly assimilated. Accordingly, you should be the speaker in the major portion of your paper, giving proper credit, of course, wherever credit is due.

Direct quotation is necessary with primary sources. You must cite the poem or novel in a literary study, the presidential speech in a political science paper, the computer data in a business paper, or a case study in a sociology paper. With secondary sources, direct quotation is useful as support for an assertion now and then; therefore, look for the secondary material that is the best evidence on the subject and that is written with special clarity.

You will have success with quotation note cards if you:

1. Place quotation marks around material that is directly quoted onto your note cards; you must later be able to distinguish the quotes from paraphrases.
2. Copy the exact words of the author, even to the retention of any errors in the original (see *sic* used on 134) or what might appear to be errors. *Sic* is a term used within brackets to show that a quoted passage is reproduced precisely.
3. For special problems that you may encounter, see "Handling Reference Material," 125–140.

The following note card demonstrates quotation from a secondary source:

TV as breeding violence   from Zigler 40

"One finds violence, hostility and aggression everywhere, including TV, the movies, and in many of our everyday social relations. So long as this preoccupation with and even glorification of aggression is tolerated, so long can we expect the abuse of children both at home and in school."

For the example of how one student worked these two quoted sentences into her paper, see below. Note especially that rather than lump the sentences together as one long indented quotation, she works them separately into a meaningful paragraph that fits her style:

What's more, the television age may breed its own
violence. Zigler laments, "One finds violence, hostility
and aggression everywhere, including TV, the movies, and in
many of our everyday social relations" (40). Violence
observed perhaps becomes violence practiced by parents on
the children as well as by children on their brothers and
sisters and even against their own parents. As one authority puts it, "So long as this preoccupation with and even
glorification of aggression is tolerated, so long can we
expect the abuse of children both at home and in the school"
(Zigler 40).

In the case of direct quotation from a primary source, just be certain that
you quote exactly as printed. Two samples follow:

Images of frustration   Eliot's "Prufrock" 5

"For I have known them all already,
    known them all:—
Have known the evenings, mornings,
    afternoons,
I have measured out my life with
    coffee spoons;
I know the voices dying with a
    dying fall
Beneath the music from a farther room.
So how should I presume?"

From: T. S. Eliot, "The Love Song of J. Alfred Prufrock."

Note in the sample item above that the student has copied an entire verse; he or she may use only a line or two, but having an entire sentence or entire verse assures accuracy in handling the quotation within the body of the research paper.

The following item quotes a novel:

> Awakening like being born   Renzo Rosso 43
>
> "There was the morning's penumbra, the room, the wind that beat its swollen hands against the walls; and it was as if he had just then risen to the surface, his eyes barely opened. Immersed in something liquid, This was the sensation he still had, as if he had floated up from a deep abyss. Was it an interrupted dream?"

From: Renzo Rosso, *The Hard Thorn*. Trans. William Weaver. London: Alan Ross, 1966, 43.

Additional examples of handling quoted materials may be found on 125–38 and a discussion of technical matters on 150–69.

AVOIDING PLAGIARISM

Plagiarism (the improper use of source materials) is a serious breach of ethics. Many instances of plagiarism are more often the result of ignorance of rules than a deliberate effort on the part of the student to deceive instructors and other readers of the research paper.

Purpose of Documentation of Source Materials

Thomas Edison once said that he began where other men left off; he built upon the beginnings of others. How fortunate he was that his predecessors recorded their experiments. The basic ingredient of business and professional life is research, whether you are a lawyer, boot maker, or hospital nurse. Your future role in middle to upper management level positions will demand research expertise as well as the ability to examine critically and to write effectively about an issue: from the architectural design of a new building to the chemical treatment of algae in the water supply. That is why college professors expect you to perfect these skills.

Scholarship is the sharing of information. The primary reason for a research paper is to announce and publicize your findings. A botanist explains her discovery of a new strain of ferns in Kentucky's Land Between the Lakes. A medical scientist reports the results of his cancer research. A sociologist announces the results of a two-year pilot study on Appalachian Indians. In like manner, the college student explains his or her findings in a biology experiment, or discloses research into shoplifting, or discusses the results of an investigation into schizophrenia of preschool children.

Like Thomas Edison, your research in any area begins where others have left off, for you must examine source materials in the library, the laboratory, or in the field. Whether or not somebody continues your research after you will depend upon two factors: the quality of your research and the accuracy of your written document. Your undergraduate paper probably will not be circulated beyond the immediate classroom; yet the central purpose remains the same as if it were intended for publication—to disclose your findings and to share them with your fellow students and instructor. In the process, you will learn the conventions of scholarship, you will discover the multiple resources of the library, and you will learn more about your topic than you ever thought possible.

Conventions of Scholarship Documentation

Dr. Jonas Salk is credited with the discovery of a vaccine that has almost eradicated polio as a health menace to America's children. Yet Dr. Salk would be the first to credit other researchers who preceded him and laid the groundwork for his laboratory findings. Without their research and the careful documentation of it, Dr. Salk would surely have failed.

The lesson should be clear: documentation serves those who follow. The conventions of research documentation enable others to follow, refine, and augment previous findings. Some students mistakenly believe an instructor wants a list of works cited so that the student's work can be double-checked. Such an assumption is usually false. In truth, the student who quotes a source and documents it properly follows conventions of scholarship. Otherwise, the student shows clear disregard for the conventions and probably commits plagiarism. Instructors double-check your sources only when something blatant in the paper causes suspicions about careless or dishonest practices.

An Explanation of Plagiarism

Fundamentally, plagiarism is the offering of the words or ideas of another person as one's own. While the most blatant violation is the use of another student's work, the most common is the unintentional misuse of your reference sources. Since you will be working with the writings of others, it is important that you learn and adhere to the scholarly conventions of documentation. In particular, you want to avoid unintentional error.

An obvious form of plagiarism is copying any direct quotation from your source material without providing quotation marks and without crediting the source. A more subtle form, but equally improper, is the paraphrasing of material or use of an original idea that is not properly introduced and documented. Remember that another author's ideas, interpretations, and words are his or her property; in fact, they are protected by law and must be acknowledged whenever you borrow them. Consequently, your use of source materials requires you to conform to a few rules of conduct:

1. Acknowledge borrowed material within your text by introducing the quotation or paraphrase with the name of the authority from whom it was taken. This practice serves to indicate where the borrowed materials begin.
2. Enclose within quotation marks all quoted materials.
3. Make certain that paraphrased material is rewritten into your own style and language. The simple rearrangement of sentence patterns is unacceptable.
4. Provide specific documentation for each borrowed item. Remember the previous discussion: another researcher may follow in your steps and need the same source.
5. Provide a bibliography entry in "Works Cited" for every book or journal that is referred to in your paper.

The examples provided below should reveal the difference between genuine research writing and plagiarism. First is the original reference material; it is followed by student versions, two of which would be labeled plagiarism and two of which would not.

Original Material:

> The extended family is now rare in contemporary society, and with its demise the new parent has lost the wisdom and daily support of older, more experienced family members. Furthermore, many parents are not as well equipped for parenthood as were their parents before them, since over the years most children have been given less responsibility in helping to care for younger siblings.

> —From: Edward F. Zigler, "The Unmet Needs of America's Children," *Children Today* 5.3 (1976): 42.

STUDENT VERSION A (UNACCEPTABLE)

Today's society and shifting patterns of social order may

dictate, then, a climate for abuse. Many parents are just

not equipped today for parenthood. For instance, the extended family is rare in contemporary society, and because
of its disappearance new parents have lost the wisdom and
daily support of the wise grandparents. In truth, a family
such as that portrayed by the Waltons on television seldom
exists today with grandparents, parents, and many children
all living together under one roof. Therefore, today's
young parents are not well equipped because as children
they were given less responsibility in helping care for
younger brothers and sisters.

This piece of writing is plagiarism in a most deplorable form. Material stolen
without documentation is obvious, and the instructor will spot it immediately
because of radical differences in the student's style and that of the source. The
student has simply borrowed abundantly from the original source, even to the
point of retaining the essential wording. The student has provided no documentation whatever, nor has the student named the authority. In truth, the student
implies to the reader that these sentences are entirely his or her original creation
when, actually, only two sentences belong to the student, and the rest belong to
the source.

The next version is better, but it still demonstrates blatant disregard for
scholarly conventions.

STUDENT VERSION B (UNACCEPTABLE)

Too many parents are not equipped today for parenthood. The
extended family with three or more generations under one
roof is now rare. Thus parents have lost the wisdom of
older, experienced persons. In truth, a family such as that
portrayed by the Waltons on television seldom exists today

with grandparents, parents, and many children living all

together under one roof. Therefore, young parents of today

do a poor job because as youngsters they did not help care

for younger brothers and sisters (Zigler 42).

Although this version provides a citation to the authority, it contains two serious errors. First, as readers we cannot know that the citation refers to most of the paragraph; we can only assume that the citation refers to the final sentence. Second, the paraphrasing is careless and includes wording and phrasing of the authority, words that should be enclosed by quotation marks or rephrased into the student's language and style, such as: "not equipped for parenthood," "extended family," and "lost the wisdom of older."

The next version is correct and proper.

STUDENT VERSION C (ACCEPTABLE)

Today's society and shifting patterns of social order may

dictate, then, a climate for abuse. Edward Zigler argues

that many parents are just not equipped today for parent-

hood (42). He says, for instance, that the "extended family

is now rare in contemporary society, and with its demise

the new parent has lost the wisdom and daily support of

older, more experienced family members" (Zigler 42). In

truth, a family such as that portrayed by the Waltons on

television seldom exists today with grandparents, parents,

and many children all living together under one roof. No

wonder Zigler argues that "many parents are not as well

equipped for parenthood as their parents before them, since

over the years most children have been given less respon-

sibility in helping care for younger siblings" (42).

This version represents a satisfactory handling of the source material. The authority is acknowledged at the outset, and key phrases are directly quoted so as to give full credit where credit is due. The student has been wholly honest to her source material.

Let's suppose, however, that you do not wish to quote Zigler directly nor to use as much material as shown above. The following version shows how a condensed paraphrase of Zigler's ideas can be worked into the paper.

STUDENT VERSION D (ACCEPTABLE)

Today's society and shifting patterns of social order may

dictate, then, a climate for abuse. Edward Zigler argues

that many parents are just not equipped today for parent-

hood (42). He insists that the "extended family" with

several generations under one roof no longer exists and

parents, who have little experience and no wise adults

around, are therefore ill equipped to handle their duties

toward family members (Zigler 42). In truth, a family such

as that portrayed by the Waltons on television seldom ex-

ists today with grandparents, parents, and many children all

living together under one roof.

This shortened version also represents a satisfactory handling of the source material. In this case, no direct quotation is employed, other than "extended family," the authority is acknowledged, and the substance of the commentary is presented in the student's own language.

Finally, consider the typical complaint: "When I started this research, I didn't know *anything* about child abuse. Does that mean I must document every sentence in the paper?" No, relax, and think a moment. Your invention, organization, personal notes, synthesis are your own, along with your thesis, topic sentences, analysis, as well as the opening and closing. All you are borrowing is evidence from primary and secondary sources, and only that specific evidence must be documented.

4
Writing Your Paper

During the course of your research, you have been making judgments and comparisons, putting details into order, and compiling information on note cards. Now you are ready to synthesize all research materials in order to give your paper and your reader the greatest possible clarity, orderliness, and meaning for your findings. However, before beginning the actual writing, you need a plan of attack: a thesis sentence and a final outline that will bring your notes into order and bring your thoughts and arguments into focus. To repeat, your preliminary thesis helped control your note-taking; now the final thesis will control your essay argument and guide your reader.

DETERMINING YOUR FINAL THESIS SENTENCE

The thesis, as the heart of your argument, dictates your title, your outline, and the actual writing of the paper. Your investigative approach to the topic (see 6–8) guided the early stages of your work. Now you must reevaluate your approach and frame your thesis sentence.

For example, the child abuse paper, 170–193, began with an investigative approach (some call it a preliminary thesis) that stated: "A need for a cure to child abuse faces society each day." After investigation of the available literature, the final thesis became: "Parents who abuse their children should be treated as victims, not criminals." The student moved to a specific position, arguing finally that social organizations need to reach out to help the parents both before and after they abuse the children, not just provide aid to the children after abuse occurs.

The final thesis sentence should conform to several conventions:

1. It declares your main issue in a full, declarative sentence, which is not a question or a statement of purpose or merely a topic.
2. It limits your subject to a narrow focus.
3. It establishes an investigative, inventive edge to your discovery, interpretation, or argument.

4. It points forward to your conclusion.
5. It conforms to your note card evidence and your title.

The following examples have served effectively as thesis sentences for student papers:

Title: The Theme of Black Matriarchy in *A Raisin in the Sun*
Thesis: Hansberry uses the sociological concept of black matriarchy to create dramatic conflict among the members of the Younger family.

Title: Computer Control: Safeguard Against Computer Theft
Thesis: A company should program the computer to safeguard its own software.

Title: Geological Predictions: Sinkholes
Thesis: It is possible within certain parameters to predict the location of new sinkholes.

The sample theses above all have three things in common: (1) a declarative sentence that (2) focuses the argument toward an investigative issue that (3) will be resolved in the paper's general discussion and conclusion.

WRITING A TITLE

The title should describe clearly the contents of the paper. Fancy literary titles fail to describe the issues under discussion. A title such as "Let There Be Hope" offers no clue for the reader about the nature of the work. Granted, a good title serves as part of the appeal to attract readers, but a better title would be "Let There Be Hope: A View of Child Abuse Victims." A more scientific title would be: "Child Abuse: A View of the Victims." You might imagine that somebody must catalog, file, or index your paper by its title; then provide key words of identification, as with the following:

Poor: Gothic Madness
Better: Gothic Madness in Three Southern Writers
         Key Words: Southern Writers

Poor: Melville and the Bible
Better: An Interpretation of Melville's Use of Biblical Characters in *Billy Budd*
         Key Words: Biblical Characters and *Billy Budd*

Poor: Saving the Software
Better: Computer Control: Software Safeguard and Computer Theft
         Key Words: Computer Theft and Computer Software

A precise title with specific key words is best. Therefore, use imaginative titles but do not be overly fancy or cute.

THE OUTLINE FOR WRITING

This step in your work classifies the segments of your argument into clear divisions. You must now abandon your rough preliminary outline or restructure it into clear logical stages to guide the writing of your paper. Understand that not all instructors require the formal outline. Nor do some students need one. In fact, the very best of outlines should be modified during the writing of the rough draft. After all, the draft is a preliminary step to discovering what you actually want to say. It is difficult to plan a paper completely in advance of actually writing the first draft. Nevertheless, an outline will order the issues and guide your note card arrangement. Needed adjustments can be made as your write. The following conventions will assist you in outline development.

Use Standard Outline Symbols

You may wish to use standard outline symbols (as shown here) because they clearly delineate the major categories and the supporting or subsidiary issues:

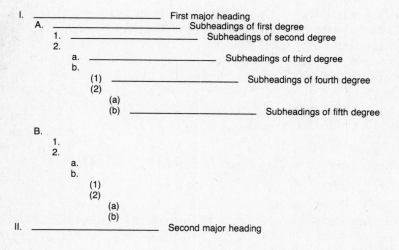

Your indentation of each heading will indicate the importance of the material; that is, you will progress from major concepts to minor ones. The degree to which you continue the subheads will depend, in part, upon the complexity of your subject; but, as a general rule, you should seldom find it necessary to carry the subheads beyond the first series of small letters.

Use Balanced and Parallel Form

Headings of like rank on the same margin should have equal importance. As you establish ideas, give them parallel form. Note the mistake in the following:

I. Spring sports

    A. To swing a baseball bat

    B. Tennis

    C. Golf

Obviously, the infinitive phrase "To swing a baseball bat" is not parallel with the nouns "Tennis" and "Golf." If A is a noun, then make B and C nouns also, or if you prefer, make them all infinitives; however, do not mix the grammatical forms.

When you indent outline headings, subordinate your ideas. Thus, if you find yourself attempting to enter a single subhead, you obviously have one major idea and not several subordinate ones. Note the following:

I. Spring sports

    A. Baseball

        1. Swinging the bat

    B. Tennis

        1. Swinging the racket

    C. Golf

        1. Swinging the golf club

This writer probably intends to discuss one aspect of these spring sports: the swing necessary for hitting a baseball, tennis ball, or golf ball. Therefore, the writer might rearrange the entries in the following manner:

CLASSIFIED BY SPORT

Spring Sports: Swinging the Bat, Racket, or Club

I. The Baseball Swing

    A. Setup

    B. Mechanics of the swing

    C. Follow through

```
    II. The Tennis Swing
        A. Setup
        B. Mechanics of the swing
        C. Follow through
   III. The Golf Swing
        A. Setup
        B. Mechanics of the swing
        C. Follow through
```

All parts now balance in well-ordered sequence with possibilities for full development of the paper. However, classifying the outline by the three elements of the swing provides another effective outline:

CLASSIFIED BY ELEMENTS OF THE SWING

```
    Spring Sports: Swinging the Bat, Racket, or Club
     I. Setup
        A. Balance
           1. Baseball
           2. Tennis
           3. Golf
        B. Addressing the ball
           1. Baseball
           2. Tennis
           3. Golf
        C. Grip and hand position
           1. Baseball
           2. Tennis
           3. Golf
    II. Mechanics of the swing
        A. Backswing
           1. Baseball
           2. Tennis
           3. Golf
```

        B. Hand-eye contact

            1. Baseball

            2. Tennis

            3. Golf

        C. Acceleration

            1. Baseball

            2. Tennis

            3. Golf

    III. Follow through

        A. Steady head

            1. Baseball

            2. Tennis

            3. Golf

        B. Body rotation

            1. Baseball

            2. Tennis

            3. Golf

        C. Extension

            1. Baseball

            2. Tennis

            3. Golf

Again, the balance of parts in ordered sequence should lead to control of the paper's flow and sense of direction.

Avoid General Headings

Avoid the terms ''introduction'' and ''conclusion'' in your outline. You can do this by keeping both your ''introduction'' and your ''conclusion'' *content* oriented, labeling them specifically just as you do other parts of the outline. For example, the outline on 171–173 lists ''The Cry of the Children'' in the introduction position and ''The Necessary Treatment'' as the conclusion, thereby avoiding the vague headings, ''Introduction'' and ''Conclusion.''

List the Thesis Separately Above the Outline

Because the thesis is the main idea of the entire paper, you should not label your thesis sentence as Item I in the outline. Otherwise, you may find yourself searching fruitlessly for a parallel idea to put in II, III, and IV. Instead, you should write your thesis sentence separately, placing it above the outline proper. Then, as you write the rough draft, the thesis develops naturally as the motivating part of the paper.

The Dynamic Order of the Outline

The outline as a guide to your writing should trace your argument by laying out a trail to defend and support your thesis. That is, the general categories of the preliminary outline should be replaced by a dynamic progression of issues and concepts as you point forward to your conclusions. Note the differences between an early preliminary outline and a final outline:

PRELIMINARY OUTLINE (WITH LITTLE OR NO DYNAMIC ORDER)

```
The Battered Child
      Discipline
      Physical abuse
      Psychological abuse
Short Term Effects
Long Term Effects
Public Response
      Government Agencies
      Private Organizations
Spotting the Unfit Parent
```

FINAL OUTLINE (WITH DYNAMIC ORDER)

```
Thesis: Parents who abuse their children should be treated as
        victims, not criminals
The Issues of Child Abuse
      The problems
      Statistics and Examples
      A Possible Answer
```

```
    The Causes and Cycles of Abuse

        The Potentials for Abuse

        Cycles of Child Abuse

    Focusing on the Parents as Victims

        A Look at the Evidence

        Therapy and Study Groups

    The Necessary Treatment

        Community Involvement Programs

        The Parent as Victim

        The Character of the Community
```

Although these outlines carry only the major headings (see 171–173 for the full outline), the sense of argument flows through the material. The first outline has major headings that might aid note-taking, but the second outline, by its progressive structure, carries the basic stages of the student's thesis development and will therefore aid writing of the paper: from the issues, to the causes, to a focus on the parents, and finally to the need for treatment of parents before they abuse their children. The final outline, then, should carry the flow of your thesis toward a conclusion. If you have trouble creating an outline, arrange your notes by categories, then arrange the categories into a dynamic order that carries the flow of the information into logical, progressive sequence. It should require slight adjustment during the writing of your first draft, but the dynamic order of the outline helps maintain the orderly sequence of the discourse.

Choosing an Outline Form

You may write your outline in topic, sentence, or paragraph form, remembering, of course, that you cannot alternate forms within a given outline. With the topic outline, every heading is a noun phrase (''Prevention of abuse'') or its equivalent, a gerund phrase (''Preventing abuse'') or an infinitive phrase (''To prevent abuse''). In the sentence outline, either all headings are sentences or the major headings are nouns and the subheads are sentences. With the paragraph outline, every section is a paragraph or the major headings are nouns with full paragraphs under each noun heading.

Reproduced below is a portion of the outline from the sample research paper, ''Child Abuse: A View of the Victims'' (see 171–173 for the complete topic outline) in topic, sentence, and paragraph forms.

```
    Thesis: Parents who abuse their children should be treated as

            victims, not criminals.
```

TOPIC OUTLINE

This form of outline is the most popular; it establishes succinctly and precisely the main areas of investigation:

```
II. The Issues of Child Abuse

    A. The Problems

       1. Recognition that there is a problem

       2. Myth that America is child-oriented

       3. Problems of discovery of potential child abuse

       4. Help after the fact is limited help at best

    B. Statistics and Examples of Abuse

       1. Abuse on the increase

       2. Specific examples

       3. Absence of professional help before the abuse

       4. Prevention of rather than coping with
```

SENTENCE OUTLINE

Many students and their instructors prefer the sentence outline because it establishes full sentences that you may transcribe into the rough draft. Many of these entries serve as topic sentences for paragraphs, thereby speeding the writing process by offering you ready beginnings for many paragraphs. The logic of your development is easier to check in a sentence outline where a predicate establishes the direction of your thinking (for example, the topic outline word "myth" becomes "We must avoid myths and distortions"). However, major problems with the sentence outline usually become ones of time and effort.

```
II. The issues of child abuse are multiple and complex.

    A. The problems center on recognition and discovery of
       abuse.

       1. First, we need to recognize that there is a prob-
          lem.

       2. Next, we must avoid myth and distortions.

       3. We should discover potential abusers.

       4. Help after the fact is limited help at the very
          best.
```

```
      B. Statistics reveal the extent of the problem.

         1. Abuse is increasing yearly.

         2. All types of abuse take place daily.

         3. There is an absence of professional help before

            abuse occurs.

         4. We cope with abuse more than we prevent it.
```

PARAGRAPH OUTLINE

The paragraph outline provides an opportunity for developing a unity of thought for each major section of the paper. The dangers of the paragraph outline are twofold: you may try to write the paper when developing only an outline or you may carry weak, undeveloped outline paragraphs directly into the rough draft.

```
     II. The Issues

         A. Experts say public recognition of the degree of child

            abuse is a serious problem. Too many myths and distor-

            tions of the truth exist in the public mind. Gener-

            ally, we think everybody should love their children.

            Therefore, the discovery of abuse after a child is

            battered arrives too late. We need a way to discover

            potential abusers.

         B. Statistics are startling by revealing the increase an-

            nually in reported cases of all types--beatings, burn-

            ings, neglect, etc. There is an absence of profes-

            sional help before abuse. Thus, we cope with it rather

            than prevent it.
```

DECIMAL OUTLINE

Various outline forms exist that deviate from the classic models with respect to indenting, spacing, numbers, and so on. The most popular alternative, especially in business and the sciences, is the decimal outline (also known as the industrial numerical outline):

```
2. The issues of child abuse

   2.1 The problems

       2.1.1 Recognition that there is a problem

       2.1.2 Myth that America is child-oriented

       2.1.3 Problems of discovery of potential child abuse

       2.1.4 Help after the fact is limited help at best

   2.2 Statistics and examples of abuse

       2.2.1 Abuse on the increase

       2.2.2 Specific examples

       2.2.3 Absence of professional help before the abuse

       2.2.4 Prevention rather than coping
```

Use this decimal system for scientific and business reports. It breaks the material down into specific elements with every segment a numerical item.

PREPARING TO WRITE

If you begin the actual writing of your paper at least two full weeks before it is due, you should have sufficient time for writing, revising, and rewriting. Prior to the final two weeks, you should not rush into the writing; instead, you should (1) examine your thesis sentence and outline to see that they provide you with a well-rounded, logically organized plan of procedure; (2) examine your approach to the topic; and (3) review your note cards.

Reviewing the Thesis Sentence and Outline

Ask yourself, "Do I know my main idea and supporting ideas?" If in doubt, you must reread your thesis sentence and study your outline. You should examine your ideas and their logical progression through the outline objectively. At this point you cannot afford confusion because each of your paragraphs must develop and expand your thesis sentence.

For example, you may decide with the sample topic "child abuse" that unemployment in a community may cause an increase in the abuse of children. Such a thesis concept must be clear in your mind before you begin writing. Obviously, you must defend and document the generalization that loss of a job causes family stress and that parental frustrations may eventually cause a parent to abuse his or her child. In other words, control of your thesis sentence will maintain the unity of your writing.

Reviewing Your Approach to the Topic

Next ask yourself, "Do I know my purpose?" To answer this question, you must consider both the intellectual framework (what you want the reader to understand) and the emotional framework (what you feel and want the reader to feel).

For example, your intellectual choice about child abuse will be to condemn the practice, but your emotional framework becomes more sensitive. You may select a detached approach and, with a degree of objectivity, give accurate, well-ordered presentations of all sides of the issue, declaring your conclusions with controlled logic. If, on the other hand, you assume an involved position, either pro or con, your presentation will be persuasive and, usually, will offer directives for action.

An objective writer reports and offers facts while the involved writer analyzes the issues and argues towards a conclusion, an answer, a principle, or a finding. For example, suppose your topic is the world energy crisis. Obviously, you face an intellectual choice: you may defend or condemn the energy policies of the Department of the Interior. Complete objectivity is unlikely in your research paper which is, in fact, a form of argument. Your emotional tone will be affected by your intellectual position. For example, the writer who either condemns or supports agency actions might use examples and case studies that trigger emotions; moreover, other conclusions generally demand, direct, or insist. Other writers may maintain a quiet prose style, offer rational reasons, and cite precedents. The lesson to be learned is that moderation of your voice and tone, even during argument, suggests to the listener that you have control of the situation—both emotionally and intellectually.

At all costs you should avoid bias and prejudice, but you may express subjective feelings by condemning falsehoods, by destroying misconceptions, by rallying your audience to your cause, and by supporting your ideas with examples and comparisons that vividly portray the circumstances.

Moreover, with some topics you might consider the possibility of a humorous or a satiric approach, by which you relate, with tongue-in-cheek, the absurdity of a situation. Or, you may ridicule the foolishness of a condition, intending, thereby, to bring a new awareness of a problem to your reader. However, such papers are very rare in scholarly writing, and you should consult your instructor before launching such a venture.

Reviewing Your Note Cards

Ask yourself, "Do I have sufficient support from several sources for my contention?" Since many undergraduates attempt to rely upon one major source, this question is a vital one. Remember, especially, that relying heavily on one source shows that your research has been too restricted in its scope. A long string of citations to the work of one scholar over a length of several paragraphs reflects a lack of industry and initiative on your part. Moreover, reliance on one major source invites plagiarism because, knowing that you depend too heavily on the one source, you may be tempted to sneak in a few borrowed sentences without documentation. The works cited in your text, as well as the text itself, will reflect the quality of your research. Your instructor expects you to synthesize anywhere from eight to twenty-five sources into a readable and effective whole.

After arranging your note cards according to your outline, you will have a clear picture of note card strengths and failings. Often, one more trip to the library is necessary to fill out any gaps in your research.

WRITING THE ROUGH DRAFT

First, be certain that you write a rough draft. You cannot create a quality paper in one pass. Systematically, you must write your way through the outline and your note cards.

Write the paper using your own words and ideas. Use the note cards from source material as evidence or support. Avoid quoting from one source after another; instead rephrase most of the source material into your style, giving credit for any paraphrased ideas, of course. (See the sample paper, 170–193, for examples of the way one student maneuvered through paraphrase, quotation, and her own words.)

In general, you should cite only one source at a time in order to control the flow of your essay and to maintain proper documentation. Blanket citations to several sources are acceptable, but they generally require a content endnote (see 141–145).

Feel free to cite more than one source in a paragraph; in fact, you are encouraged to cite two or three supporting sources for a generalization. Note the following:

Each year more and more children suffer the trauma of phys-

ical and emotional abuse. Although the exact number remains

unknown, the Education Commission of the States reports that

some 60,000 cases occur annually (Cohen and Sussman 433).

Boys outnumber girls as victims of abuse until the teen

years (Chase 104). The death rate from cruelty exceeds that

from infectious disease (Fontana 196). In truth, few young

This example displays two points: each source is cited separately, one at a time, and three different sources provide support for the student's generalization.

Keep your purpose in mind as you write the various paragraphs. You will be arguing, proving, or supporting a thesis, not merely stringing together research information. Study the following suggestions for handling your reference material carefully before you write the rough draft of your paper.

Writing with Appropriate Language

Many words and phrases are peculiar to a certain topic. Therefore, while reading and note-taking, record words and phrases that you should use in your study. Get comfortable with them and use them effectively. In short, employ the language of the discipline. For example, the child abuse topic would improve your acquaintance with such terms as the following:

social worker	maltreatment
aggressive behavior	poverty levels
behavioral patterns	incestuous relations
hostility	stress
battered child	formative years
recurrence	guardians

As a writer on child abuse, you might need these terms, plus others. After all, a sociology paper must use terminology from the field. In fact, many writers compose a terminology list for use during writing to strengthen their noun and verb usage. Every discipline and every topic has a vernacular; you will be ahead if you learn it. Can you imagine writing a poetry paper without using such terms as *symbolism, imagery, rhythm,* or *rhyme?*

However, on a cautionary note, do not throw around specialized words if you are unfamiliar with their proper meanings and usage. Nothing betrays a lack of command of the subject matter more quickly than awkward, distorted usage of technical terminology. For example, the following sentence demonstrates an awkward, fumbling usage of big words; it is one that wholly distorts any meaning:

> The impediment maltreatment documents the national compulsion toward crippling economic children.

The words may be large, but what does the passage mean?

Writing with Unity, Coherence, and Clarity

After many hours of considerable effort, you are ready to give expression to your ideas, to share them with others, and to convince your readers of the validity of your findings. Therefore, you should construct your paper carefully, always seeking unity, coherence, and clarity.

Unity. Your paper will have unity if it explores one topic in depth, with each paragraph carefully expanding upon a single aspect of the thesis and/or topic. Your outline helps with unity (see above, ''Choosing an Outline Form,'' 107–110).

Coherence. Your paper will have coherence if your controlling ideas and your research evidence all flow together and function as an interrelated whole. Coherence requires that quotations and paraphrases be logical extensions of your writing, not intrusions or mere padding. Coherence also demands clear transitions that highlight the logical progression of your ideas: repetition of key words, pronouns, and synonyms, and other transitional words and phrases (for example, *also, furthermore, therefore, in addition,* and *thus*). Therefore, when writing or rewriting the first draft, pay special attention to transitions between major segments of your argument and to the smooth incorporation of quoted material, as shown in the following sample piece:

The most delicate members of our society, the children, appear the most likely affected by family problems. A recognition of causes for their mistreatment and a need for a cure face this society each day if we are to defeat what one authority calls "the greatest crippler and killer of our children--child abuse and neglect" (Fontana xvi). In fact, another writer argues that the "single greatest impediment to our improving the lives of America's children is the myth that we are a child-oriented society" (Zigler 39). This sociologist suggests that too many Americans will not respond to documented findings about child abuse (39). However, a growing concern among many segments of the population has spurred laws for protecting the rights of children, but even these new laws are difficult to enforce because, according to several sources, the families and the children themselves often lie to protect the abuse from being exposed in order to protect the family unit.[1]

Clarity. Your paper will have clarity if you use precise prose that avoids excessive rhetorical splendor and, at the other extreme, vague, abstract, and general words. Research writing is exact writing, employing concrete, specific words and featuring well-balanced sentences with proper subordination of minor elements. Note the exactness of the following sample paragraph:

Depression also causes a parent to beat a child, but
E. Milling Kinard suggests that treating the parent for
depression without removing the social problems of economic
poverty and emotional stress will probably have only limited success (403-06). The causal chain leading to abuse
may be complex to the point that social workers need to dip
into the life history of the parent/abuser, asking always,
"How is this adult a victim who needs help as much as his
or her battered child?"

Writing in the Proper Tense

When you are dealing with an event or concept of the past, your overall approach to the material should be in the past tense, as in the following example:

Perhaps an answer lies in preventing abuse, not in
makeshift remedies after the fact. For instance, let's
look at one example as summarized from a case study by
Leontine Young (76-77). Jane Neilson was the oldest of
ten children of an alcoholic father and promiscuous mother.
Jane became a prostitute and her mother shared the income. Along with three of her sisters, Jane was arrested
and spent time at the state correctional school. Later,

```
Jane had six children of her own, two of whom were illegit-

imate.  She married a man with a criminal record who abused

her and her children.  Jane and her husband frequently

separated; after he was arrested again, she began to drink

heavily.  Three of her children were placed under the care

of agencies.
```

Clearly, the use of the past tense is required for the case history of Jane Neilson, above. But note the use of present tense in the same paragraph:

```
Three of her children were placed under the care of agen-

cies.  Young points out that Jane Neilson's entire life has

been "dreary misery, a saga of exploitation, deprivation,

indifference, and hate" (76).  Then Young concludes: "What

she could have given any child is hard to see" (76).  In

truth, Jane Neilson is a victim of her own background; lit-

tle wonder that her children would suffer.
```

The words of the student and of Young are concerned with the present; therefore, the present tense is required. That is, a writer uses the historical present tense to indicate what is true at the present time and will remain true in the future.

You should use the present tense for most comments or observations by authorities about an issue under examination because the criticism is still in print and continues to be true in the present. Good usage demands ''Richard Ellmann argues,'' ''Professor Thompson writes,'' or ''T. S. Eliot stipulates,'' rather than the past tense verb forms: ''argued,'' ''wrote,'' or ''stipulated.''

Note the use of the historical present by both the student writer and the authority in this segment:

```
Today's society and shifting patterns of social class may

dictate, then, a climate for abuse.  Edward Zigler argues

that many parents are just not equipped today for parent-

hood (42).  He says, for instance, that the "extended fam-
```

```
ily  is  now rare in contemporary society, and with its

demise the new parent  has lost  the wisdom and daily support

of older, more experienced family members" (Zigler 42).
```

Follow this general rule: write your paper in the historical present tense except for those instances when you report historic happenings:

```
John F. Kennedy, who was assassinated in 1963,  serves  as

a trumpet of challenge to all Americans when he  says  in his

famous inaugural address: "And so, my fellow Americans: ask

not what your country can do for you--ask what you can do for

your country."
```

Writing an Introduction

Your opening must establish four things within the first three to six paragraphs:

Subject. You must identify or define your specific topic, especially as limited and narrowed to one issue.

Significance. Convince the reader that he or she *needs* to read what you have to say on this topic. For example, stress an issue such as the influence of specialized magazines or stress a writer as one of the premier short story writers in America. By quoting and paraphrasing an authority or two, or by citing other evidence in the opening, you establish a critical focus for the paper's reader.

Appeal. Attract the attention of your audience. In general, your reader has an intellectual interest in the topic, but he or she often needs motivation beyond a ho-hum, dry opening. See below for samples featuring appeal (especially "Relate to the Well Known" and "Challenge an Assumption").

Thesis. Early in the study, within the first few paragraphs, you should state your position in order to establish the direction of the study and to point to a conclusion.

How you work these essential elements into the framework of your opening will depend upon you and your style. They need not appear in this order. Also, you need not cram into the opening paragraph all these items at once. For instance, with the sample research paper on child abuse, 170–193, the thesis is not stated until the sixth paragraph, after the student has opened with a quotation, established child abuse as an issue, then moved to her focus upon the parents as victims.

The following techniques are effective individually as opening paragraphs, and when you combine several of these you can build a full introduction several paragraphs in length.

RELATE TO THE WELL KNOWN

> Television flashes images into our living rooms, radios invade the confines of our automobiles, and local newspapers flash their headlines to us daily. However, one medium that has gained great strength and influence within the past decade is the specialized magazine.
>
> NOTE: This type of opening automatically suggests the *significance* of the subject as it *appeals* to interests of the reader.

PROVIDE BACKGROUND INFORMATION

> In 1941 Eudora Welty published her first book of short stories, <u>A Curtain of Green</u>. That group of stories was followed by <u>The Wide Net</u> (1943) and <u>The Bride of the Innisfallen</u> (1955). Each collection brought her critical acclaim, but taken together the three volumes establish her as one of America's premier short story writers.
>
> NOTE: Avoid providing a truckload of background information. Offer only the essentials necessary for the reader to understand the thesis. Later, in the body of the discussion, you may bring in additional background information when and where necessary to clarify a premise of your argument.

USE A BRIEF QUOTATION

See the opening of the sample research paper, 174.

CHALLENGE AN ASSUMPTION

> Christianity dominates the religious life of most Americans to the point that many assume that it dominates the world population as well. However, despite the denominational missionaries who have reached out to every corner of the globe, only one out of every four people on the globe is a Christian, and far fewer than that practice their faith.

PROVIDE A BRIEF SUMMARY

Ernest Hemingway's novel <u>The Old Man and the Sea</u> narrates the ordeal of an old Cuban fisherman, Santiago, who manages to endure a test of strength when locked in a tug of war with a giant marlin that he hooks and against the sharks who later attack his small boat. The heroic and stoic nature of this old hero reflects the traditional Hemingway code.

REVIEW OF THE LITERATURE

The most delicate members of our society, the children, appear the most likely to be affected by family problems. A recognition of causal elements and a need for a cure face this society each day if we are to defeat what one critic calls "the greatest crippler and killer of our children—child abuse and neglect" (Fontana xvi). Yet we fail to act. In fact, one writer argues that "the single greatest impediment to our improving the lives of America's children is the myth that we are a child-oriented society" (Zigler 39). This sociologist suggests that too many Americans will not respond to documented findings about child abuse (39). Yet the death rate from cruelty exceeds that from infectious disease (Fontana 196). Worse, one critic argues that many parents are just not equipped today for parenthood (Zigler 42). The situation is so bad that one authority warns parents to prepare for their children to turn on them and to become parent abusers (Kratcoski 437).

USE DATA, STATISTICS, AND STARTLING EVIDENCE

Severe abuse is on the rise. Each year many children suffer the trauma of physical and emotional abuse. Although the exact number remains unknown, the Education Commission of the States reports that some 60,000 cases occur annually (Cohen and Sussman 433). Boys outnumber the girls in suffering

from abuse until the teen years (Chase 104). The death rate
from cruelty exceeds that from infectious disease (Fontana
196). In truth, few young persons reach maturity without a
severe spanking from an angry parent.

SPIN OFF FROM OR TAKE EXCEPTION TO CRITICAL VIEWS

Lorraine Hansberry's popular and successful <u>A Raisin in
the Sun</u>, which first appeared on Broadway in 1959, is a problem play that tells the story of a black family's determination to move out of the ghetto to a better life. Most critics have said that this escape theme explains the drama's
forceful dramatic conflict and its importance to the black
movement in general. Yet another issue lies at the heart of
the drama. Hansberry develops a modern view of the sociological aspects of black matriarchy in order to examine the co-
hesive and, more importantly, the conflict-producing effects
it has on the individual members of the Younger family.

COMBINE YOUR THESIS WITH CRITICAL SOURCE MATERIALS

<u>Billy Budd</u> possesses many characteristics of the Bible.
According to Newton Arvin, Melville centers his story around
the "fall of man and the loss of Paradise" (294). Raymond
Weaver sees it as a gospel story filled with crime, sin, punishment, love, and innocence, or of virtue versus vice, in
which evil and horror are given their fullest play (37-38).
Throughout this tale, Melville intentionally uses biblical
references as a means of portraying and distinguishing various characters, ideas, and symbols, and of presenting different moral principles by which we should govern our lives. On
that point, E. L. Grant Watson insists that Melville uses his
characters to hint at a "deep and solemn purpose . . . "
(319). The reader, therefore, discovers below the surface of
the story the struggles and passions that good and evil in-
volve.

DELAYED THESIS (From paragraph six:)

Perhaps an answer lies in preventing abuse, not in make-shift remedies after the fact. Parents who abuse their children should be treated as victims, not criminals. Child abuse is a symptom of the parent's condition. Reaching out to the parent before a child appears in the emergency room may prove difficult, but our solving the causes of abuse may be the only way to stop this escalating maltreatment of America's precious children.

> NOTE: Delay is appropriate when the reader is likely to be surprised by or be hostile to your thesis or when the inductive process by which you thought out the problem is a vital part of your opening. Otherwise, the thesis should appear fairly early.

THESIS OPENING

Parents who abuse their children are victims and should be treated as such, not as criminals. Granted, they are not battered like the youngsters, but society must understand that child abuse is a symptom of the parent's economic condition and social background. Reaching out to the parent before a child appears in the emergency room may prove difficult, but our solving the causes of abuse may be the only way to stop this escalating maltreatment of America's precious children.

> NOTE: Unless you are writing a scientific or technical paper, the thesis will rarely appear as the first sentence of the paper because it short-circuits the other functions of a complete introduction.

DEFINITION OPENING

Black matriarchy, a sociological concept with origins in slavery, is a family situation, according to E. Earl Baughman, in which no husband is present or, if he is present, in which the wife and/or mother exercises the main influence over family affairs (80—81). Hansberry develops a modern view of black matriarchy in order to examine the conflict-producing effects it has on the individual members of the Younger family.

THINGS TO AVOID IN THE OPENING

Avoid a purpose statement, such as "The purpose of this study is. . . ."

Avoid repetition of the title, since the title should appear on the first page of the text anyway.

Avoid complex or difficult questions because you want to draw the reader into your paper, not force him or her away. However, general rhetorical questions are acceptable.

Avoid simple dictionary definitions, such as "Webster defines monogamy as marriage with only one person at a time." See immediately above for an effective definition opening.

Avoid humor, unless your subject deals with humor or satire, because research studies, in general, are serious examinations of issues and scholarly literature.

Avoid artwork and cute lettering unless the paper's nature requires it (for example, "The Circle as Advertising Symbol").

Writing the Body of Your Paper

In brief, the body of your paper should feature a logical development of the subdivisions of your outline. If your outline has a dynamic order (see 106–107), then your body should develop fully along the lines of that basic argument in defense of your thesis sentence. Your primary concern should be clarification and amplification of your topic as you defend your thesis with well-reasoned statements, documented wherever necessary. The sample paper, 170–193, will be especially helpful in demonstrating how one student clarified and amplified upon the child abuse topic.

Do not label separate sections of your text with subtitles, centered headings, or Roman numerals (although scientific papers usually *do* label separate sections with numerals or headings). In the humanities such division markers are generally reserved for much longer works. Therefore, normal paragraphing for the body is adequate.

Writing the Conclusion

Your conclusion should neither be a summary nor a mere restatement of your thesis. Instead, it must go beyond the thesis to reach a judgment, to express your approval of one side of an issue, to discuss your findings, or to offer directives. To put it succinctly, you should say something worthwhile. After all, your readers have stayed with you through eight or nine pages: you owe them a concluding statement.

The following techniques are effective as closing paragraphs; you may employ several to build a longer, more involved conclusion.

RESTATE THE THESIS AND REACH BEYOND IT

Let us face the problem straight on and try to erase it in the best way we can rather than throw up our hands and say that all we can do is help the victims and merely label the abuser a "black sheep." Let us look to the parent or guardian as a victim as well and try, difficult though it may be, to show love, warmth, and concern to these people who too often silently cry out of loneliness, isolation, and alienation. Their violent beating of a child, though we cannot condone it, may be a cry for help. People, whether young or old, rich or poor, healthy or sick, need love and the warmth that family life accomplishes. Unfortunately, those children who lack love fall victims to hostile, aggressive physical abuse and probably, because they cannot give love, grow up to be abusers themselves.

CLOSE WITH AN EFFECTIVE QUOTATION

Billy Budd, forced to leave the Rights of Man, goes aboard the Bellipotent where law, not morality, is supreme. His death is an image of the crucifixion, but the image is not one of hope. William Braswell best summarizes the mystery of the novel by suggesting that the crucifixion, for Melville, "had long been an image of human life, more suggestive of man's suffering than of man's hope" (146).

RETURN THE FOCUS OF A LITERARY STUDY TO THE AUTHOR

By her characterization of Walter, Lorraine Hansberry has raised the black male above the typical stereotype. Walter is not a social problem, a mere victim of matriarchy. Rather, Hansberry creates a character who breaks out of the traditional sociological image that dehumanizes the black male. Creating a character who struggles with his fate and rises above it, Hansberry has elevated the black male. As James Baldwin puts it, "Time has made some changes in the Negro face" (24).

OFFER A DIRECTIVE OR SOLUTION

The four points above demonstrate a central issue: the troubled parents who were victims in their own right and those who are victimized by circumstances today must be helped to recognize their real potential as human beings. The responsibility falls on all health professionals to provide the necessary treatment. Major cities across the nation and many rural communities are establishing child abuse centers and parental self-help groups. A few of the most successful community involvement programs are the Child Abuse Prevention Center in Toledo, the Johnson County Coalition for Prevention of Child Abuse in Kansas City, and the Council for Prevention of Child Abuse and Neglect in Seattle. More cities should establish such programs.

COMPARE PAST TO PRESENT

In the traditional patriarchal family, the child was legal property of the parents. But the idea that children are the property of the parents and, therefore, may receive whatever punishment seems necessary, no longer holds true. Social organizations and governmental agencies now help young victims in their search for preventive measures. Unlike the past, children today have rights too!

DISCUSSION OF TEST RESULTS

The results of this experiment were similar in nature to expectations, but perhaps the statistical significance, because of the small subject size, was biased toward the de-

```
layed conditions of the curve.  The subjects were, perhaps,

not representative of the total population because of their

prior exposure to test procedures.  Another factor that may

have affected the curves was the presentation of the data.

The images on the screen were available for five seconds, and

that amount of time may have enabled the subjects to store

each image effectively.  If the time period for each image

sequence were reduced to one or two seconds, there could be

lower recall scores, thereby reducing the differences between

the control group and the experimental group.
```

THINGS TO AVOID IN THE CONCLUSION

Avoid afterthoughts or additional ideas; now is the time to end the paper, not begin a new thought. However, scientific papers often discuss options and possible alterations that might affect test results (see above, "Discussion of Test Results," 124).

Avoid the use of closing transitional words such as "thus," "in conclusion," or "finally" at the beginning of your last paragraph where the reader can see the end of the paper. However, such tags are often advisable when your conclusion begins several paragraphs before the final one.

Avoid first person "I," especially such phrases as "I am convinced that" or "I believe" or "I have thereby proved." Keep the reader's attention focused on your subject, not you. However, use of "I" in textual discussion and explanation is acceptable.

Avoid stopping at an awkward spot or trailing off into meaningless or irrelevant information.

Avoid questions that raise new issues, but rhetorical questions that restate the issues are acceptable.

Avoid fancy artwork.

Handling Short Prose Quotations and Paraphrases

There are two basic forms for incorporating quoted matter into your text. First, if the quotation will take up no more than four lines in your paper, you should place it within the body of your text and enclose it within quotation marks. If longer than four lines, the quotation should be set off from the main text (see 137–138 for details about long, indented quotations).

Plan your short paraphrases and quotations as one-sentence units so that your transitions from source material to personal thoughts will be clear to the reader. Also provide plenty of signals for the reader, who must know the sources for quoted and paraphrased materials. Brief introductions of the quotations and paraphrases, usually with the authority's name, will meet this requirement.

In addition, your text must include within parentheses a citation for the source of each quotation and every paraphrase. Remember that the entries in "Works Cited" (see 194–219) will list only general information on the book or article; your citation within the text must name a specific *page* in the book or journal. Conform to these rules:

SIGNAL THE BEGINNING OF QUOTATIONS AND PARAPHRASES

Introduce each paraphrase or quotation, whenever convenient, with the name of the authority:

    Edward Zigler argues that many parents are just not

    equipped today for parenthood (42).

> NOTE: Describe or identify the source if such information is available: for example, "Adam B. Ulam, prominent political scientist, writes. . . ."

PROVIDE PAGE NUMBERS

Include a page number immediately after the paraphrase or quotation (as shown immediately above) or immediately after the name of the authority:

    Edward Zigler (42) argues that many parents are just not

    equipped for parenthood.

> But providing the page number at the end provides a clear indication to the reader as to when the paraphrase ends.

INCLUDE AUTHORITY'S NAME IN THE CITATION

When you do not use the authority's name to introduce the material, include his or her name within parentheses along with a specific page number:

    He says "the new parent has lost the wisdom and daily

    support of older, more experienced family members" (Zigler

    42).

CITE EVERY BORROWED SENTENCE

Every borrowed sentence needs citation of some sort. Especially avoid quoting or paraphrasing a full paragraph with only one citation to the source at the very end. That is, every sentence with borrowed materials must contain a signal to the reader: an authority's name, quotation marks, page number, or pronoun reference. The following sample is acceptable because one authority is clearly credited for the first two sentences, the student has obviously written the third, another authority gets credit for the fourth, and the fifth again belongs to the student:

> Zigler, for example, advocates an expanded effort to educate young people for parenthood. He supports the program of the Office of Child Development and the Office of Education which offers to schools and other organizations several courses on parenthood that were prepared specifically for adolescents (42). Such a program makes sense because it seeks prevention and not remedies after the act of child abuse. Another sociologist concurs, saying, "A central notion in the treatment model is the building of a social responsibility, the realization that each of us is an important element of society" (Giarreto 5). Youngsters who are future parents should be helped toward responsible social behavior.

KEEP A BIBLIOGRAPHY CARD FOR EVERY SOURCE CITED

For each in-text citation be certain that you have a bibliography card that contains full information on the source, as follows:

> Kinard, E. Milling. "Child Abuse and Depression: Cause or Consequence?" Child Welfare 61 (1982): 402-13.

You will need this card later for your "Works Cited" page because every in-text citation *must* be presented there with a full bibliography entry (see "Works Cited," 194–219).

KEEP CITATIONS SHORT

Keep in-text citations short while providing necessary information in the text and/or in the parenthetical citation. For example, the following is acceptable when only one work by Fontana appears in your "Works Cited":

Vincent J. Fontana devotes an entire book to the subject

of child abuse.

If Fontana has two works listed, then say:

Vincent J. Fontana, who has written two books and numer-

ous articles on the subject, devotes his Somewhere a Child Is

Crying to the crucial side effects of abuse upon the chil-

dren.

Remember, however, to cite a page number if you refer not to the book as
a whole but to a specific part:

According to Fontana, the death rate from cruelty ex-

ceeds that from infectious disease (196).

or

According to Fontana (196), the death rate from cruelty

exceeds that from infectious disease.

NOTE: Only the first example provides *clear* evidence for both the beginning and ending of the Fontana citation.

INCLUDE TITLE OF WORK WHENEVER NECESSARY

When more than one work by an author is cited, the author's name alone, with appropriate page number, becomes unacceptable because "Works Cited" will contain two references to this same writer. In this case, provide a shortened version of the title. In the humanities, the title of the work, rather than the date, is usually more informative (however, the date becomes important to the sciences; that is, citing "Russell and Thompson, 1983" suggests recent scientific findings while "Jones, 1962" suggests dated and therefore suspect findings). Note the following example:

In her 1980 preface to a collection of her stories, Eudora Welty makes this observation, "What I do in writing of any character is to try to enter into the mind, heart, and skin of a human being who is not myself" (Collected Stories xi). She stipulates further that "time has to move through a mind" . . . in order to call forth "some crucial recognition" (Eye of the Story 166).

> NOTE: Complete titles of the two works cited above are: *The Collected Stories of Eudora Welty* and *The Eye of the Story: Selected Essays and Reviews.*

Note this next example:

As he stresses the nobility of man, Joseph Campbell suggests that the mythic hero is symbolic of the "divine creative and redemptive image which is hidden within us all . . ." (Hero 39). He elevates the human mind to an "ultimate mythogenetic zone—the creator and destroyer, the slave and yet the master, of all the gods" (Masks 472).

> NOTE: Complete titles of the two works by Campbell cited above are: *The Hero With a Thousand Faces* and *The Masks of God.*

COMBINE PARAPHRASE WITH QUOTATION

Combine paraphrase and quotation in the same paragraph as necessary to mold them into one unified whole. Let the reader know who says what. Note how this next passage moves the reader smoothly through the diverse materials yet also cites accurately each source:

A recognition of causes for their mistreatment and a need for a cure face this society each day if we are to defeat what one authority calls "the greatest crippler and killer of our children—child abuse and neglect" (Fontana xvi). In fact, another writer argues that "the single greatest impediment to our improving the lives of America's children is the myth that we are a child-oriented society" (Zigler 29). This sociologist suggests that too many Americans will not respond to documented findings about child abuse (39).

You cannot paraphrase and synthesize such material into the desired context without intelligent, thoughtful effort.

USE DIFFERENT TYPES OF INTRODUCTIONS

Seek variety with introductions and citations of short quotations and paraphrases. As you work your way through the rough draft, you will find ways of constructing fluent sentences with only minimal documentation to the sources. The citations must be precise but not disruptive. The following examples demonstrate a few methods. You will discover many others throughout this chapter and will create many of your own:

```
Others, like Campbell (461) and Frazer (xix), hold an oppo-
site point of view.
Others hold an opposite point of view (e.g., Campbell 461 and
Frazer xix).
Lewis Mumford has argued this point before (313).
One critic (Newton Arvin 21-22) has argued this point before.
In this sense, according to Dr. Clifford Sager, the marriage
contract becomes "a therapeutic and educational concept that
tries to spell out the vague and intuitive" (48).
"The marriage contract," says Dr. Clifford Sager, "becomes a
therapeutic and educational concept that tries to spell out
the vague and intuitive" (48).
In this sense, Dr. Clifford Sager (48) envisions the marriage
contract as both therapeutic and educational.
Another critic's proposal creates a fitting conclusion to a
discussion of the creative marriages of the future: "It is
fallacious, then, even to speak of 'the future of marriage.'
We should rather speak of the 'marriage in the future'" (Ber-
nard 302).
```

ALTER INITIAL CAPITALS IN QUOTED MATTER

Alter initial capital words of quoted material in certain instances. In general, you should reproduce quoted materials exactly; yet one exception is permitted for logical reasons: if the quotation forms a grammatical part of the sentence in which it occurs, you need not capitalize the first word of the quotation, even though it is capitalized in the original, as in:

```
Another writer argues that "the single greatest impedi-
ment. . . ."
```
even though the original states:

```
"The single greatest impediment. . . ."
```

Restrictive modifiers, such as "that" or "because," limit and make the information essential to the sentence. Therefore, a comma is inappropriate before the quotation, and without a comma the capital letter is unnecessary.

However, if the quotation follows a formal introduction set off by a comma or colon, you should capitalize the first word as in the original:

```
Another writer argues, "The single greatest impedi-
ment. . . ."
```
or

```
Zigler states: "The single greatest impediment. . . ."
```

USE ELLIPSIS DOTS CORRECTLY

Omit quoted material with ellipses when you want to omit a word or words that would complete the total construction of a sentence. There will be instances when you will quote only part of a sentence. Ellipses must *not* be used to change the spirit or essential meaning of the original, for example, to remove a word such as *not*. Quote sources exactly in correct grammatical structure even when using ellipses. In many cases, incorporating fragments of the quotation into your prose will be the most effective. Note the following:

```
The long-distance marriage, according to William Nichols,
"works best when there are no minor-aged children to be con-
sidered," the two people are "equipped by temperament and
personality to spend a considerable amount of time alone,"
and both are able to "function in a mature, highly indepen-
dent fashion" (54).
```

In the sample above, the omissions are handled smoothly by the writer's grammatical styling of the material. The phrases are worked into the sentence smoothly and ellipsis dots would only disturb the reader. In other cases, however, you may need to indicate an omission by the use of ellipsis dots (three spaced dots for an omission and a fourth, if necessary, as the period to end the sentence). The situations usually occur with longer quotations or in places where the quoted matter does not mesh smoothly with your own style.

Material omitted from the middle of a source

Phil Withim objects to the idea that "such episodes are in-

tended to demonstrate that Vere . . . . has the intelligence

and insight to perceive the deeper issue" (118).

Material omitted from the end of a source

R. W. B. Lewis declares that "if Hester has sinned, she has

done so as an affirmation of life, and her sin is the source

of life . . . ." (215).

> NOTE: Parenthetical documentation in each of the last two examples is placed inside the fourth period because the page citation is part of the context of the sentence. Such is not the case with long indented quotations (see 137–38). Also, should there be no documentation at the end of the quotation, use a period first and then the ellipsis dots:

Furthermore, Zigler (42) cautions us that "the abusing mother

in such homes experiences considerable stress which is exac-

erbated by her sense of isolation. . . ."

> NOTE: Snug the period up next to the final word and then add the ellipsis in the above instance.

Material omitted from the beginning of a source

He states: ". . . the new parent has lost the wisdom and

daily support of older, more experienced family members"

(Zigler 42).

However, *avoid* such ellipsis dots at the beginning of any quotation by recasting the structure to eliminate the dots and thereby improve the reading of the material:

He states that "the new parent has lost the wisdom. . . ."

Complete sentence(s) omitted from the middle of a source (use four dots)

Zigler reminds us that ''child abuse is found more frequently

in a single (female) parent home in which the mother is work-

ing . . . . The unavailability of quality day care can only

make this situation more stressful'' (42).

> NOTE: The fourth period signals omission of a sentence or two within the middle of this quoted material.

Line(s) of poetry omitted

>   Do ye hear the children weeping, O my brothers,
>
>   Ere the sorrow comes with years?
>
>   They are leaning their young heads against their mothers,
>
>   And <u>that</u> cannot stop their tears.
>
> . . . .
>
>   They are weeping in the playtime of the others,
>
>   In the country of the free.   (Browning 382)

>   NOTE: A complete line of spaced periods indicates omission of a complete
>   line or several lines of verse.

Paragraphs omitted (but avoid omitting entire paragraphs by recasting the sentences, if possible)

>   Zigler makes this observation:
>
>   With many others, I am nevertheless optimistic that
>
>   our nation will eventually display its inherent great-
>
>   ness and successfully correct the many ills that I have
>
>   touched upon here.
>
> . . . .
>
>   Of course, much remains that could and should be
>
>   done, including increased efforts in the area of family
>
>   planning, the widespread implementation of Education for
>
>   Parenthood programs, an increase in the availability of
>
>   homemaker and child care services, and a re-examination
>
>   of our commitment to doing what is in the best interest
>
>   of every child in America. (42)

USE BRACKETS FOR INTERPOLATIONS

Add to quotations with the use of brackets when you find it necessary, on rare occasions, to insert personal comment within a quotation. You should enclose such an interpolation within brackets. Note the following:

Use brackets to clarify

>   One critic indicates that "we must avoid the temptation to
>
>   read it [The Scarlet Letter] heretically."

Use brackets to correct grammatical structure

"John F. Kennedy . . . [was] an immortal figure of courage
and dignity in the hearts of most Americans."

Use brackets to note the addition of underlining

He says, for instance, that the "extended family is now rare
in contemporary society, and with its demise the new parent
has <u>lost the wisdom</u> [my emphasis] and daily support of older,
more experienced family members" (Zigler 42).

Indicate errors in the original with *sic*

Use the brackets with "sic" to indicate that an error in the original is
quoted exactly as it appeared in the original. The word "sic" is Latin for "thus."
Its usage means that you are aware of the error or unusual usage and that you are
not responsible for it, as in the following:

"John F. Kennedy, assassinated in November of 1964 [sic] became overnight an immortal figure of courage and dignity in
the hearts of most Americans."
NOTE: The assassination occurred in 1963.

However, do not burden your text with the use of "sic" for historic material in which misspellings are obvious:

Faire seemely pleasaunce each to other makes,
With goodly purposes there as they sit:
And in his falsed fancy he her takes
To be the fairest wight that lived yit. . . .

Most typewriters do not have brackets; therefore, you should leave extra space for
the brackets and write them in with ink.

PUNCTUATE QUOTATIONS PROPERLY

Punctuate short quotations by placing commas and periods *inside* the quotation marks in every instance, with the one exception shown below. Place semicolons and colons *outside* the quotation marks in every instance. Place the question mark and the exclamation mark inside the quotation marks if the mark is part
of the quoted material; otherwise, place it outside the quotation marks. Place
single quotation marks around short quotations set within longer quotations.

Place commas and periods inside quotation marks

For example, if the original material states:

"They are weeping in the playtime of the others,
In the country of the free."   (Browning 382)

Then note the following variations that, with one exception, keep the periods and commas inside the quotation marks:

"They are weeping in the playtime of the others," says Elizabeth Browning (382), "In the country of the free."

"They are weeping," says Elizabeth Browning (382), "in the
playtime of the others / In the country of the free."
> NOTE: The comma after weeping does not appear in the original, but it must
> be added for grammatical clarity. The slash mark (virgule) separates two
> lines of poetry.

"They are weeping," says Elizabeth Browning, "in the playtime
of the others . . ." (382).
> EXCEPTION: The period must follow a page citation.

"They are weeping in the playtime of the others," says Elizabeth Browning, who urges also that the weeping unfortunately
occurs in "the country of the free" (382).

> NOTE: The period must go outside the parenthetical documentation *unless*
> the quotation is set off separately and indented (see 137–138).

Place semicolons and colons outside quotation marks

For example, if the original material states:

The extended family is now rare in contemporary society, and
with its demise the new parent has lost the wisdom and daily
support of older, more experienced family members. (Zigler 42)

Then note the following possibilities:

Zigler (42) admits that "the extended family is now rare in
contemporary society"; however, he stresses the greatest loss
as the "wisdom and daily support of older, more experienced
family members."

Zigler's meaning seems quite clear when he laments the demise
of the "extended family": that is, the loss of the "wisdom
and daily support of older, more experienced family members"
(42).

Arranging question marks and exclamation marks

Question marks and exclamation marks should be arranged with your in-
text citations so that they do not interfere with one another. Note the following
examples:

The philosopher Thompson (118) asks, "How should we order our
lives?"

How should we order our lives, asks Thompson (118), when we
face "hostility from every quarter?"

Thompson (118) in the passion of his address to union members, shouted, "We must bring order into our lives even
though we face 'hostility from every quarter'"!

Then Thompson (118) shouted, "I shall face down hostility
from every quarter!"

> NOTE: The marks go inside the quotation mark only when the quotation
> demands it; otherwise, the larger sentence receives the mark.

Place single quotation marks inside quotation marks

Note the following examples:

George Gilder (32) believes that "monogamy is central to any
democratic social contract, designed to prevent a breakdown
of society into 'war of every man against every other man.'"

Remember: The period always goes inside quotation marks with the one exception shown below:

George Gilder believes that "monogamy is central to any democratic social contract, designed to prevent a breakdown of
society into 'war of every man against every other man'"
(32).

USE SHORTENED CITATIONS FOR FREQUENT REFERENCES

Frequent references to the same work require abbreviated citations to page or line only. If you base your paper solely on a single work (novel, drama, short story, long poem, or document) and if this fact is obvious to the reader, you need not repeat the author's name in every instance. A specific page reference is adequate, or provide act, scene, and line if appropriate. Note the following:

> When the character Beneatha denies the existence of God in
> Hansberry's <u>A Raisin in the Sun</u>, Mama slaps her in the face
> and forces her to repeat after her, "In my mother's house
> there is still God" (37). Then Mama adds, "There are some
> ideas we ain't going to have in this house. Not long as I am
> at the head of the family" (37). Thus Mama meets Beneatha's
> challenge head on. The other mother in the Younger household
> is Ruth who does not lose her temper, but through kindness
> wins over her husband (79–80). In fact, she refuses Walter's
> plea that she use her influence to convince Mama to buy the
> liquor store, saying, "Walter, that ain't none of our money"
> (15).

As long as the references obviously cite the same work, you need not repeat the author's name because a page number will suffice. For example, after you have established one major work, then simple references to act, scene, and line(s) are sufficient, as shown:

> The king cautions Prince Henry:
> Thy place in council thou hast rudely lost,
> Which by thy younger brother is supplied,
> And art almost an alien to the hearts
> Of all the court and princes of my blood.
>
> (3.2.32–35)
>
> NOTE: Your instructor may request traditional Roman numerals for this citation, in which case you would write "III.ii.32–35" (see also 165).

Handling Long Indented Quotations

Quotations that will exceed four lines in your paper should be indented and no quotation marks should be used. But do not overuse long quotations. The obvious fact is that most readers tend to skip over long, indented material unless it

is strongly introduced and unless such quotations occur infrequently. The proper
method for such quotations is shown below:

    long-distance nature of their marriage as temporary and not a

    fixed lifestyle, according to one source (124).   In his crit-

    ical article Nichols makes this conclusion:

        Whether long-distance marriage will facilitate or

        retard growth and deepening of the relationship be-

        tween husband and wife is an unknown, and probably

        depends a great deal on the individuals, their ma-

        turity, and on the degree of their commitment to

        their careers—and to each other. (54)

    Another creative marriage alternative evolving in our society

    is the idea of sharing roles.

As indicated in this example, you should observe the following rules:

1. Make certain that the quotation is properly introduced. Use a colon to link
   the quotation with its introduction.
2. Double-space the quotation and separate the quotation from the text by
   triple-spacing.
3. Do not employ quotation marks with a long quotation that is indented
   except for quotations within the quotation.
4. Indent the material ten spaces from your regular margin, but the right
   margin needs no special indentation.
5. If quoted matter begins with the opening of a paragraph in the original
   source, then indent the first line fifteen spaces from the left margin—the
   quotation, that is, carries its own paragraph indentation. Otherwise, there
   is no extra indentation of the first line.
6. Place the in-text citation flush right after the last word of the quotation and
   on the same line if possible; otherwise, drop down and place the citation
   flush right one double-space below the last line of the quotation (for
   example, see the Shakespeare quotation above).

Handling Poetry Quotations

Short passages of quoted poetry (one or two lines) should be incorporated
into your text as in the following:

Eliot's "The Waste Land" (1922) remains a springtime search for nourishing water: "Sweet Thames, run softly, for I speak not loud or long" (3.12) says the speaker in the "The Fire Sermon," while in Part 5 the speaker of "What the Thunder Said" yearns for "a damp gust / Bringing rain" (5.73–74).

As these examples indicate, you should conform to certain conventions:

1. Set off the quotation with quotation marks.
2. Indicate separate lines of the poetry text by the use of a virgule (/) with a space before and after the slash mark.
3. Place documentation within parentheses immediately following the quotation and inside the period because the reference, like the quotation, is part of the basic sentence.
4. Use Arabic numerals whenever possible for books, parts, volumes, and chapters of works; acts, scenes, and lines of plays; cantos, stanzas, and lines of poetry. In your text write:

Act 1 of Antony and Cleopatra

Part 2 of Goethe's Faust

Chapter 16 of Far From the Madding Crowd

Book 2 of The Faerie Queene

Volume 3 of Dryden's Works

In your documentation, write:

(Ant.1.1.12–13)	for act 1, scene 1, lines 12–13
(Faust 2.114)	for part 2, line 114
(Madding 211–12)	for pages 211 and 212
(FQ 1.9.3.23–27)	for book, canto, stanza, and lines
(Matthew 2.5–6)	for chapter 2, lines 5–6
(II Kings 8.12)	for Second Kings, chapter 8, line 12
(4:434–35; 66–75)	for volume 4, pages 434–35, lines 66–75

If there is danger that your reader might misunderstand your citation, then by all means add clarifying words or abbreviations:

(5.pt.2:16–17; lines 201–02)

or

(Pt. 2 of vol. 5: 16–17; lines 201–02)

5. Retain Roman numerals for citing pages that are so numbered in the text
being cited (for example, preface, table of contents, and other preliminary
pages of books):

```
(Fontana iv-v)

(Madding ii-iv)
```

Also retain Roman numerals for identifying persons in a series, such as Henry
VIII or George I. Some instructors may request that you retain Roman numerals
for traditional documentation of poetry:

```
Oth. IV.ii.7-13

          or

FQ II.viii.14
```

Longer passages of poetry (three or more lines) are handled differently, as shown
by the following passage from Shakespeare's *Hamlet:*

```
In his famous soliloquy, Hamlet allows his emotions to over-

flow as he declares:
```

```
          To be, or not to be: that is the question:
          Whether 't is nobler in the mind to suffer
          The slings and arrows of outrageous fortune,
          Or to take arms against a sea of troubles,
          And by opposing end them? To die, to sleep--
          No more; and by a sleep to say we end
          The heart-ache and the thousand natural shocks
          That flesh is heir to. . . .  (Ham. 3.1.56-63)
```

```
Hamlet's frustration now borders on thoughts of suicide that

would remove him from the turmoil of his mother's

actions. . . .
```

Again, you should follow certain rules:

1. Indent the quotation ten spaces or, in the case of extremely short or long
lines (as above), center it on the page.
2. Type with double-spacing and without quotation marks. Separate the
quotation from the text by triple-spacing.

3. Use this method whenever poetry quotations run longer than two lines.
4. Place the page and line citation far to the right or below the quotation.
   The citation is not a contextual part of the quoted sentence of poetry and
   therefore does not go inside the period as with short quotations.
5. Do not use "1." or "ll." for "lines" because of confusion with the
   number 1. If necessary for clarity, write "lines 23–26."
6. Place the parenthetical documentation on the same line with the last line of
   verse if room permits; otherwise, place it flush right below the quotation:

> Meredith opens <u>Modern Love</u> with the lament of sorrow for his
> grieving wife:
>
>> By this he knew she wept with waking eyes:
>>
>> That, at his hand's light quiver by her head,
>>
>> The strange low sobs that shook their common bed
>>
>> Were called into her with a sharp surprise,
>>
>> And strangled mute, like little gaping snakes,
>>
>> Dreadfully venomous to him.   (1.1–6)
>
> That beginning sets the stage for the poet's. . . .

In other cases, place it below:

>> Like sculptured effigies they might be seen
>>
>> Upon their marriage tomb, the sword between;
>>
>> Each wishing for the sword that severs all.
>>
>>   (1.14–16)

CONTENT ENDNOTES

Content endnotes will be necessary on a limited basis for most undergraduate research. As a general rule, you should put important matters into the text
and should omit entirely the unimportant and marginally related items. However,
when various circumstances do call for content endnotes, they should conform to
these rules:

1. Content endnotes are *not* documentation notes. References to sources are
   now made by in-text citations and the full entries in "Works Cited."
2. Place endnotes on a separate page(s) following the last page of your text.
   Label the page "Notes." (See 190 for an example.)

3. Place endnote reference numerals within the text of your paper by turning the roller of the typewriter so that the Arabic numeral strikes about half a space above the line. Each numeral immediately follows the material to which it refers, usually at the end of a sentence, with no space between the superscript numeral and a word or mark of punctuation. A sample follows:

> Third, a program to advise young girls and boys about incest could prevent many children from ruining themselves and perhaps help them preserve the family unit.[2] The case of Leigh. . . .

4. Complete documentation to endnote sources must appear in your "Works Cited" just as with your in-text citations. That is, you may mention a source in a content endnote that is not mentioned in the main text; the source requires regular documentation. Do not put full documentation into the endnote. (See samples below.)

The sample endnotes below should serve as guidelines for the types of notes occasionally required of research writers:

Blanket Citation

> [1] On this point see Giarretto (2), de Young (581), Kinard (406–08), and Young (81).

or

> [2] On this point see Campbell (_Masks_ 170–225; _Hero_ 342–45), Frazer (106), and Baird (287–89).

Remember: Your "Works Cited" should provide full documentation to these sources.

Related Matters Not Germane to the Text

> [3] The problems of incest and sexual abuse are explored in Giarretto, Walters, and also de Young. These authorities cite the need for preventive measures, if possible, before damage occurs to the children; nevertheless, sexual abuse,

like a disease, is here today in horrifying case after case,
and we don't have a cure.

Suggest Literature on a Related Topic

[4] For additional study of the effects of alcoholics on
children, see especially the Journal of Studies on Alcohol
for the article by Wolin et al. and the bibliography on the
topic by Orme and Rimmer. In addition, group therapy for
children of alcoholics is examined in Hawley and Brown.

Major Source Requiring Frequent In-Text Citation

[5] All citations to Shakespeare are to the Parrott edition.

or

[6] Dryden's poems are cited from the California edition
of the Works and documented in the text with first references
to each poem giving volume, page, and lines and with subsequent references citing only lines.

Compare Textual Commentary with Another Source

[7] Cf. James Baird who argues that the whiteness of Melville's whale is "the sign of the all-encompassing God"
(257). Baird states: "It stands for what Melville calls at
the conclusion of the thirty-fifth chapter of Moby-Dick 'the
inscrutable tides of God'; and it is of these tides as well
that the great White Whale himself is the quintessential em-
blem, the iconographic representation" (257).

NOTE: the abbreviation "Cf." (confer) means "compare this source to another";
do not use in place of "see." Note this sample:

 [8] On this point see also the essay by Patricia Chaffee in which she examines the "house" as a primary image in the fiction of Eudora Welty.

Explain Tools, Methods, or Testing Procedures

 [9] Water samples were drawn from the identical spot each day at 8:00 a.m., 12:00 noon, 4:00 p.m., and 8:00 p.m. with testing done immediately on site.

 [10] The control group continued normal dietary routines, but the experimental group was asked to consume nuts, sharp cheeses, and chocolates to test acne development of its members against that of the control group.

 [11] The initial sample was complete data on all twins born in Nebraska between 1920 and 1940. These dates were selected to provide test subjects 60 years of age or older.

Provide Statistics

(See also "Illustrations & Tables," 158–62)

 [12] Database results show 27,000 pupil-athletes in 174 high schools with grades 0.075 above another group of 27,000 non-athletes at the same high schools. Details on the nature of various <u>reward structures</u> are unavailable.

Acknowledge Assistance or Support

 [13] Funds to finance this research were graciously provided by the Thompson–Monroe Foundation.

 [14] This writer wishes to acknowledge the research assistance of Pat Luther, graduate assistant, Physics Department.

NOTE: Acknowledge neither your instructor nor typist for research papers, though such acknowledgments are standard with graduate theses and dissertations.

Explain Variables or Conflicts in the Evidence

[15] Potlatch et al. (431-43) includes the following variables: the positive acquaintance, the equal status norm, the
various social norms, the negative stereotypes, and sexual
discrimination. However, racial barriers cannot be overlooked as one important variable.

[16] The pilot study at Dunlap School, where sexual imbal-
ance was noticed (62 percent males), differed sharply from
test results compared with those of other schools. The male
bias at Dunlap thereby eliminated those scores from the to-
tals.

PLANNING A "WORKS CITED" PAGE

Since your sources are alphabetically arranged on bibliography cards, you
should have little trouble typing out the entries for "Works Cited." However,
keep in mind that every source referred to in your text and/or your content endnotes must be listed in the "Works Cited." (See 191–193 for a sample.)

REVISING THE ROUGH DRAFT

After you complete your first draft, begin revising and rewriting in a critical
and exacting mood—there is no place for any complacent pride of accomplish-
ment at this point. Note the following sample:

The most delicate members of our society, the children, appear most
likely to be affected by family troubles. Our recognition of causal
elements and a cure ~~always~~ face this society each ~~every~~ day ~~of
the year~~ if we are to defeat what one ~~a real good~~ authority
calls "the greatest crippler and killer of our children--
child abuse and neglect" (Fontana xvi). In fact, Another writer

As shown above, you should conscientiously delete unnecessary material, add supporting statements and evidence, relate facts to one another, rearrange data, and rewrite for clarity. Review the earlier sections of this text, if necessary, on matters of tense, unity and coherence, handling quotations, and so on. Follow this cycle of revision until the paper meets your full approval. Check for errors in sentence structure, spelling, and punctuation; read each quotation for accuracy. In particular, check the accuracy of your terminology. Finally, check over your "Works Cited" page for correctness of both the content of each entry and also the form according to standards explained in Chapter 6, "Works Cited."

Before and during final typing of your manuscript, study Chapter 5, "Format," for tips on handling technicalities, such as margins, spacing, and pagination.

PROOFREADING THE FINAL MANUSCRIPT

After your final copy is finished, you should proofread carefully, remembering that you, and you alone, are responsible for everything within the paper. Failure to proofread is an act of carelessness that may seriously lower your final grade. Typing a paper, of course, does not remove the requirement of proofreading; if anything, it doubles your responsibility, whether you have done the typing yourself or had it done. Typographical errors will often count against the paper just as heavily as other shortcomings. Should you find errors but have no time for retyping, you should make the necessary corrections neatly in ink. It is far better to mar a page with a few handwritten corrections than to leave damaging errors in your text.

A Format for Your Paper

PREPARING THE FINAL MANUSCRIPT

In its basic organization the research paper consists of the following parts:

1. One blank sheet (optional)
2. Title page or opening page (see below)
3. Outline (if required)
4. The text of the paper
5. Notes
6. Bibliography
7. One blank sheet (optional)

Title Page or Opening Page

The title page contains three main divisions: the title of the work, the author, and the course information.

```
          An Interpretation of Melville's

          Use of Biblical Characters

               In Billy Budd




                      by

               Doris Singleton


     Freshman English II, Section 108b

               Mr. Crampton

               April 23, 1983
```

Note the following guidelines for title pages (see also the title page of the sample research paper, 170, for an example):

1. If the title requires two or more lines, position the extra line(s) in such a manner as to form an inverted pyramid.
2. Do not underline your title, capitalize it in full, or enclose it in quotation marks. Underline only published works if they appear in your title. Also, do not use a period after a centered heading.
3. Enter your own name with the word "by" centered above it.
4. Provide the class and section information and the date. Entry of the instructor's name is usually optional.
5. Employ separate lines for each item.
6. Provide balanced, two-inch margins for all sides of the title page.
7. If you omit the title page and outline (your instructor may prefer that), then place information in the upper right corner, as in the following:

                                                    Pamela Howell

                                                    Professor Rimsky

                                                    English 102c

                                                    May 17, 1979

                              Creative Marriages

Judging by recent divorce rates, it would seem that

traditional marriage is not meeting the needs of our soci-

ety. . . .

Outline

The outline follows the title page in the finished manuscript. It is on a separate page (or pages), and outline pages are numbered with small Roman numerals (for example, "iii," "iv," "v") at the top right-hand corner of the page. For full information on outlining, see 70–74 and 102–110. For a sample outline in manuscript form see 171–73.

The Text of the Paper

The heart of your paper, of course, is the text itself. The three dominant parts of the text are the opening, body, and conclusion. These parts are discussed under "Writing Your Paper," 117–25. In general, you should not use subtitles or numbered divisions to separate parts of the text, whether your paper is six, ten, or even twenty pages long; therefore, continuous paragraphing of research papers is standard.

The opening page of your text should begin with the title of the paper centered two inches below the top edge of the sheet. Quadruple-space between the title and the first line of your text. No page number appears on the opening page, though it should be counted in the numbering sequence. The opening page should contain your name and classroom information in the upper right-hand corner only if you have no title page (see 148).

The closing page of your text should end with a period and blank space on the remainder of the page. Do not write "The End" or provide artwork as a signal. Do not start "Notes" or "Works Cited" on this final page of text.

Content Endnotes Page

Label this page with the word "Notes" centered and two inches from the top edge of the sheet. Quadruple-space between this heading and the first note. Do not put a page number on this first page of notes, though it is counted in the sequence, and page numbers should appear in the upper right-hand corner of subsequent pages of the "Notes." The notes should be numbered in sequence with raised superscript numerals to match those placed within your text at appropriate locations. Double-space all entries and double-space between the entries. (See 190 for a sample "Notes" page.)

Works Cited Page

Label this page with the words "Works Cited" centered and two inches from the top edge of the sheet. Quadruple-space between this heading and the first entry. Don't put a page number on this first page of the bibliography, though it is counted in the sequence, and page numbers should appear in the upper right-hand corner of subsequent pages of the bibliography entries. The entries should be listed in alphabetical order. Double-space all entries and also double-space between the entries. For samples and additional information see "Works Cited," 194–219, and also the sample paper, 191–93.

HANDLING TECHNICALITIES OF PREPARING THE MANUSCRIPT

As you write your various drafts and type the final manuscript, you will have questions about such diverse matters as margins, pagination, and the proper form for dates and numbers. The following material, presented in alphabetical order, explains many of the immediate problems facing you. Consult the index of this text for matters not addressed below.

Abbreviations   You should employ abbreviations often and consistently in your notes and citations, although in your text you should avoid them (except "Dr.," "Esq.," "Hon.," "Jr.," "Mr.," "Ms.," "Rev.," and "St."). In citations you should abbreviate dates (for example, "Jan.," or "Dec."), institutions (for example, "Univ." or "Assn."), and states (for example, "TN" or "CA"). Finally, you may use and certainly will encounter many of the following abbreviations and reference words:

A.D. *anno Domini* 'in the year of the Lord'; *precedes* numerals with no space between letters, as in "A.D. 350"

anon. anonymous

art., arts. article(s)

B.C. 'Before Christ'; *follows* numerals with no space between letters, as in "500 B.C."

bk., bks. book(s)

ca. (*or* c.) *circa* 'about,' used to indicate an approximate date, as in "ca. 1812"

cf. *confer* 'compare' (one source with another); not, however, to be used in place of "see"

ch., chs. (*or* chap., chaps.) chapter(s)

col., cols. column(s)

comp. compiled (by) or compiler

diss. dissertation

ed., eds. editor(s), edition, or edited (by)

e.g. *exempli gratia* 'for example,' preceded and followed by a comma

enl. enlarged, as in "enl. ed."

esp. especially, as in "312–15, esp. 313"

et al. *et alii* 'and others'; "John Smith et al." means John Smith and other authors

et pas. *et passim* 'and here and there' (see "passim")

et seq. *et sequens* 'and the following'; "9 et seq." means page nine and the following page; compare "f." and "ff."

f., ff. page or pages following a given page; "8f." means page eight and the following page; but exact references are preferable, for example, "45–51, 55, 58" instead of "45 ff."

ibid. *ibidem* 'in the same place,' i.e., in the immediately preceding title

i.e. *id est* 'that is,' preceded and followed by a comma

illus. illustrated by, illustrations, or illustrator

infra 'below,' refers to a succeeding portion of the text; compare "supra." Generally, it is best to write "see below"

intro. (*or* introd.) introduction (by)

l., ll. line(s)

loc. cit. *loco citato* 'in the place (passage) cited'

MS, MSS manuscript(s); but followed by a period ("MS.") when referring to a specific manuscript

n., nn. note(s), as "23, n. 2" or "51 n."

n.d. no date (in a book's title or copyright pages)

no., nos. number(s)

n.p. no place (of publication)

op. cit. *opere citato* 'in the work cited'

p., pp. page(s), but omit and use Arabic numerals alone

passim 'here and there throughout the work,' e.g., "67, 72, et passim"

pseud. pseudonym

pt., pts. part(s)

rev. revised (by), revision, review, or reviewed (by)

rpt. reprint, reprinted

sec., secs. section(s)

sic 'thus,' placed in brackets to indicate an error has been made in the quoted passage and the writer is quoting accurately

st., sts. stanza(s)

sup. (*or* supra) 'above,' refers to a preceding portion of the text; it is just as easy to write "above"

s.v. *sub voce (verbo)* 'under the word or heading'

trans. (*or* tr.) translator, translated (by), or translation

vol., vols. volume(s), as in "vol. 3"

Abstract   An abstract is a brief summary in paragraph form of the essential ideas of the paper. Include exact terminology to specify and identify the narrow focus of your study. Provide a very *brief* digest of the paper's argument. Include within a sentence or two your conclusion(s) and/or finding(s). Place the abstract on your opening page (page 1) below the title and before the first lines of the text with the abstract set off by triple-spacing both above and below. Note this example:

                    Child Abuse: A View of the Victims

        This study examines the problems of child abuse, espe-

    cially the fact that families receive attention after abuse

    occurs, not before. With abuse statistics on the rise, ef-

    forts of prevention rather than coping should focus on

    parents in order to discover those adults most likely to

    commit abuse because of heredity, their own childhood, the

    economy, and other causes of depression. Viewing the parent

    as a victim, not just a criminal, will enable social agen-

    cies to institute preventive programs that may prevent

    abuse and hold together family units.

            Do ye hear the children weeping, O my brothers,

            Ere the sorrow comes with years?

            They are leaning their young heads against their

                mothers,

            And that cannot stop their tears.

Acknowledgments   Generally, acknowledgments are unnecessary. Place obligatory acknowledgments or explanations in a content endnote with a superscript reference numeral to your first sentence:

[1] I wish here to express my thanks to Mrs. Horace A. Humphrey for permission to examine the manuscripts of her late husband.

Usually there is no need for a preface in a research paper.

Ampersand Avoid using the ampersand symbol "&." Instead, spell out the "and" in the name of a company or organization, unless custom demands it, as in, "A & P."

Annotated Bibliography Write descriptive notes for each entry (see 41).

Apostrophe Add an apostrophe and *s* to form the possessive of one-syllable proper names that end in *s* or another sibilant (for example, "Keats's poem," "Rice's story," "Bates's *The Kinds of Man*"). In words of more than one syllable ending in a sibilant, add the apostrophe only (for example, "Rawlings' novel," "Evans' essay," "Daiches' criticism"), except for names ending in a sibilant and a final *e* (for example, "Lovelace's enduring appeal").

Appendix Place additional material in an appendix at the end of your paper. It is a logical location for numerous tables and illustrations or other accumulated data. Place it after "Notes" but before "Works Cited."

Arabic Numerals Use Arabic numerals whenever possible: for volumes, books, parts, and chapters of works; acts, scenes, and lines of plays; cantos, stanzas, and lines of poetry.

Write as numerals only those numbers that *cannot* be spelled out in one or two words (such as thirteen, twenty-one, three hundred *but* 3 1/2, 154, or 1,269).

When you begin a sentence with a number, spell out the initial number (for example, "Twelve people will be chosen from this initial group.").

Use the small "1," not a capital "I" when typing the numeral "one."

Numbers compared or contrasted should appear in the same style (for example, "6 out of 128 in the 2 1/2 to 3 age group").

Samples of correct usage within your text:

A.D. 200 *but* 200 B.C.

Art. 3

Col. 5

Vol. 7

Fig. 6

in 1974–75 *or* from 1974 to 1975, *but not* from 1974–75

32–34 or lines 32–34, *but not* ll. 32–34

121–22 *but not* pp. 121–22

161 *but not* p. 161

45, *but not* the forty-fifth page

6.213

0.5 *but not* .5

March 5, 1983 or 5 March 1983, *but not* both styles

1960's *but* the sixties

one-fifth *but* 153½ (for numbers that cannot be spelled in one or two words)

1151–53 *but* 1193–1215

6 percent

six o'clock *or* 6:00 P.M.

twentieth century

Samples of correct usage of Arabic numerals within documentation:

Oth. 5.3.16–18

Faust 2.140

2 Sam. 2.1–8

Iliad 2.121–30

Fredericks 23–24

Thompson 1132–38

4: 434–35; 66–75

17 (1981): 92–98

2 vols.

Rpt. as vols. 13 and 14

1927, 12: 231–44

MS CCCC 201

With 50 plates

2nd ed.

12 March 1979, 60–61

No. 1117 (1849): 296

15 (Winter 1974): 3–6

95th Cong., 1st sess. S. 2411

16 mm., 29 min., color

Monograph 1962–M2

Asterisks   Use Arabic numerals for note numbers and asterisks only for notes to illustrations or tables (see Fig. 47, 162).

Bible   Use parenthetical documentation for biblical references in your text—that is, place the entry within parentheses immediately after the quotation, for example, "(2 Kings 18.13)." Do not underline titles of books of the Bible. Abbreviations of most books of the Bible follow (but do not abbreviate one-syllable titles, for example, "Mark" or Acts"):

1 and 2 Chron.	1 and 2 Chronicles	Lev.	Leviticus
Col.	Colossians	Mal.	Malachi
1 and 2 Cor.	1 and 2 Corinthians	Matt.	Matthew
Dan.	Daniel	Mic.	Micah
Deut.	Deuteronomy	Nah.	Nahum
Eccles.	Ecclesiastes	Neh.	Nehemiah
Eph.	Ephesians	Num.	Numbers
Exod.	Exodus	Obad.	Obadiah
Ezek.	Ezekiel	1 and 2 Pet.	1 and 2 Peter
Gal.	Galatians	Phil.	Philippians
Gen.	Genesis	Prov.	Proverbs
Hab.	Habakkuk	Ps. (Pss.)	Psalm(s)
Hag.	Haggai	Rev.	Revelation
Heb.	Hebrews	Rom.	Romans
Hos.	Hosea	1 and 2 Sam.	1 and 2 Samuel
Isa.	Isaiah	Song of Sol.	Song of Solomon
Jas.	James	1 and 2 Thess.	1 and 2 Thessalonians
Jer.	Jeremiah	1 and 2 Tim.	1 and 2 Timothy
Josh.	Joshua	Zech.	Zechariah
Judg.	Judges	Zeph.	Zephaniah
Lam.	Lamentations		

Capitalization   Titles of books: capitalize the first word and all principal words, but not articles, prepositions, and conjunctions (for example, *The Last of the Mohicans*).

Titles of magazines and newspapers: as above, except do not treat an initial definite article as part of the title:

```
"He was referring to the Kansas City Star and. . . ."

Editorial. Kansas City Star 18 March 1978, 43D.
```

Titles of parts of a specific work: capitalize as for books (for example, Thompson's "Appendix 2," Jones's "Preface," "Writing the Final Draft").

Abbreviations: capitalize a noun followed by a numeral indicating place in sequence (for example, "Ch. 4," "No. 14," "Vol. 3").

Titles of French, Italian, and Spanish works: capitalize the first words, the proper nouns, but not adjectives derived from proper nouns.

Titles of German works: capitalize the first word, all nouns, and all adjectives derived from names of persons.

If a complete sentence follows a colon, the first word after the colon may be capitalized (although standard usage would keep lowercase):

```
The consequences of this decision will be disastrous: Each

division of the corporation will be required to cut twenty

percent of its budget within this fiscal year.
```

Capitalize the second part of a hyphenated compound word only when it is used in a heading with other capitalized words:

```
Low-Frequency Sound Equipment
```

                                   but

```
Low-frequency sound distortion results, in this instance,

from . . . .
```

Capitalize trade names:

```
Pepsi, Plexiglass, DuPont, or Dingo
```

Capitalize proper names used as adjectives *but not* the words used with
them:

```
Einstein's theory; Salk's discovery
```

Dates   You should follow these examples:

```
14 March or March 14, not the fourteenth of March
14 March 1975 or March 14, 1975, but consistently use one
style
March 1975 or March, 1975, but consistently use one style
1970's or the seventies
in 1974-75 or from 1974 to 1975, but not from 1974-75
150 B.C. but A.D. 150
fourteenth century but 14th century in notes
```

Definitions   For definitions within your text, use single quotation marks without
intervening punctuation, for example:

```
The use of foreign words, such as et alii 'and others,' has

diminished in scholarly writing.
```

Endnotes for Documentation of Sources   Your instructor may prefer that you use
the traditional superscript numerals within your text and provide documentation
notes at the end of the paper. If so, you will need to replace your in-text citations
with superscript numbers. Your citations should then appear as double-spaced
entries on the ''Notes'' page at the end of your text. Note the following portion of
a paper that uses superscript numerals rather than in-text citations:

```
In a striking parallel, Billy Budd possesses many character-

istics of the Bible. According to Newton Arvin, Melville

centers his story around the "fall of man and the loss of

Paradise."[1]  Raymond Weaver sees it as a gospel story filled
```

with crime, sin, punishment, love, and innocence, or of vir-

tue versus vice, in which evil and horror are given their

fullest play.[2]

These two references would then appear as complete documentation entries on a
separate page at the end of the paper, as follows:

Notes

[1] Herman Melville: A Critical Biography (New York: Viking Press, 1950), 294.

[2] "Introduction," The Shorter Novels of Herman Melville
(1928; rpt. New York: Premier-Fawcett, 1960), 37-38.

[3] E. L. Grant Watson, "Melville's Testament of Acceptance," New England Quarterly 6 (1933): 319-20.

[4] Watson, 321.

[5] Weaver, "Introduction," 38.

Enumeration of Items   Incorporate short items into the text, as follows:

College instructors are usually divided into four ranks:
(1) instructors, (2) assistant professors, (3) associate professors, and (4) full professors.

Present longer items in tabular form, as follows:

1. Full professors generally have 15 or more years experience, the Ph.D. or other terminal degree, and have
   achieved distinction in teaching and scholarly publications.
2. Associate professors. . . .

Etc.   *Et cetera* 'and so forth': avoid using this term in your text by listing at
least four items, as follows:

Images of color occur frequently in Crane's writing, especially blue, gold, red, and grey.

Footnotes for Documentation   Your instructor may prefer that you use footnotes.
If so, you will need to replace your in-text citations with superscript numbers.
Your citation should then appear as a footnote on the same page as do the super-

script numbers within the text. Suppose, for example, that you have five superscript citations on one page of your text; the bottom portion of that page should
contain the footnotes, as shown by this sample:

```
Melville also describes him as possessing an amiable disposi-
tion, never given offense to anyone.⁷   The author of Billy
```

```
    ³ E. L. Grant Watson, "Melville's Testament of Accep-
tance," New England Quarterly 6 (1933): 319-20.

    ⁴ Watson, 321.

    ⁵ Herman Melville, Billy Budd, Sailor (An Inside Narra-
tive), eds. Harrison Hayford and Merton M. Sealts, Jr.
(Chicago: Univ. of Chicago Press, 1962), 52.

    ⁶ Watson, 319.

    ⁷ Melville, 52.
```

These conventions prevail for footnotes: (1) place footnotes on pages with superscript citation, (2) separate the footnotes from the text by triple-spacing, (3)
single-space the footnotes, indent each as a paragraph, and double-space between
each note, (4) begin each note with a raised index numeral, followed by a space,
(5) use a shortened version of the entry for succeeding citations to author and
page and, when needed, author, shortened title, and page.

Foreign Cities   In general, use the name of foreign cities as written in the source
material for both your own text and your "Works Cited" entries. However, for
clarity you may substitute an English name or provide both:

Köln (Cologne)

München (Munich)

Braunschweig (Brunswick)

Praha (Prague)

Foreign Languages   Underline foreign words used in an English text:

```
Like his friend Olaf, he is aut Caesar, aut nihil, either
overpowering perfection or ruin and destruction.
```

Do not underline quotations:

```
Obviously, he uses it to exploit, in the words of Jean Lau-
mon, "une admirable mine de themes poetiques."
```

Do not underline titles of magazine articles:

```
    ³ Von Thomas O. Brandt, "Brecht und die Bibel," PMLA, 79
(1964): 171.
```

Do not underline places, institutions, proper names, or titles that precede proper names:

> Of course, Racine became extremely fond of Mlle Champmeslé,
>
> who interpreted his works at the Hotel de Bourgogne.

Titles of French, Italian, and Spanish works: capitalize the first word, the proper nouns, but not adjectives derived from proper nouns.

Titles of German works: capitalize the first word, all nouns, and all adjectives derived from names of persons.

Illustrations and Tables   A table is a systematic arrangement of statistical materials, usually in columns. An illustration is any item that is not a table: blueprint, chart, diagram, drawing, graph, photo, photostat, map, and so on. Note the samples here.

Fig. 42: Illustration

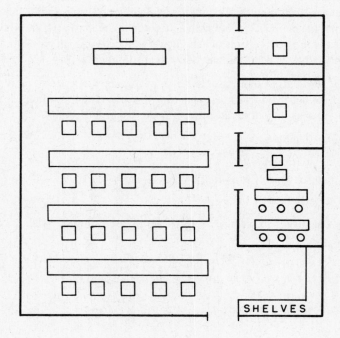

Fig. 42: Audio Laboratory with Private Listening Rooms and a
Small Group Room

Fig. 43: Table

Table 1

Response By Class on Nuclear Energy Policy

	Freshmen	Sophomores	Juniors	Seniors
1. More nuclear power	150	301	75	120
2. Less nuclear power	195	137	111	203
3. Present policy is acceptable	87	104	229	37

When presenting an illustration or table in your research paper, conform to the following stipulations:

1. Present only one kind of information in each illustration, making it as simple and as brief as possible; frills and fancy artwork may distract rather than attract the reader.
2. Place small illustrations within your text. Large illustrations should go on a separate page. If you have numerous illustrations or long, complex tables, these should be placed in an appendix at the end of your paper.
3. Place the illustration as near to your textual discussion as possible, although the illustration should not precede your first mention of it.
4. Make certain that your textual discussion adequately explains the significance of the illustration. Follow two rules: (1) write the illustration so that your reader can understand it without reference to your discussion; and (2) write your discussion of the illustration so that your reader may understand your observations without reference to the illustration. But avoid giving too many numbers and figures in your text.
5. In your textual discussion refer to illustrations by number (for example, "Figure 5" or "Table 4, 16"), not by a vague reference (for example, "the table above," "the following illustration," or "the chart below").
6. Number illustrations consecutively throughout the paper with Arabic numbers, preceded by "Fig." or "Figure" (for example, "Figure 4"), placed one double-space above the caption and centered on the page *below* the illustration.
7. Number tables consecutively throughout the paper with Arabic numerals, preceded by "Table" (for example, "Table 2"), placed one double-space above the caption and centered on the page *above* the table.
8. Always insert a caption that explains the illustration, placed *above* the table and *below* the illustration, centered, in full capital letters or in capitals and lowercase, but do not mix forms in the same paper. An alternative is to place the caption on the same line with the number (see Fig. 44 below).

9. Insert a caption or number for each column of a table, centered above the column or, if necessary, inserted diagonally or vertically above it.

10. When inserting an explanatory or reference note, place it below both a table and an illustration; then use an asterisk as the identifying superscript, not an Arabic numeral (for example, see Figs. 46 and 47, 162).

The charts and illustrations on the following pages are examples of what you might use in a research paper.

Fig. 44: Illustration

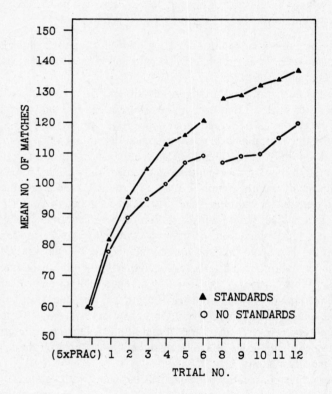

Fig. 44: Mean Number of Matches by Subjects with and without Standards (By Trial). From Locke and Bryan (289).

Fig. 45: Illustration

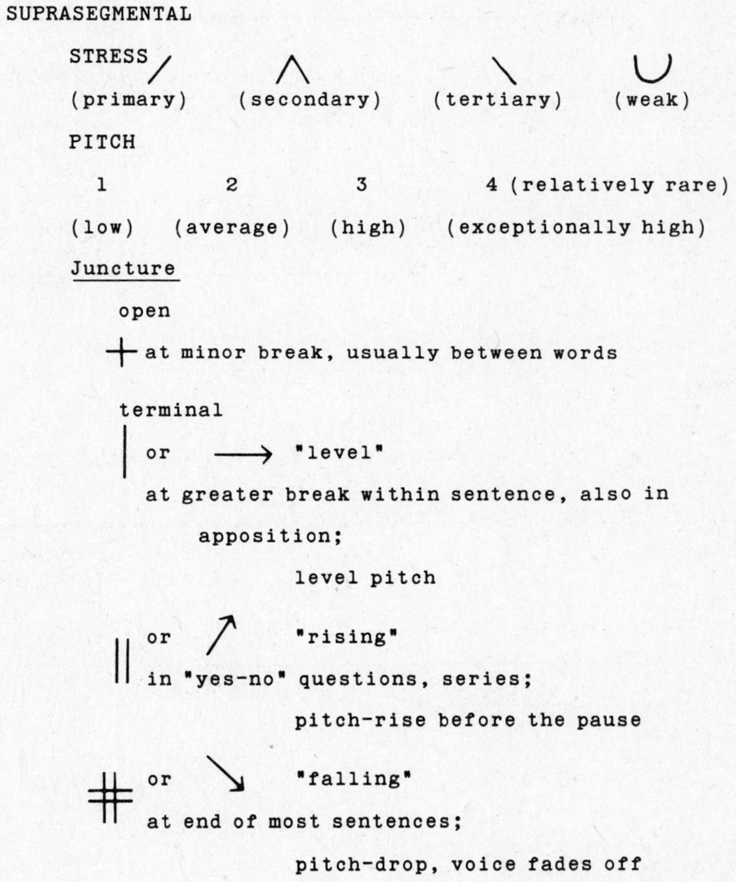

```
SUPRASEGMENTAL
    STRESS  /         /\              \           U
    (primary)    (secondary)     (tertiary)      (weak)
    PITCH
       1          2          3          4 (relatively rare)
    (low)    (average)    (high)    (exceptionally high)
    Juncture
       open
      —+—  at minor break, usually between words

       terminal
       |   or    ——→    "level"
          at greater break within sentence, also in
              apposition;
                      level pitch

       ||  or    ↗     "rising"
       ||  in "yes-no" questions, series;
                      pitch-rise before the pause

       #   or    ↘     "falling"
       #   at end of most sentences;
                      pitch-drop, voice fades off
```

Fig. 45: Phonemes of English. Generally, this figure follows
the Trager-Smith system, used widely in American linguistics.
From Anna H. Live (1,066).

Fig. 46: Table

Table 2*

Mean Scores of Six Values Held by College Students According to Sex

All Students		Men		Women	
Pol.	40.61	Pol.	43.22	Aesth.	43.86
Rel.	40.51	Theor.	43.09	Rel.	43.13
Aesth.	40.29	Econ.	42.05	Soc.	41.62
Theor.	39.80	Rel.	37.88	Pol.	38.00
Econ.	39.45	Soc.	37.05	Econ.	36.85
Soc.	39.34	Aesth.	36.72	Theor.	36.50

*From Carmen J. Finley, et al. (165).

Fig. 47: Table

Table 3

Inhibitory effects of sugars on the growth of Clostridium histolyticum (11 strains) on nutrient agar*

Sugar added (2%)	Aerobic incubation (hr)		Anaerobic incubation (hr)	
	24	48	24	48
None	11**	11	11	11
Glucose	0	0	11	11
Maltose	0	0	11	11
Lactose	1	1	11	11
Sucrose	3	6	11	11
Arabinose	0	0	0	0
Inositol	0	0	11	11
Xylose	0	0	0	0
Sorbitol	2	7	11	11
Mamnitol	9	10	11	11
Rhamnose	0	0	11	11

*From Shoki Nishida and Masaaki Imaizumi. 1966. Toxigenicity of Clostridium histolyticum. J. Bacteriol. 91: 481.

**No. of strains which gave rise to colonies in the presence of the sugar.

Italics Indicate italics in a typed manuscript by underlining; see "Underlining," 167.

Length of the Research Paper Your instructor may set definite restrictions concerning the length of the paper. Various factors make it difficult to set an arbitrary length, which may vary with the nature of the topic, the reference material available, the time allotted to the project, and the initiative of the student. However, if your instructor offers no guidelines on length, then plan a paper of 2,000 or 3,000 words, about ten typewritten pages, excluding the title page, outline, endnotes, and bibliography pages.

Margins A basic one inch margin on all sides is recommended. Place your page number one inch down from the top edge of the paper and one inch in from the right edge. You should then triple-space (leave two spaces) between the page number and text. For pages with a major heading (such as the opening page, "Notes" page, or "Works Cited" page) use a two inch margin at the top of the page without a page number, though these pages are counted in the numbering sequence. (See also "Spacing," 166.)

Monetary Units

$10 *or* ten dollars

$14.25 *but not* fourteen dollars and twenty-five cents

$4 billion *or* four billion dollars

$10.3 billion *or* $10,300,000,000

$63 or sixty-three dollars

The fee is one hundred dollars ($100). *or* The fee is one hundred (100) dollars.

Names of Persons Formal titles (Mr., Mrs., Dr., Hon.) are usually omitted in textual and note references to distinguished persons, living or dead. As a general rule, first mention of a person requires the full name (for example, Ernest Hemingway or Margaret Mead) and thereafter requires only usage of the surname (Hemingway or Mead).

Convention suggests that certain prominent figures (Lord Byron, Dr. Johnson, Dame Edith Sitwell) require the title while others, for no apparent reason, do not (for example, use Tennyson, Browne, and Hillary rather than Lord Tennyson, Sir Thomas Browne, or Sir Edmund Hillary). Where custom dictates, you may employ simplified names of famous authors (for example, use "Dante" rather than his surname "Alighieri" and use "Michelangelo" rather than "Michelangelo Buonarroti"). You may also use pseudonyms where custom dictates (for example, George Eliot, Maxim Gorky, Mark Twain).

Numbering (Pagination) Number pages in the upper right-hand corner of the page, one inch down from the top edge of the paper and one inch from the right edge. Pages preceding your opening require lowercase Roman numerals. Pages following your opening page require Arabic numerals. All pages are counted, but place no number on those pages with major headings: title page, first page of outline, opening page, first page of "Notes," and first page of "Works Cited."

Paper Type on one side of white bond paper, sixteen- or twenty-pound weight, eight and one-half by eleven inches. If you write your final manuscript in longhand, use ruled theme paper.

Percentages In the humanities, arts, and social sciences, use numerals only when they cannot be spelled out in one or two words:

> one hundred percent *but* 150 percent
>
> a two point average *but* a 2.5 average
>
> one metric ton
>
> 0.907 metric ton
>
> 3.150 metric tons
>
> percent *not* per cent
>
> forty-five percent *but* 45 1/2 percent

In business, scientific, and technical writing that requires frequent use of percentages, write all percentages as numerals with appropriate symbols:

> 100% 45 1/2% 15¢ £92 3 @ $1.95

Punctuation Consistency is a key to punctuation for research writing. Careful proofreading of your paper for punctuation errors will generally improve the clarity and accuracy of your writing.

1. *Commas* are used in a series of three or more before "and" and "or." Never use a comma and a dash together. The comma follows a parenthesis (such as this), if your text requires the comma. The comma goes inside single quotation marks as well as double quotation marks (for example, "The Sources of Franklin's 'The Ephemera,' ").
2. *Dashes* are formed with your typewriter by typing two hyphens with no blank space before or after.
3. *Exclamation marks* are seldom used in research writing. A forceful declarative sentence is preferable.
4. *Hyphens* to separate words at the end of a typed line are acceptable in research papers. However, you should always double-check word division by consulting a dictionary. If possible, do not separate by a hyphen two letters at the end or beginning of a line (for example, use "depend-able," not "de-pendable"). If possible, avoid hyphenating proper names.
5. *Periods* end complete sentences of the text, endnotes or footnotes, and all bibliography entries. The period normally follows the parenthesis. (The period is placed within the parenthesis only when the parenthetical

statement is a complete sentence, as in this instance.) See also "Ellipsis," 132, for explanation of the period in conjunction with ellipsis dots.

6. *Brackets* should be inserted by hand if these figures are not on your typewriter. Brackets are used to enclose a parenthesis within a parenthesis, to enclose phonetic transcription, and to enclose interpolations in a quotation (see "Brackets," 133).

7. *Words discussed,* such as slang, words cited as words, or words purposely misused, should be enclosed within quotation marks. Also use quotation marks for English translations of foreign words. However, linguistic studies require that you underline all linguistic forms (letters, words, phrases) that are subjects of discussion and also require that you employ single quotation marks for definitions, without intervening punctuation (for example, nosu 'nose').

8. *Quotation marks* should enclose all quotations used as part of your text. For quotations within quotations, use single marks. You should put all commas or periods inside quotation marks, whether double or single, unless a parenthetical reference intervenes. Other marks of punctuation go inside the quotation marks only when such items (question mark, dash, exclamation) are actually part of the quoted materials. Semicolons and colons generally fall outside the quotation marks.

Roman Numerals   Use capital Roman numerals for titles of persons (Elizabeth II) and small Roman numerals for preliminary pages of text, as for a preface or introduction (iii, iv, or viii). Otherwise, use Arabic numerals (for example: Act 2, Vol. 5, Ch. 16, Plate 32).

A list of Roman numerals:

	Units	Tens	Hundreds
1	i	x	c
2	ii	xx	cc
3	iii	xxx	ccc
4	iv	xl	cd
5	v	l	d
6	vi	lx	dc
7	vii	lxx	dcc
8	viii	lxxx	dccc
9	ix	xc	cm

Shakespearean Plays   For use in parenthetical documentation, the editorial board of the *Shakespeare Quarterly* has approved the following abbreviations of titles of Shakespearean works: *Ado; Ant.; AWW; AYL; Cor.; Cym.; Err.; Ham.; 1H4; 2H4; H5; 1H6; 2H6; 3H6; H8; JC; Jn; LLL; Lr.; Mac.; MM; MND; MV; Oth.; Per.; R2; R3; Rom.; Shr.; TGV; Tim.; Tit.; Tmp.; TN; TNK; Tro.; Wiv.; WT; LC; Luc.; PhT; PP; Son.; Ven.*

Short Titles in the Text   Shorten titles of books and articles mentioned often in the text after a first, full reference. For example, *English as Language: Backgrounds, Developments, Usage* should be shortened, after initial usage, to *English as Language* both in the text and notes (see 128–29). See also "More Than One Work by an Author," 201.

Slang   Enclose in double quotation marks any words to which you direct attention.

Spacing   Double-space the body of the paper, all indented quotations, and both the endnote and bibliography entries. Triple-space between your text and indented quotations. Quadruple-space between major headings and the text. (If your instructor requests footnotes, they should be single-spaced and set off from the text by triple-spacing.) Note the following:

```
                 The Theme of Black Matriarchy

               in A Raisin in the Sun



       Lorraine Hansberry's popular and successful A Raisin

   in the Sun, which first appeared on Broadway in 1959, is

   a problem play that tells the story of a black family's

   determination to move out of the ghetto to a better life.

   Most critics have said that this escape theme explains the

   drama's forceful dramatic conflict and its importance to

   the black movement in general.  As Grier and Cobbs point

   out, the black family is often in serious trouble:


           It is coming apart and it is failing to provide

           the nurturing that black children need.  In its

           failure the resulting isolated men and women fail

           generally to make a whole life for themselves in

           a nation designed for families. . . . (83)


   Thus another issue lies at the heart of the drama.
```

```
Hansberry develops a modern view of the sociological

aspects of black matriarchy in order to examine the cohe-

sive and, more importantly, the conflict-producing effects

it has on the individual members of the Younger family.
```

Spelling   Spell accurately. When in doubt, always consult a dictionary. If the dictionary says a word may be spelled in two separate ways, be consistent in the form employed, as with *theater* and *theatre,* unless the variant form occurs in quoted materials. Use American (as opposed to English) spelling throughout. In addition, proofread carefully for errors of hyphenation.

Superscript Numerals in the Text for Endnotes   Place the raised note numerals, like this,[14] into the text by turning the roller of the typewriter so that the Arabic numeral strikes about half a space above the line. Each numeral immediately follows the quotation or material to which it refers with no space between a word or a mark of punctuation, like this.[15] (See also "Content Endnotes," 144.)

Typing   Preferably, you should submit the paper in typed form, although some instructors will accept handwritten manuscripts, if neat, legible, and written in blue or black ink on ruled paper. Also, before typing the final draft, remember to clean the type carefully and insert a new ribbon if necessary.

   If you produce the paper by a word processor or computer, keep in mind that you are responsible for correct pagination and accuracy of the manuscript. Schedule your time so that you may print out your document one day early, revise and proofread it, then call up the document for final revisions before you print the version that will go to the instructor. Also, print the research paper on a daisy-wheel, typewriter quality printer rather than a high speed printer whenever possible.

Underlining   Underlining takes the place of italics in a typed manuscript. Use a continuous line for titles with more than one word. Always underline titles of the following types of works:

aircraft	Enola Gay
ballet	The Nutcracker
book	Earthly Powers
bulletin	Production Memo II
drama	Desire Under the Elms
film	Treasure of the Sierra Madre
journal	Journal of Sociology
magazine	Newsweek

newspaper   The Nashville Banner

novel   The Scarlet Letter

opera   Rigoletto

painting   Mona Lisa

pamphlet   Ten Goals for Successful Sales

periodical   Scientific American

play   Cat on a Hot Tin Roof

poem   Idylls of the King (only if book length)

radio show   Grand Ole Opry

sculpture   David

ship   Titanic

short novel   Billy Budd

symphony   Beethoven's Symphony No. 3

television show   Tonight Show

yearbook   The Pegasus

By contrast, place quotation marks around: articles, essays, chapters, sections, short poems, stories, songs, lectures, sermons, reports, and individual episodes of television programs.

If separately published, underline titles of essays, lectures, poems, proceedings, reports, sermons, and stories. However, these items are usually published as an anthology of sermons or a collection of stories, in which cases you would underline the title of the anthology or collection.

Underlining for Emphasis   On occasion, underlining is used to emphasize certain words or phrases in a typed paper, such as in these examples:

```
This example, however, prompts this thought: if people like
the Jane Neilsons of our society could be identified and
given help in a timely fashion, then perhaps children would
not be victimized.  Perhaps an answer lies in preventing
abuse, not in makeshift remedies after the fact.  Parents who
abuse their children should be treated as victims, not crimi-
nals.
```

There may be occasions when you wish to emphasize certain words within quoted materials. Handle such underlining as in the following example:

```
Then Mama adds, "There are some ideas we aint going to have

in this house.  Not long as I am at the head of this family"

(37, my emphasis).
```

Follow this rule: You may underline another person's words only if you stipulate within parentheses or brackets that you have done so. (See also ''Adding to a Quotation With Brackets,'' 134–135.)

Remember that a little underlining goes a long way. Like too many neon signs, too much underlining for emphasis (and too many exclamation marks, for that matter) distracts your reader and gives the impression that nearly everything in your paper is of the utmost importance, a practice the reader will quickly grow tired of.

Word Division   When necessary, divide a word with a hyphen so that the break comes between two syllables, but avoid one-letter and two-letter division (for example, ''o-ver'' or ''separate-ly''). When in doubt about the proper division of a word, always consult a dictionary.

Sample Research Paper

The following
marginal comments
clarify the form of
the research paper
and explain specific
problems you may
encounter.

Child Abuse: A View of the Victims

by

Jo Walker

Note that the title
page is a three part
balance of title,
student, and course
information.

English 102j

Dr. Marsh

May 16, 1983

Outline

4 lines

Child Abuse: A View of the Victims *interesting but short*

3 lns.

Thesis: Parents who abuse their children should be
treated as victims, not criminals.

The title is repeated
at the beginning of
the outline.

Place the thesis
sentence at the
beginning of the
outline, though it
may take a different
form in the paper
itself.

I. The Cry of the Children

   A. Quote from E. B. Browning

   B. Commentary on quote

II. The Issues of Child Abuse

   A. The Problems

      1. Recognition that there is a problem

      2. Myth that America is child-oriented

      3. Problems of discovery of potential child
         abuse

      4. Help after the fact as limited help at best

   B. Statistics and Examples of Abuse

      1. Abuse on the increase

      2. Specific examples

      3. Absence of professional help before the
         abuse

      4. Prevention of rather than coping with

      5. Case study of Jane Neilson

Employ standard
outline symbols.

C. A Possible Answer

    1. Help for the Jane Neilsons before, not after

    2. Prevention of abuse before the fact

    3. Thesis: Parents as victims

    4. Reaching parents before abuse

III. The Causes and Cycles of Abuse

  A. Potentials for abuse

    1. Parents who abuse as having been abused themselves

    2. Predisposition to be abusive

    3. Social levels offer climates for abuse

    4. Absence of the extended family

    5. Television breeds violence

    6. Depression as a causal element

  B. Cycles of Child Abuse

    1. High unemployment in 1982

    2. Increase in child abuse in 1982

    3. Declines in work force and increases in child abuse

    4. Sample of scenario of unemployed father

    5. The cycle as escalating even more in years to come

    6. The cycle breeds itself: the abused become abusive

iv

IV. Focus on the Parents as Victims

    A. A Look at the Evidence

        1. Help for the parents, not just the children

        2. Facts to be faced

    B. Therapy and Study Groups

        1. Parents Anonymous

        2. Courses on parenthood

        3. Warnings against incest

        4. Aid for alcoholics

V. The Necessary Treatment

    A. Community involvement programs

    B. The parent as well as the child as victims

    C. The character of the community

The introduction (I)
and the conclusion
(V) are treated as
other parts of the
outline with no
special labels.

The title is repeated
on the first page of
the body of the
paper.

Child Abuse: A View of the Victims

Quotation opening
for effect; note the
line of spaced dots
to indicate omission
of several lines of
poetry.

Do ye hear the children weeping, O my

brothers,

Ere the sorrow comes with years?

. . . .

They are weeping in the playtime of the

others,

In the country of the free.   (Browning 383)

Elizabeth Barrett Browning wrote this poem con-

cerning child labor in factories of England. Today,

America has laws preventing child labor, but unfortu-

nately the poem can still apply today, mainly the third

line: "They are weeping in the playtime of the oth-

The writer identifies
the issue, but thesis
will come later (see
paragraph 7).

ers." If the poem were applied to conditions today,

it could reflect the horrors of abuse and neglect.

The most delicate members of our society, the

children, appear the most likely to be affected by

family problems. A recognition of causes for their

mistreatment and a need for a cure face this society

each day if we are to defeat what one authority calls

"the greatest crippler and killer of our children--

2

child abuse and neglect" (Fontana xvi). In fact,

another writer argues that "the single greatest im-

pediment to our improving the lives of America's

children is the myth that we are a child-oriented

society" (Zigler 39). This sociologist suggests that

too many Americans will not respond to documented

findings about child abuse (39). However, a growing

concern among many segments of the population has

spurred laws for protecting the rights of children,

but even these new laws are difficult to enforce

because, according to several sources, the families

and the children themselves often lie to protect the

abuse from being exposed in order to protect the

family unit.[1]

     In addition, social agencies find it difficult

to prevent abuse when they can't discover it until a

battered child is brought into an emergency room.

The police then must enter the picture and, as often

as not, a judge splits up the family structure and

the child no longer has a father or a mother or, in

the worst of cases, either parent. At this point the

parent is treated as a criminal. It becomes a cycle

which Giarretto describes like this: The father is

usually convicted on a felony charge and spends

Note the use of in-text citations to references in "Works Cited."

Superscript numerals are used for content endnotes only, not for documentation of source material.

Student narrows and narrows toward parent as criminal.

months, perhaps years, in jail; the mother is left in
shock and terror and feels herself a failure; and the
child, now under protective custody, feels banished
and punished even though he or she is the victim
(2-3). Surely the child's loss at that point is severe. Help after the fact of criminal abuse is limited help at best.

Even worse, severe abuse is on the rise. Each
year more and more children suffer the trauma of
physical and emotional abuse. Although the exact
number remains unknown, the Education Commission of

Use of statistics
reinforces
generalizations.

the States reports that some 60,000 cases occur annually (Cohen and Sussman 433). Boys outnumber girls
as victims of abuse until the teen years (Chase 104).
The death rate from cruelty exceeds that from infectious disease (Fontana 196). In truth, few young
persons reach maturity without a severe spanking from
an angry parent.

In the face of ever increasing incidents of abuse,
can our social organizations not do better? One
critic, who argues that child abuse has become "pan-
demic" in the United States, puts it this way:

> More often than not an object such as a
> hairbrush, switch, belt, or ironing cord

4

is used to inflict pain on the child. In
some instances children suffer a whip, fan
belt, clotheslines, steam, fire, cigarette
burns, or a blowtorch. Some spend long
hours tied to a bed, in basements or attics,
or locked out of the house. Some are not
fed. Relatively few die, however, yet most
who do are young, very young. Few parents
who abuse their children are reported to
the authorities, and most of those who are
reported deny the abuse. Few are prose-
cuted and few are treated by professionals.

(Walters 3)

Long quotations are introduced by colon, indented, without quotation marks, double-spaced, with source set flush right outside the final period.

It is important that we note the last phrase above,
that few are treated by professionals either after
or before the abuse. After abuse takes place, we
cope with it rather than work to prevent this pain-
ful menace.

For instance, let's look at one example as summarized from a case study by Leontine Young (76-77).
Jane Neilson was the oldest of ten children of an
alcoholic father and promiscuous mother. Jane became a prostitute and her mother shared the income.
Along with three of her sisters, Jane was arrested

The shift into past tense is correct, but student's regular text is historical present.

and spent time at the state correctional school.

Later, Jane had six children of her own, two of whom

were illegitimate. She married a man with a criminal

record who abused her and her children. Jane and her

husband frequently separated; after he was arrested

again, she began to drink heavily. Three of her chil-

dren were placed under the care of agencies. Young

points out that Jane Neilson's entire life has been

"dreary misery, a saga of exploitation, deprivation,

indifference, and hate" (76). Then Young concludes:

"What she could have given any child is hard to see"

(76). In truth, Jane Neilson is a victim of her own

background; little wonder that her children would

suffer.

The thesis sentence
is stated late in the
opening, after the
issue is well
developed.

        This example, however, prompts this thought: If

people like the Jane Neilsons of our society could be

identified and given help in a timely fashion, then

perhaps children would not be victimized. Perhaps

an answer lies in preventing abuse, not in makeshift

remedies after the fact. Parents who abuse their

children should be treated as victims, not criminals.

Child abuse is a symptom of the parent's condition.

Reaching out to the parent before a child appears in

the emergency room may prove difficult, but our solv-

ing the causes of abuse may be the only way to stop
this escalating maltreatment of America's precious
children.

Most people agree that parents who abuse children were abused themselves as children. Many abusive parents had poor role models as parents and did
not experience the love between parent and child that
most of us know. Julianne Wayne and Nancy Avery stipulate that some parents do not see themselves as people with real potential, and they even believe
themselves to be the "black sheep" of the family (10).
In addition, Young states that "a number of psychi-
atrists believe that there is an organic or constitu-
tional factor involved" with parents who abuse a child
(78). That is, for unknown reasons some people have
"a predisposition toward this kind of [violent] personality" (Young 78). Environment may determine or
encourage such personality development, but the seeds
are planted in the future abuser. Young explains that
this psychic disorder causes "the gap in communications so often experienced with abusive parents, as
if they acted on different premises than other people" (78). Thus, society and the abusive parent are
in discord, as this expert points out:

The blending of paraphrase and quotation flows smoothly with proper introductions and citations.

First lines of long
quotations receive
extra paragraph
indentation only
when the original
begins a new
paragraph.

> Social class, by the behavioral standards it
> imposes and enforces, permits or prohibits
> what the individual family acts out in view
> of the community. Both society and classes
> which compose it set a certain climate in
> which specific kinds of behavior may flour-
> ish or wither.   (Young 81)

Today's society and shifting patterns of one's social
class may dictate, then, a climate for abuse. Edward
Zigler argues that many parents are just not equipped
today for parenthood (42). He says, for instance,
that the "extended family is now rare in contemporary
society, and with its demise the new parent has lost
the wisdom and daily support of older, more experienced family members" (Zigler 42). In truth, a family
such as that portrayed by the Waltons on television
seldom exists today with grandparents, parents, and
many children all living together under one roof. No
wonder Zigler argues that "many parents are not as
well equipped for parenthood as their parents before
them, since over the years most children have been
given less responsibility in helping care for young
siblings" (42).

What's more, the television age may breed its

own violence. Zigler laments, "One finds violence,

hostility and aggression everywhere, including TV,

the movies, and in many of our everyday social rela-

tions" (40). Violence observed perhaps becomes vio-

lence practiced by parents on the children as well as

by children on their brothers and sisters and even

against their own parents. As one authority puts it,

"So long as this preoccupation with and even glorifi-

cation of aggression is tolerated, so long can we

expect the abuse of children both at home and in the

school" (Zigler 40).

 Depression also causes a parent to beat a child,

but E. Milling Kinard suggests that treating the

parent for depression without removing the social

problems of economic poverty and emotional stress will

probably have only limited success (403-06). The

causal chain leading to abuse may be complex to the

point that social workers need to dip into the life

history of the parent/abuser, asking always, "How is

this adult a victim who needs help as much as his or

her battered child?"

 Cycles of child abuse appear regularly on a com-

munity-wide level, even on a national level. The

year 1982 saw an increase in child abuse all across

Even paraphrased material should be introduced and documented in the text.

the nation. The year 1982 was also one of extremely

high unemployment. Experts are quick to note the cor-

relation that unemployment in a town or a nation may

endanger the well-being of the children as well as

Even three authors
may be listed in the
citation.
their very lives (Steinberg, Catalano, and Dooley

975). This same source reaches rather distressing

conclusions:

> Declines in the work force are significantly
>
> related to reported child abuse in two
>
> metropolitan communities. This finding is
>
> consistent with the hypothesis that undesir-
>
> able economic change causes family stress,
>
> resulting subsequently in child abuse. (982)

On an individual basis the family scenario might go

like this: the father loses his job so the mother

enters the job market, leaving the children to a man

without the experience or the patience for managing

and properly disciplining the children. Thereafter,

the entire family is victimized. In the worst of

cases the children are harmed physically, even sex-

ually molested, the father is placed in jail, the

children are split up for placement in foster homes,

and the mother struggles to hold together what is

10

left--all events triggered by the loss of a job.

These cycles of child abuse may be expected to esca-

late for years to come as more and more children are

raised in violent, hostile environments.

Student effectively
summarizes the
basic problem, then
moves to additional
issues.

On that point, Peter Kratcoski suggests that

childhood experiences help form basic personalities

that "shape the individual's relationship with his or

her own children" (436). Kratcoski makes this signif-

icant point:

This paragraph
blends short
quotation of a line or
two with a longer,
indented quotation.

> Children reared with love and respect
>
> mature adequately and become loving, respon-
>
> sible, and productive parents and spouses,
>
> while children who are disliked and abused
>
> by their parents may turn out to be abus-
>
> ers.   (436-37)

Kratcoski reaches a rather obvious conclusion, saying

that children who experience violence as children

tend to incorporate such behavior into their own pat-

terns for handling stress (437).

In truth, troubled parents must be treated as

victims of their heritage and social conditioning.

Health professionals and social support organizations

need to rededicate themselves to a focus on the

The writer reasserts
the thesis and
begins the move
toward a conclusion.causes, not just on remedies after the fact. We may

help the child after he gets battered, but we are

probably too late to help the parent. As a conse-

quence, child abuse is growing more and more every

day. The main reason for the increasing number of

cases might be our "unwillingness to accept the

truth, look ugliness in the eye, to draw upon our

reserves of courage, and fight back" (Fontana xii).

All the people who fail to get involved or who

don't report case of abuse say to themselves--if I

don't look, if I don't get involved, if I don't think

about it, abuse will go away. But the truth of the

matter is, it does not go away, the problem of abuse

just gets bigger and bigger.

    Therefore the time has arrived for several

The writer begins
enumeration of four
steps.
positive steps. First, the idea of group therapy

and self-help sessions for adults seems sound.

Marlin Blizinsky reports that group sessions may be

the only answer for some persons because a group

session might be the only program in which an abusive

person will participate (311). For instance,

Blizinsky reports that Parents Anomymous, a self-help

group, has begun to gain national attention (305). He

reports that community efforts, such as Seattle's

12

Children's Home Society, are being duplicated around

the country (307). Also, Zigler cites a successful

program of emergency services to families in Nash-

ville where the number of children institutionalized

because of abuse dropped from 324 in 1969-70 to only

50 in 1973-74: "The Nashville program is an excel-

lent one and there is no reason that it cannot be im-

plemented in every community in America" (41). Sec-   The second step is
                                                           explained.
ond, parenthood courses for adolescents are positive

actions. Zigler, for example, advocates an expanded

effort to educate young people for parenthood. He

supports the program of the Office of Child Develop-

ment and the Office of Education which offers to

schools and other organizations several courses on

parenthood that were prepared specifically for ado-

lescents (42). Such a program makes sense because

it seeks prevention and not remedies after the act

of child abuse. Another sociologist concurs, say-

ing, "A central notion in the treatment model is the

building of social responsibility, the realization

that each of us is an important element of society"

(Giarretto 5). Youngsters who are future parents

should be helped toward responsible social behavior.

Third, a program to advise young girls and boys about   Step three is
                                                          advanced next.

incest could prevent many children from ruining themselves and perhaps help them preserve the family

unit.[2] The case of Leigh, as described below, seems

an excellent case study of the abused child feeling

personally responsible for the abuse and developing

hatred for her own body:

This description may
seem bizarre but the
message is effective
under conditions of
the paper.

> Leigh, now 25, had been sexually abused by
> her father for five years. He continually
> told her that if she would only stop act-
> ing like such a "slut" he would quit having
> sex with her. Early attempts to tell her
> mother what was happening only reinforced
> her father's claim: her mother told her
> that only a "whore" would accuse her
> father of such things. "So here I was,
> 11 years old, standing in front of a mir-
> ror thinking, 'You filthy slut! You de-
> serve everything you get!' Then I'd go
> into a trance almost, and cut my arms and
> legs with a razor blade. Later I cut my
> breasts and even my genitals because I
> learned that those were the parts of my
> body that made me a whore." (de Young 581)

14

Counseling for a person like Leigh at twenty-five may
help her to adjust today and to be a good parent to-
morrow, but how much better it would be if women like
Leigh were counseled as children before self-
injurious behavior marred their bodies, their lives,
and the manner in which they eventually treat their
own children.   Fourth, in a related area, identifying

The fourth step is
presented.

and offering aid to alcoholic parents and their
children may serve to reduce child abuse because
studies demonstrate that a high percentage of abused
children have alcoholic parents or guardians.[3]

The four points above demonstrate a central
issue: the troubled parents who were victims in their

The conclusion now
officially begins.
Note how the
student develops a
full judgment on the
issue and does not
merely summarize
the paper.

own right and those who are victimized by circumstances today must be helped to recognize their real
potentials as human beings.   The responsibility falls
on all health professionals to provide the necessary
treatment.   Major cities across the nation and many
rural communities are establishing child abuse centers and parental self-help groups.   A few of the
most successful community involvement programs are
the Child Abuse Prevention in Toledo, the Johnson
County Coalition for Prevention of Child Abuse in
Kansas City, and the Council for Prevention of Child

Abuse and Neglect in Seattle. More cities should
establish such programs.

 Let us face the problem straight on and try to
erase it in the best way we can rather than throw up
our hands and say that all we can do is help the victims and merely label the abuser a "black sheep."
Let us look to the parent or guardian as a victim as
well and try, difficult though it may be, to show
love, warmth, and concern for these people who too
often silently cry out of loneliness, isolation, and
alienation. Their violent beating of a child, though
we cannot condone it, may be a cry for help. Let
there be hope; may it never cease. People, whether
young or old, rich or poor, healthy or sick, need
love and the warmth that family life accomplishes.
Unfortunately, those children who lack love fall
victims to hostile, aggressive physical abuse and
probably, because they cannot give love, grow up to
be abusers themselves. Repeatedly, our social agencies destroy family life by institutionalizing family
members after abuse occurs even though warning signals have been noticed by neighbors, relatives, and
even the social workers themselves. We participate
in the crime by our failure with preventive measures.

16

If we have love and tolerance in our national and
community social programs, so that we touch effectively the lives of children, teenagers, and aggressive adults, we might succeed in reversing the
present growing trend in child abuse.

Content notes are
on a separate page.

Notes

A blanket reference
to several sources.

[1] On this point see Giarretto (2), de Young (581),
Kinard (406-08), and Young (81).

A reference to
sources on a related
area of the topic.

[2] The problems of incest and sexual abuse are ex-
plored in Giarretto, Walters, and also de Young.
These authorities cite the need for preventive measures, if possible, before damage occurs to the children; nevertheless, sexual abuse, like a disease, is
here today in horrifying case after case, and we
don't have a cure.

A reference to
additional literature
on a point.

[3] For additional study of the effects of alcoholics on children see especially the Journal of Studies
on Alcohol for the article by Wolin et al., and the
bibliography on the topic in Orme and Rimmer. In
addition, group therapy for children of alcoholics
is examined in Hawley and Brown.

Works Cited

Blizinsky, Marlin. "Parents Anomymous and the Pri-

    vate Agency: Administrative Cooperation." <u>Child</u>

    <u>Welfare</u> 61 (1982): 305-11.

Browning, Elizabeth Barrett. "The Cry of the Chil-

    dren." In <u>Poetry of the Victorian Period</u>. Ed.

    J. H. Buckley and G. B. Woods. Glenview, Ill.:

    Scott, Foresman, 1965, 382-84.

Chase, Naomi Feigelson. <u>A Child Is Being Beaten</u>.

    New York: Holt, Rinehart and Winston, 1975.

Cohen, Stephan J., and Alan Sussman. "The Incidence

    of Child Abuse in the United States." <u>Child</u>

    <u>Welfare</u> 54 (1975): 432-43.

de Young, Mary. "Self-Injurious Behavior in Incest

    Victims: A Research Note." <u>Child Welfare</u> 61

    (1982): 577-84.

Fontana, Vincent J. <u>Somewhere a Child Is Crying</u>.

    New York: Macmillan, 1973.

Start the "Works Cited" on a new page.

A typical entry for a journal article.

An entry for the component part of a book.

Standard book form.

Giarretto, Henry. "The Treatment of Father-Daughter

   Incest: A Psycho-Social Approach." Children

   Today 5.4 (1976): 2-5.

Hawley, N. P., and E. L. Brown. "Use of Group

   Treatment with Children of Alcoholics." Social

   Casework 62 (1981): 40-46.

Kinard, E. Milling. "Child Abuse and Depression:

   Cause or Consequence?" Child Welfare 61 (1982):

   403-13.

Kratcoski, Peter C. "Child Abuse and Violence

   Against the Family." Child Welfare 61 (1982):

   435-44.

Orme, T. C., and J. Rimmer. "Alcoholism and Child

   Abuse: A Review." Journal of Studies on Alcohol

   42 (1981): 273-87.

Steinberg, Laurence D., Ralph Catalano, and David

   Dooley. "Economic Antecedents of Child Abuse

   and Neglect." Child Development 52 (1981):

   975-85.

Walters, David R. Physical and Sexual Abuse of Chil-

   dren: Causes and Treatment. Bloomington: Indi-

   ana Univ. Press, 1975.

20

Wayne, Julianne L., and Nancy C. Avery. <u>Child Abuse:</u>

   <u>Prevention and Treatment Through Social Group</u>

   <u>Work</u>. Charleston, MA: Charles Rivers Books,

   1980.

Wolin, S. J., L. A. Bennett, D. L. Noonan, and M. A.

   Teitebaum. "Disrupted Family Rituals: A Factor

   in the Intergenerational Transmission of Alco-

   holism." <u>Journal of Studies on Alcohol</u> 41

   (1980): 199-214.

Young, Leontine. <u>Wednesday's Children: A Study of</u>

   <u>Child Neglect and Abuse</u>. New York: McGraw-Hill,

   1964.

Form for two
authors.

Form for more than
two authors.

6
Works Cited

THE BIBLIOGRAPHY

After writing your paper, you should prepare a selected bibliography, entitled "Works Cited," listing the source materials actually used in writing your manuscript and including any sources mentioned within your content endnotes. Some instructors may request that you label it "List of References Cited" or "Selected Bibliography." Whatever the title, it offers the reader a limited list of the literature used in developing your paper. Yours will not be a comprehensive or exhaustive list because it will contain only those works referred to within your text and notes.

If you carefully developed your early working bibliography cards (35–40), you will find that preparation of the final list is a relatively simple process. In fact, the final list is really not a new assignment at all because your bibliography cards, arranged alphabetically, already provide the necessary information if, of course, you have kept the cards up-to-date during note-taking by adding new sources and by disposing of cards that you found to be irrelevant.

Again, you should include in the bibliography list all works actually mentioned in your text and endnotes. Therefore, works pertinent to the paper, such as an article that strongly influenced your thinking, although you did not quote or paraphrase it, should be mentioned with appropriate commentary in a content endnote (141–45); thereafter, you may list it within the "Works Cited." Other unused or irrelevant bibliography cards gathered during your study should be discarded.

FORMAT FOR "WORKS CITED" PAGE

You should arrange the items of the bibliography in alphabetical order by the surname of the author. Place the first line of each entry flush with the left margin and indent succeeding lines five spaces. Double-space each entry and also double-space between entries. Set the title "Works Cited" two inches down from the top of the sheet and quadruple-space between it and the first entry. Study carefully the following sample page:

Works Cited

The Bible. Revised Standard Version.

Bulfinch, Thomas. Bulfinch's Mythology. 2 vols. New York:
        Mentor, 1962.

Campbell, Joseph. The Hero With a Thousand Faces. Cleve-
        land: Meridian Books, 1956.

--------. The Masks of God. 4 vols. New York: Viking-
        Compass, 1970.

Henderson, Joseph L., and Maud Oakes. The Wisdom of the Ser-
        pent: The Myths of Death, Rebirth, and Resurrection.
        New York: Collier, 1971.

Homer. The Iliad. Trans. Richmond Lattimore. Chicago:
        Univ. of Chicago Press, 1951.

Laird, Charlton. "A Nonhuman Being Can Learn Language."
        College Composition and Communication 23 (1972): 142–54.

Lévi-Strauss, Claude. "The Structural Study of Myth." In
        Myth: A Symposium. Ed. A. Sebeok. Bloomington: Indiana
        Univ. Press, 1958.

McFadden, George. "'Life Studies'—Robert Lowell's Comic
        Breakbrough." PMLA 90 (1975): 96–106.

Robinson, Lillian S. "Criticism—and Self-Criticism." Col-
        lege English 36 (1974): 436–45.

NOTE: Enter anonymous works alphabetically by the first important word of
the title. Imagine lettered spelling for unusual items, such as "#2 Red Dye
& Cancer" (entered as though "Number 2 Red Dye") or "6 Million Die in
Earthquake" (entered as "Six Million").

Bibliography Form—Books

When entering references to books, you should use the following order, omitting unnecessary items:

Name of the Author(s)

The author's name, surname first, followed by given name or initials, followed by a period:

```
Baxter, John.  The Bidders.  New York: Lippincott, 1979.
```

Always give authors' names in the fullest possible form: for example, "Cosbey, Robert C." rather than "Cosbey, R. C." unless, as indicated on the title page of the book, the author prefers initials.

If an author has two or more works in the bibliography, do not repeat his or her name with each work. Rather, insert a continuous, seven-dash line flush with the left margin, followed by a period:

```
Hansberry, Lorraine.  A Raisin in the Sun.  New York: Random

    House, 1959.

———————.  To Be Young, Gifted and Black.  Ed. Robert Nemi-

    roff.  Englewood Cliffs, N.J.: Prentice-Hall, 1969.
```
An alternative is that of extending the line of dashes the length of the author's name.

Use the following form for an author who has two or more works in the bibliography when one is written in collaboration with someone else:

```
Lagarsfeld, Paul F., and others, eds.  Continuities in the

    Language of Social Research.  Rev. ed.  New York: Free

    Press, 1972.

———————, and E. Katz.  Language of Social Research: A Reader

    in the Methodology of Social Research.  New York: Free

    Press, 1965.
```

A Chapter or Part of a Book

A chapter or a part of a book is placed before the title, within quotation marks or underlined, and followed by a period. The word "In" usually follows this period to specify the anthology or collection in which this piece appears:

```
Elder, Lonne.  "Ceremonies in Dark Old Men."  In New Black

    Playwrights: An Anthology.  Ed. William Couch, Jr.

    Baton Rouge: Louisiana State Univ. Press, 1968.

Aristophanes.  The Birds.  In Five Comedies of Aristophanes.

    Trans. Benjamin B. Rogers.  Garden City, N.Y.: Double-

    day, 1955.
```

List the chapter or part of a book in "Works Cited" only when it is separately edited, translated, written, or demands special attention. For example, if you quote from a specific chapter of a book, let's say Lewis Thomas' chapter entitled "The Music of This Sphere" from his book *The Lives of a Cell,* the entry should read:

> Thomas, Lewis. <u>The Lives of a Cell</u>. New York: Viking, 1974.
> NOTE: Your in-text citation will list specific page numbers; there is no reason to list a specific chapter even though that might be the only portion of Thomas' book that you read.

The primary author of a part of a book or the editor(s) of the collection should be listed first, according to your in-text citation:

> Child, Harold. "Jane Austen." In <u>The Cambridge History of</u>
> <u>English Literature</u>. Ed. A. W. Ward and A. R. Waller.
> London: Cambridge Univ. Press, 1927, 12:231–44.
> Use the above form if your textual citation reads,
> "Child's essay on Jane Austen. . . ."
>   but
> Ward, A. W., and A. R. Waller, eds. <u>The Cambridge History of</u>
> <u>English Literature</u>. 15 vols. London: Cambridge Univ.
> Press, 1927.
> Use this form when the textual citation reads,
> "The history of Ward and Waller. . . ."

The Title of the Book

Show the title of the work, underlined, followed by a period:

> Lagercrantz, Olof. <u>From Hell to Paradise: Dante and His Com-</u>
> <u>edy</u>. Trans. Alan Blair. New York: Washington Square
> Press, 1966.
> NOTE: Separate the subtitle from the primary title by a colon, even though the title page may have no mark of punctuation or the card catalog entry may have a semicolon.

When a title of a book includes the title of another book, do not underline the latter:

> Schilling, Bernard N. <u>Dryden and the Conservative Myth: A</u>
> <u>Reading of</u> Absalom and Achitophel. New Haven: Yale
> Univ. Press, 1961.
> See also periodical entries that feature titles within titles, 213.

For additional samples of title entries see 207.

Name of the Editor or Translator

Show the name of the editor or translator, preceded by "Ed." or "Trans.":

> Mirandola, Giovanni Pico della. On the Imagination. Trans.
>
> and notes Harry Caplan. 1930; rpt. Westport, Conn.:
>
> Greenwood, n.d.

However, if the work is a collection, or if the editor's or translator's work rather than the text is under discussion, place the editor's or translator's name first, followed by a comma, followed by "ed." or "eds." or "trans." without further punctuation:

> Bevington, David, ed. The Complete Works of Shakespeare.
>
> 3rd ed. Glenview, Ill.: Scott, Foresman, 1980.
>
> Use the above form because the work is a collection. See 139–41 for
> methodology of in-text citations.

> Ciardi, John, trans. The Purgatorio. By Dante. New York:
>
> New American Library, 1961.
>
> Use the above form if your in-text citation says, for example:
>
> "Ciardi's explanation in his introduction (iv—vii) indi-
>
> cates. . . ."

Edition of the Book

Indicate the edition used, whenever it is not the first, in Arabic numerals (for example, "3rd ed."), without further punctuation:

> Beyer, Robert, and Donald J. Trawicki. Profitability
>
> Accounting: For Planning and Control. 2nd ed. New
>
> York: Ronald, 1972.

Name of a Series

Show the name of the series, without quotation marks and not underlined, followed by a comma, followed by the number of this work in the series in Arabic numerals (for example, "vol. 3," "no. 3" or simply "3"), followed by a period:

> Fowler, David. Piers the Plowman. Univ. of Washington Pub-
>
> lications in Lang. and Lit., 16. Seattle: Univ. of
>
> Washington Press, 1961.

Number of Volumes with this Title

Show the number of volumes with this particular title, if more than one, in Arabic numerals (for example, "6 vols."):

Horacek, Leo, and Gerald Lefkoff. Programmed Ear Training.

4 vols. New York: Harcourt, 1970.

Place, Publisher, and Date

Indicate the place, publisher, and date of publication:

Steinbeck, John. The Grapes of Wrath. New York: Viking,

1939.

If more than one place of publication appears on the title page, the first city mentioned is usually sufficient, although in some cases a foreign publisher might be listed along with the American publisher:

Ruskin, John. The Works of Ruskin. Ed. E. T. Cook and Alex-

ander Wedderburn. 39 vols. London: George Allen; New

York: Longmans, Green, 1903.

If successive dates of copyright are given, the most recent is usually sufficient (unless your study is specifically concerned with an earlier, perhaps definitive, edition. A new printing does not constitute a new edition nor demand usage of its corresponding date. If the text has a 1940 copyright date but a 1975 third printing, use 1940 unless you have other information, such as: "1975 Diamond Printing," "1975 third printing rev.," or "1975 reprint of original 1940 edition" (see immediately below).

Weaver, Raymond. Introduction. The Shorter Novels of Herman

Melville. 1928; rpt. New York: Premier-Fawcett, 1960.

Lewes, George Henry. The Life and Works of Geothe (1855). 2

vols. Rpt. as vols. 13 and 14 of The Works of J. W. von

Goethe. Ed. Nathan Haskell Dole. 14 vols. London:

Francis A. Nicolls, n.d.

Such detailed publication information as shown above may be necessary on occasion because you want your reader to be able to locate the source if necessary.

Include the name of the state if necessary for clarity:

Forliti, John E. Program Planning for Youth Ministry. Wi-

nona, Minn.: St. Mary's College Press, 1975.

If the place, publisher, or date of publication is not provided, insert either "n.p." or "n.d.":

```
Bouret, Jean.  The Life and Work of Toulouse Lautrec.  Trans.

     Daphne Woodward.  New York: Abrams, n.d.

Lowell, James Russell.  Democracy.  N.p., 1886.
```

Provide the publisher's name in a slightly shortened form whenever possible, for example: Macmillan; Doubleday; Free Press; Scott, Foresman; Norton; Dell; Little, Brown; Wiley; Knopf.

But list university presses in full to distinguish between a publication of the university and that of a university press: Harvard Univ. Press, Louisiana State Univ. Press, Yale Univ. Press, Oxford Univ. Press.

Volume Number of the Book

Show the volume number, in Arabic numerals, preceded by a comma and followed by a colon and page numbers, only if you find it necessary to specify such information:

```
Child, Harold.  "Jane Austen."  The Cambridge History of En-

     glish Literature.  Ed. A. W. Ward and A. R. Waller.

     London: Cambridge Univ. Press, 1927, 12: 231–44.

Macaulay, Thomas Babington.  "John Dryden."  In Critical,

     Historical, and Miscellaneous Essays.  New York: A. C.

     Armstrong and Son, 1860, 1: 321–75.  Originally pub-

     lished in The Poetical Works of John Dryden.  1826.
```

Page Numbers to a Section of a Book

Show page numbers of the entire selection, in Arabic numerals, preceded by a volume number and colon (see immediately above) or by a date and comma and followed by a period. Again, supply this information only upon rare occasions.

```
Knoepflmacher, U. C.  "Fusing Fact and Myth: The New Reality

     of Middlemarch."  In This Particular Web: Essays on Mid-

     dlemarch.  Ed. Ian Adam.  Toronto: Univ. of Toronto

     Press, 1975, 55–65.
```

SAMPLE BIBLIOGRAPHY ENTRIES—BOOKS

Author

Baxter, John. The Bidders. New York: Lippincott, 1979.

Author, *anonymous*

The Song of Roland. Trans. Frederick Bliss Luquines. New
York: Macmillan, 1960.
You should alphabetize this entry by the "S" of the first important word of
the title.

Author, *anonymous but name supplied*

[Madison, James.] All Impressments Unlawful and Inadmissi-
ble. Boston: William Pelham, 1804.

Author, *pseudonymous but name supplied*

Slender, Robert [Freneau, Philip]. Letters on Various and
Important Subjects. Philadelphia: D. Hogan, 1799.

Author, *more than one work by the same author*

Hansberry, Lorraine. A Raisin in the Sun. New York: Random
House, 1959.

————. To Be Young, Gifted and Black. Ed. Robert Nemi-
roff. Englewood Cliffs, N.J.: Prentice-Hall, 1969.
Rather than repeat the author's name in succeeding entries, insert seven
continuous typewriter dashes, or extend a line of dashes the length of the
author's name.

Authors, *two*

Hooper, Henry O., and Peter Gwynne. Physics and the Physical
Perspective. New York: Harper & Row, 1977.

Authors, *three*

Richardson, Charles E., Fred V. Hein, and Dana L. Farnsworth.
Living: Health, Behavior, and Environment. 6th ed.
Glenview, Ill.: Scott, Foresman, 1975.

Authors, *more than three*

Baugh, Albert C., Tucker Brooke, Samuel C. Chew, Kemp Malone,
and George Sherburn. A Literary History of England.
2nd ed. New York: Appleton, 1967.
An alternative to this form is the use of "et al." or "and others," as follows:

Lewis, Laurel J., et al. <u>Linear Systems Analysis</u>. New York:
McGraw—Hill, 1969.

Alphabetized Works (Encyclopedias and Biographical Dictionaries)

When your text refers to the work as a whole:

<u>DAB</u> (1928). Dumas Malone. 20 vols.

When your in-text citation mentions the writer Edmund K. Alden, for example,
"Alden is described by one historian as. . . ."

A[lden], E[dmund] K. "Alden, John." <u>DAB</u> (1928).

See also "Encyclopedia" 204.

The Bible

Your in-text citation should provide book and chapter, for example,

(1 Samuel 6:12—14).

The Bible, Revised Standard Version

The King James version is assumed unless you specify another version.

<u>The Geneva Bible</u>. 1560; facsim. rpt. Madison: Univ. of Wis-
consin Press, 1961.

Classical Works

Homer. <u>The Iliad</u>. Trans. Richmond Lattimore. Chicago:
Univ. of Chicago Press, 1951.

Shorey, Paul, trans. <u>The Republic</u>. By Plato. Cambridge,
Mass.: Harvard Univ. Press, 1937.
Use the translator's name first only if his or her work rather than Plato's text
is the focus of your study (see 198).

Committee Report

<u>The Church and the Law of Nullity of Marriage</u>. Report of a
commission appointed by the archbishops of Canterbury
and York in 1949. London: Society for Promoting Christian Knowledge, 1955.

Component Part of a Book

Hoy, Cyrus. "Fathers and Daughters in Shakespeare's Romances." In <u>Shakespeare's Romances Reconsidered</u>. Ed.

Carol McGinnis Kay and Henry E. Jacobs. Lincoln: Univ.
of Nebraska Press, 1978, 77—90.

Lévi—Strauss, Claude. "The Structural Study of Myth." In
Structural Anthropology. Garden City, N.Y.: Anchor—
Doubleday, 1967, 202—28.

Harvey, W. J. "The Intellectual Background of the Novel:
Casaubon and Lydgate." In Middlemarch: Critical Ap—
proaches to the Novel. Ed. Barbara Hardy. New York:
Oxford Univ. Press, 1967, 25—37.

Scott, Nathan, Jr. "Society and Self in Recent American Lit—
erature." In his The Broken Center. New Haven: Univ.
Press, 1966. Rpt. in Dark Symphony: Negro Literature in
America. Ed. James A. Emanuel and Theodore L. Gross.
New York: Free Press, 1968, 539—54.

Corporate Authorship

Committee on Telecommunications. Reports on Selected Topics
in Telecommunications. New York: National Academy of
Sciences, National Research Council, 1970.

Cross Reference

Eliot, George. "Art and Belles Lettres." Westminster Re—
view, U.S.A. ed., April 1856: partly rpt. Eliot, A Writ—
er's Notebook.

————————. A Writer's Notebook, 1854—1879, and Uncollected
Writings. Ed. Joseph Wiesenfarth. Charlottesville:
Univ. Press of Virginia, 1981.

The first entry to Eliot makes reference to the one that follows.

Edition

Keith, Harold. Sports and Games. 6th ed. Scranton, Penn.:
Crowell, 1976.

Laslett, Peter. The World We Have Lost. 2nd ed. 1965; rpt.
London: Methuen, 1971.

Nordloh, David J. et al. A Hazard of New Fortunes. Vol. 16
of A Selected Edition of W. D. Howells. Gen. ed. Don L.
Cook. Bloomington: Indiana Univ. Press, 1976.

The Statutes of the Realm. London: Record Commissions,

1820–28; facsim. ed. 1968.

Stone, Lawrence. The Crisis of the Aristocracy: 1558–1660.

Abridged ed. London: Oxford Univ. Press, 1971.

Editor

Bevington, David, ed. The Complete Works of Shakespeare.

3rd ed. Glenview, Ill.: Scott, Foresman, 1980.

Evans, G. Blakemore, ed. The Riverside Shakespeare. Boston:

Houghton, 1974.

If the work is a collection, or if the editor's work rather than the text is under
discussion, place the editor's name first. Otherwise, place the editor's
name after the title, as follows:

Brackenridge, Hugh Henry. Modern Chivalry. Ed. Claude M.

Newlin. New York: American Book, 1962.

Encyclopedia

Dickinson, Robert E. "Norman Conquest." The World Book

Encyclopedia. 1976 ed.

N[aess], A[rne] D. "Martin Heidegger." Encyclopedia Britan-

nica: Macropaedia. 1974 ed.

Illustrations

Venturi, Lionello. Botticelli. With 50 Plates. Greenwich,

Conn.: Fawcett, n.d.

Honoré Daumier: Drawings and Watercolors. Selected and with

introduction by Jean Adhemar. With 58 Illustrations.

New York: Macmillan, 1954.

Introduction

Webb, Walter Prescott. The Great Frontier. Introd. Arnold

J. Toynbee. Austin, Texas: Univ. of Texas Press, 1964.

Lowell, Robert. Foreword. Ariel. By Sylvia Plath. New

York: Harper & Row, 1966.

Use the above form only if your subject is Lowell's work, not the poetry of
Plath.

Manuscript collections

British Museum. <u>Cotton Vitellius</u>. A. XV.

Corpus Christi College, Cambridge. MS CCCC 201.

Bodleian Library, Oxford. MS Tanner 346.

Monograph

LeClercq, R. V. "Crashaw's Epithalamium: Pattern and Vision." <u>Literary Monographs</u>, 6. Madison: Univ. of Wisconsin Press, 1975, 73—108.

Play, *classical*

Parrott, T. M., ed. <u>Shakespeare: Twenty-Three Plays and the Sonnets</u>. New York: Scribner's, 1953.

> but also

Shakespeare, William. <u>Macbeth</u>. In <u>Shakespeare: Twenty-Three Plays and the Sonnets</u>. Ed. T. M. Parrott. New York: Scribner's, 1953.

> See 198 and 204.

Play, *modern*

Greene, Graham. <u>The Complaisant Lover</u>. New York: Viking, 1959.

Poem, *classical*

Dante, <u>The Divine Comedy</u>. Trans. Lawrence Grant White. New York: Pantheon, 1948.

Ciardi, John, trans. <u>The Purgatorio</u>. By Dante. New York: New American Library, 1961.

> Use the translator's or editor's name first only if his or her work rather than the primary text is under discussion (see 198).

Poem, *modern*

Warren, Robert Penn. <u>You, Emperors, and Others: Poems 1957—1960</u>. New York: Random House, 1960.

Keats, John. "Ode to a Nightingale." In <u>Beginnings in Poetry</u>. Ed. William J. Martz. 2nd ed. Glenview, Ill.: Scott, Foresman, 1973, 302.

Reprint

Lowes, John Livingston. <u>The Road to Xanadu: A Study in the
Ways of the Imagination</u>. 2nd ed. 1930; rpt. New York:
Vintage–Knopf, 1959.

Hooker, Richard. <u>Of the Lawes of Ecclesiasticall Politie</u>.
1594; fascim. rpt. Amsterdam: Theatrum Orbis Terrarum,
1971.

Arnold, Matthew. "The Study of Poetry." In <u>Essays: English
and American</u>. Ed. Charles W. Eliot. 1886; rpt. New
York: P. F. Collier and Son, 1910. Originally published
as the General Introduction to <u>The English Poets</u>. Ed.
T. H. Ward. 1880.

Series, *Numbered and Unnumbered*

Fowler, David. <u>Piers the Plowman</u>. Univ. of Washington Pub–
lications in Lang. and Lit., 16. Seattle: Univ. of
Washington Press, 1961.

Gibson, Lawrence Henry. <u>The Coming of the Revolution: 1762–
1775</u>. Ed. Henry Steele Commager and Richard B. Morris.
The New American Nation Series. New York: Harper & Row,
1954.

Commager, Henry Steele. <u>The Nature and the Study of History</u>.
Social Science Seminar Series. Columbus, Ohio: Merrill,
1965.

Wilson, Howard E. "Education, Foreign Policy, and Interna–
tional Relations." In <u>Cultural Affairs and Foreign
Relations</u>. Ed. Robert Blum. The American Assembly
Series. Englewood Cliffs, N.J.: Prentice–Hall, 1963.

Jefferson, D. W. "'All, all of a piece throughout': Thoughts
on Dryden's Dramatic Poetry." In <u>Restoration Theatre</u>.
Ed. John Russell Brown and Bernard Harris. Stratford-
upon–Avon Studies, 6. London: Edward Arnold, 1965,
159–76.

Wallerstein, Ruth C. Richard Crashaw: A Study in Style and
    Poetic Development. Univ. of Wisconsin Studies in Lang.
    and Lit., no. 37. Madison: Univ. of Wisconsin Press,
    1935.

Sourcebooks and Casebooks

Ellman, Richard. "Reality." In his Yeats: The Man and the
    Masks. New York: Macmillan, 1948; rpt. in John Unter-
    ecker, ed. Yeats: A Collection of Critical Essays.
    Twentieth Century Views. Englewood Cliffs, N.J.:
    Prentice-Hall, 1963, 163–74.

Title

Brownell, Thomas Church, ed. The Family Prayer Book; or, the
    Book of Common Prayer according to the Use of the Prot-
    estant Episcopal Church. New York: Stanford and Swords,
    1853.
    Separate two titles by a semicolon and the word "or"; see immediately
    below for another example of how to handle a title that includes the title of
    another book.

Schilling, Bernard N. Dryden and the Conservative Myth: A
    Reading of Absalom and Achitophel. New Haven: Yale
    Univ. Press, 1961.
McFadden, George. Dryden: The Public Writer, 1660–1685.
    Princeton: Princeton Univ. Press, 1978.
    Underline dates that are part of the title.

Title, *Foreign*

Brombert, Victor. Stendhal et la voie oblique. New Haven:
    Yale Univ. Press, 1954.
    Use lower case lettering for foreign titles except for the first major word
    and proper names.

André, Robert. Ecriture et pulsions dans le roman stendha-
    lien. Paris: Klinksieck, 1977.
Levowitz-Treu, Micheline. L'Amour et la mort chez Standhal.
    Aran: Editions due Grand Chêne, 1978.

Castex, P–G. Le Rouge et le noir de Stendhal. Paris: Sedes,
1967.

> Another example of one title within the title of the book from which you are
> quoting.

Translator

Eliade, Mircea. The Sacred and the Profane. Trans. Willard
R. Trask. New York: Harcourt, 1959.

Homer. Iliad. Trans. Robert Fitzgerald. Garden City, N.Y.:
Anchor, 1974.

Ciardi, John, trans. The Purgatorio. By Dante. New York:
New American Library, 1961.

> When the translator's work rather than the text is under discussion, place
> the translator's name first (see 198).

Lévi–Strauss, Claude. The Elementary Structures of Kinship.
Trans. James Harle Bell. Ed. John Richard von Sturmer
and Rodney Needham. Paris, 1949; rpt. Boston: Beacon,
1969.

Volumes, a work of several volumes

Ruskin, John. The Works of Ruskin. Ed. E. T. Cook and Alexander Wedderburn. 39 vols. London: George Allen; New
York: Longmans, Green, 1903.

Parrington, Vernon L. Main Currents in American Thought. 3
vols. New York: Harcourt, Brace, 1927–32.

Dryden, John. The Works of John Dryden. Vol. 1: Poems 1649–
1680. Ed. Edward Niles Hooker et al. Univ. of California Press, 1956. Vol. 2: Poems 1681–1684. Ed. H. T.
Swedenberg, Jr. et al. Berkeley: Univ. of California
Press, 1972. Vol. 3: Poems 1685–1692. Ed. Earl Miner
et al. Berkeley: Univ. of California Press, 1969. Vol.
4: Poems 1693–1696. Ed. A. B. Chambers et al. Berkeley: Univ. of California Press, 1974.

Volumes, one of several volumes

Stendhal. "La Comédie est impossible en 1836." In Mélanges
de littérature. Ed. Henri Martineau. Paris: Divan,
1933. Vol. 3.

Emerson, Ralph Waldo.   "Poetry and Imagination." In <u>Letters</u>
    <u>and Social Aims</u>.   Vol. 8 of <u>The Complete Works of Ralph</u>
    <u>Waldo Emerson</u>.   Boston: Houghton, 1865.

Volumes, component part of one of several volumes

Child, Harold.   "Jane Austen."   In <u>The Cambridge History of</u>
    <u>English Literature</u>.   Ed. A. W. Ward and A. R. Waller.
    London: Cambridge Univ. Press, 1927, 12: 231—44.

Daiches, David.   <u>A Critical History of English Literature</u>.
    2nd ed.   New York: Ronald, 1970, 2: 117—186.

Macaulay, Thomas Babington.   "John Dryden."   In <u>Critical,</u>
    <u>Historical, and Miscellaneous Essays</u>.   New York: A. C.
    Armstrong and Son, 1860, 1: 321—75.   Originally pub-
    lished in <u>The Poetical Works of John Dryden</u>.   1826.

Bibliography Form—Periodicals

When entering references to journals or magazine articles, you should use
the following order, omitting unnecessary items:

Name of the Author(s)

Show the author's name flush with the left margin, without a numeral and with
succeeding lines indented five spaces. Enter the surname first, followed by a
comma, followed by a given name or initials, followed by a period:

Shade, B. J. "Social—Psychological Traits of Achieving Black
    Children."   <u>Education Digest</u> 44 (1978): 38—40.

Title of the Article

Show the title within quotation marks followed by a period inside the closing
quotation marks:

Chiasson, Elias J.   "Dryden's Apparent Scepticism."   <u>Harvard</u>
    <u>Theological Review</u> 54 (1961): 207—21.

Publication Information

The name of the journal or magazine, underlined, followed by a volume number,
followed with a space and the year of publication within parentheses, followed
by a colon and page numbers for the entire article, not for specific pages cited:

Boose, Lynda E. "Othello's Handkerchief: 'The Recognizance
   and Pledge of Love.'" English Literary Renaissance 5
   (1975): 360-74.

Journals with separate pagination for each issue will require the issue number
following the volume number, separated by a period:

Frey, John R. "America and Her Literature Reviewed by Post-
   war Germany." American-German Review 20.5 (1954): 4-6.

You may add the month if more information would ease the search for the article:
"20.5 (Nov. 1954): 4-6."

If the article is paged here and there throughout the issue (for example,
pages 46, 48, 50, and 81), the following are possible methods of page citation:

46 et passim.	which means page 46 and several pages here and there throughout the work
46, 48, 50, 81.	which designates each page; use this method if only three or four pages are involved

In other circumstances the following forms might be appropriate:

46ff.	which means page 46 and several immediately follow-ing pages
46 et seq.	which means page 46 and the following page
46f.	which means page 46 and the following page (same as "46 et seq.")

Magazines that publish weekly or monthly require only the date without a
volume number listed:

"Chaos in Television." Time, 12 March 1979, 60-61.

Sontag, Susan. "Baby." Playboy, Feb. 1974, 74 et passim.

Sample Bibliography Entries—Periodicals

Address

Humphries, Alfred. "Computers and Banking." Address to
   Downtown Kiwanis Club, Nashville, TN. 30 Aug. 1981.
   Rpt. in part The Tennessean, 31 Aug. 1981, B3-B4.

U. S. President. "Address to Veterans of Foreign Wars." 19
   Aug. 1974. Rpt. in Weekly Compilation of Presidential
   Documents, 10 (26 Aug. 1974): 1045-50.

Author, anonymous

"Commodities: Sweet and Sour." Time, 16 Dec. 1974 32.

Authors, multiple

Libby, Roger W., Alan C. Acock, and David C. Payne. "Config-
urations of Parental Preferences Concerning Sources of
Sex Education of Adolescents." Adolescence 9 (1974):
73–80.

Bulletin

U.S. Dept. of Treasury. "Financial Operations of Government
Agencies and Funds." Treasury Bulletin. Washington,
D.C.: Government Printing Office, June 1974, 134–41.

"Spotlight on Crime." World of Politics Monthly, Nov. 1974,
10–11.

Critical review

Clignet, Remi. Rev. of Urban Poverty in a Cross–cultural
Context, by Edwin Eames and Judith Granich Goode (New
York: Free Press, 1973). American Journal of Sociology
80 (1974): 589–90.

Lewes, George Henry. Rev. of "Letters on Christian Art," by
Friedrich von Schlegel. Athenaeum, No. 1117 (1849):
296.

Gardner, John. Rev. of Falconer, by John Cheever. Saturday
Review, 2 April 1977, 20.

Interview

Hanks, Nancy, Chairperson, National Endowment of the Arts.
Interview. U.S. News and World Report, 7 Oct. 1974,
58–60.

Journal, with continuous pagination

Dyke, Vernon Van. "Human Rights and the Rights of Groups."
American Journal of Political Science 18 (1974): 725–41.

Kilchenmann, Ruth. "Traum und Wirklichkeit in den Werken
Friedrich Schnacks." German Quarterly 34 (1961): 257–
63.

Journal, with separate pagination

Mangan, Doreen. "Henry Casselli: Superb Contradictions."

American Artist 38.2 (1974): 39–43.

Because each issue of the journal is paged separately, you should include
the issue number (month or season of the issue is also acceptable; see
immedately below). Issue number is necessary because page numbers
alone will not locate the article within a volume of twelve issues when each
issue has separate pagination.

Stuart, Jesse. "Love Affair at the Pasture Gate." Ball

State University Forum 15 (Winter 1974): 3–6.

McDavid, Raven I. "Sense and Nonsense About American Dia-

lects." PMLA 81.2 (1966): 9–11.

PMLA normally pages continuously, but this issue is paged separately,
necessitating the issue number.

Journal, volume number embracing two years

Brooks, Peter. "Freud's Masterplot." Yale French Studies

55–56 (1977–78): 280–300.

Magazine, monthly

Crickmer, Barry. "Can We Control Spending?" Nation's Busi-

ness, April 1982, 22–24.

Magazine, weekly

von Hoffman, Nicholas. "The White House News Hole." The New

Republic, 6 Sept. 1982, 19–23.

Pileggi, Nicholas. "A Long Smoldery Summer?" New York, 21

June 1982, 28–31.

Notes, Queries, Reports, Comments

"Professional Notes and Comment." PMLA 97 (1982): 724 et

pas.

Robinson, Ken. "Does Otway Ascribe Sodom to Rochester? A

Reply." Notes and Queries New Series 29 (1982): 50–51.

Seymour, Thom. "Faulkner's The Sound and the Fury." The

Explicator 39.1 (1980): 24–25.

Stoppelmann, Ron. "Letters." New York, 23 Aug. 1982, 8.

Reprint of journal article

Hope, A. D. "Anne Killigrew; or, The Art of Modulating."
Southern Review: An Australian Journal of Literary Studies 1 (1963): 4–14. Rpt. in Hope, The Cave and the
Spring: Essays on Poetry. Adelaide, Australia: Rigby,
1965, 129–43.

Series

Hill, Christopher. "Sex, Marriage and the Family in England." Economic History Review, 2nd ser., 31 (1978):
450–63.

Title, *omitted*

Berkowitz, David. Renaissance Quarterly 32 (1979): 396–493.
But include title of the article any time it is available.

Title, *quotation within the title*

Ranald, Margaret Loftus. "'As Marriage Binds, and Blood
Breaks': English Marriage and Shakespeare." Shakespeare
Quarterly 30 (1979): 68–81.

Frey, Charles. "'O sacred, shadowy, cold and constant
queen': Shakespeare's Imperiled and Chastening Daughters
of Romance." South Atlantic Bulletin 43 (1978): 125–40.

Title, *within the article's title*

Dundes, Alan. "'To Love My Father All': A Psychoanalytic
Study of the Folktale Source of King Lear." Southern
Folklore Quarterly 40 (1976): 353–66.

Kearful, Frank J. "''Tis Past Recovery': Tragic Conscious-
ness in All for Love." Modern Language Quarterly 34
(1973): 227–46.

Title, *foreign*

Stivale, Charles J. "Le Vraisemblable temporel dans Le Rouge
et le noir." Stendhal Club 84 (1979): 299–313.

Barthes, Roland. "Introduction à l'analyse structurale des
récits." Communications 8 (1966): 1–27.

Title, *two titles listed*

Hope, A. D. "Anne Killigrew; or, The Art of Modulating."
Southern Review: An Australian Journal of Literary Studies 1 (1963): 4–14. Rpt. in Hope, The Cave and the
Spring: Essays on Poetry. Adelaide, Australia: Rigby,
1965, 129–43.

Bibliography Form—Public Documents

Since the nature of public documents is so varied, the form of the entry
cannot be standardized. Therefore, you should provide sufficient information so
that the reader can easily locate the reference. As a general rule, place information in the bibliography entry in this order: Government. Body. Subsidiary
body. Title of document. Identifying numbers.

Congressional papers

U.S. Cong. Cong. Rec. 6 March 1974, S2916–28.

U.S. Cong. Senate. Transportation System for Alaskan Natural
Gas. 95th Cong., 1st sess. S. 2411. Washington, D.C.:
GPO, 1977.

U.S. Cong. House. Committee on Interstate and Foreign Commerce. Federal Cigarette Labeling and Advertising Act.
89th Cong., 1st sess. H. Rept. 449 to accompany H.R.
3014. Washington, D.C.: GPO, 1965.

U.S. Cong. Senate. The Constitution of the United States of
America: Analysis and Interpretation. 82nd Cong., 2nd
sess. S. Doc. 170. Washington, D.C.: GPO, 1952.

Executive branch documents

U.S. President. Public Papers of the Presidents of the
United States. Washington, D.C.: Office of the Federal
Registrar, 1978.

U.S. President. Alternative to Drugs: A New Approach to Drug
Education. Pr Ex 13.2:D84/3/1972. Washington, D.C.:
GPO, 1972.

U.S. Dept. of State. <u>Foreign Relations of the United States:</u>
<u>Diplomatic Papers, 1943</u>. 5 vols. Washington, D.C.:
GPO, 1943–44.

Legal citations

U.S. Const. Art. II, sec. 1.

California, Const. Art. II, sec. 4.

15 U.S. Code. Sec. 78h (1964).

Noise Control Act of 1972. Statutes at Large. LXXXVI. Pub–
lic Law 92–574 (1972).

Gold Coin and Gold Bullion Act. 31 U.S. Code. Supp. III,
sec. 442 (1970).

Environmental Protection Agency et al. v. Mink et al. U.S.
Reports, CDX (1972).

Illinois, Revised Statutes Annotated. Sec. 16–7–81 (1980).

People v. McIntosh. California 321 P.3d 876, 2001–6 (1970).

State v. Lane. Minnesota 263 N. W. 608 (1935).

Bibliography Form—Other Sources

Art Work

Raphael. <u>School of Athens</u>. The Vatican, Rome. Illus. in
<u>The World Book Encyclopedia</u>. 1976 ed.

Use this form for art works reproduced in other books or journals. If you
actually experience the work itself, use the following form.

Remington, Frederic. <u>Mountain Man</u>. Metropolitan Museum of
Art, New York.

Bulletin

Economic Research Service. <u>Demand and Price Situation</u>.
Washington, D.C.: Dept. of Agriculture, Aug. 1974, DPS–
141, 14 pp.

French, Earl. <u>Personal Problems in Industrial Research and</u>
<u>Development</u>. Ithaca, N.Y., 1963. (Bulletin of the New
York State School of Industrial and Labor Relations, No.
51.)

For examples of bulletins published within periodicals, see 211.

Bib Form—Other

Computer Data

"Statistics on Child Abuse—Montgomery County, Tennessee."
Diskette 12. Clarksville, TN: Harriett Cohn Mental
Health Center, 1983.

Sears, Robert O. "Trends in Women's Sports: Factual Data on
Participation and Revenue." VAX—1419. Bowling Green:
Western Kentucky State Univ., 1983.

"Scipax." Series 3 software. Cleveland: Hunt Information
Services, 1982.

"Purchase Ledger." CPM C—Basic for Apple II. Chamberley,
England: Graham Doreian Software, 1982.

Data Base Sources

"Alexander Hamilton." Academic American Encyclopedia. 1981
ed.; rpt. Columbus: CompuServe, 1983, Record No. 1816.

Nevin, John J. "Doorstop to Free Trade." Harvard Business
Review 61 (1983): 88—95; rpt. Palo Alto: Dialog Information Services, 1983, Record No. 83—N43.

Dissertation, *published*

Nykrog, Per. Les Fabliaux: Etude d'histoire littéraire et de
stylistique mediévale. Diss. Aarhus 1957. Copenhagen:
Munksgaard, 1957.

Dissertation, *unpublished*

Phillips, Emmett Loy. "A Study of Aesthetic Distance in Tho-
reau's Walden." Diss. Univ. of Oklahoma 1970.

Film

Last Tango in Paris. United Artists, 1972.

Wilets, Bernard. Environment. Santa Monica, Calif.: BFA
Educational Media, 1971. (16 mm., 29 min., color.)

Interview

Turrentine, Robert, President, Acme Boot Co. Personal Interview. Clarksville, TN, 11 Feb. 1983.

Letter, *personal*

Weathers, Winston. Letter to author. 5 March 1979.

Manuscripts (MS) and typescripts (TS)

Glass, Malcolm. Journal 3, MS. M. Glass Private Papers.

Clarksville, Tenn.

Glass, Malcolm. The Hardlanders, TS. M. Glass Private

Papers. Clarksville, Tenn.

Microfilm or Microfiche

Tuckerman, H. T. "James Fenimore Cooper." North American

Review, 89 (1859): 298–316. (Microfilm.)

Indicate at the end of your entry that your source is on microfilm or microfiche.

Mimeographed material

Smith, Jane L. "Terms for the Study of Fiction." Cleveland,

1975. (Mimeographed.)

Monograph

NEA Research Division. Kindergarten Practices, 1961. Wash-

ington, D.C., 1962. (Monograph 1962–M2.)

Veeder, William R. W. B. Yeats: The Rhetoric of Repetition.

Univ. of California English Studies, 34. Berkeley:

Univ. of California Press, 1968.

Musical composition

Mozart, Wolfgang A. Jupiter. Symphony No. 41.

Newspaper

Bryant, Alice Franklin. "U.N. Role." Letter to the Editor.

Chattanooga Times, 15 Dec. 1974, B7, cols. 6–7.

Use this form for special newspaper articles, such as editorials, letters to
the editor, cartoons, and so on.

"Egypt Demands That Israel Put Limit on Population Growth."

Los Angeles Times, 14 Dec. 1974, 1.

When an item is unsigned, the title comes first and all subsequent information remains the same.

Sperling, Godfrey, Jr. "Ford's Plan to Spur Republican

Revival." Christian Science Monitor, 29 Nov. 1974, 20.

The basic form for signed newspaper articles.

"How to Measure Justice." Editorial. The Tennessean [Nash--

ville], 18 Aug. 1979, 8.

Pamphlet

U.S. Civil Service Commission. <u>The Human Equation: Working</u>
<u>in Personnel for the Federal Government</u>. Pamphlet 76.
Washington, D.C.: GPO, May 1970.

Public address or lecture

Sarnoff, David. "Television: A Channel for Freedom." Address presented at the University of Detroit Academic
Convocation. Detroit, 1961.

Quotation, as quoted in a book

Symington, Stuart. As quoted in Victor Marchetti and John D.
Marks. <u>The CIA and the Cult of Intelligence</u>. New York:
Knopf, 1974.

Recording on record or tape

"Chaucer: The Nun's Priest's Tale." In his <u>Canterbury Tales</u>.
Narrated in Middle English by Robert Ross. Caedmon, TC
1008, 1971.

John, Elton. "This Song Has No Title." In his <u>Goodbye Yel-</u>
<u>low Brick Road</u>. MCA, MCA 2-10003, 1974.

Statler Brothers. Jacket Notes. <u>The Originals</u>. Mercury,
SRM-1-5016, 1979.

Report

Linden, Fabian. "Women: A Demographic, Social and Economic
Presentation." Report by The Conference Board. New
York: CBS/Broadcast Group, 1973.

Panama Canal Company. <u>Annual Report: Fiscal Year Ended June</u>
<u>30, 1968</u>. Panama: Canal Zone Government, 1968.
Reports in the form of books or pamphlets require underlining.

<u>Womanpower</u>. Brookline, Mass.: Betsy Hogan Associates, 1974.

Reproductions and photographs

Blake's <u>Comus</u>, Plate 4. Photograph reproduced in Irene Tay-
ler. "Blake's <u>Comus</u> Designs." <u>Blake Studies</u>, 4 (Spring
1972): 61.

Michener, James A. "Structure of Earth at Centennial, Colo-
   rado." Line drawing in <u>Centennial</u>. New York: Random
   House, 1974.

Table or illustration

Corbett, Edward P. J. Syllogism graph. <u>Classical Rhetoric
   for the Modern Student</u>. New York: Oxford Univ. Press,
   1965.

   Because the graph has no title, the descriptive heading should not be
   placed within quotation marks.

Helmich, Donald L. "Organizational Growth and Succession
   Patterns." <u>Academy of Management Journal</u>. 17 (Dec.
   1974): 773, Table 2.

Television or radio program

<u>The Commanders: Douglas MacArthur</u>. New York: NBC–TV, 17
   March 1975.

Shakespeare, William. <u>As You Like It</u>. Nashville: Nashville
   Theatre Academy, WDCN–TV, 11 March 1975.

Thesis

   See "Dissertation, unpublished," 216.

Transparency

Sharp, La Vaughn, and William E. Loeche. <u>The Patient and
   Circulatory Disorders: A Guide for Instructors</u>. 54
   Transparencies, 99 overlays. Philadelphia: Lippincott,
   1969.

Unpublished paper

Elkins, William R. "The Dream World and the Dream Vision:
   Meaning and Structure in Poe's Art." (Unpublished
   paper.)

Videotape

Thompson, Paul. "W. B. Yeats." Lecture on Videotape VHS–MSU
   160. Memphis: Memphis State Univ., 1982.

Sevareid, Eric. <u>CBS News</u>. New York: CBS–TV, 11 March 1975;
   Media Services Videotape 1975–142. Nashville: Vanderbilt Univ., 1975.

7
Form and Style for Other Disciplines

The research style advocated by this text, as based upon principles of the Modern Language Association, should be adequate for most undergraduate assignments. Philosophically, the style focuses upon the author and the work, especially the title and page number (for example, "Jones 342" or "Campbell, *Masks* 23"). Language and literary scholars seek the work itself, not the date, as the key element. However, the sciences focus upon "date" because scientific data change dramatically and rapidly year by year. For instance, an essay on new findings in psychology or computer science becomes dated quickly. Therefore, the sciences call attention to the date by placing it within the textual citations and by positioning it for attention in bibliography entries.

However, shifts of stylistic emphasis by discipline should not cause problems if you know the MLA style. You will be able to convert your manuscript format to other systems with little difficulty. If asked to convert to the author-date system, you need only alter the in-text citations to include the date (for example, "Jones, 1983, p. 342" or "Campbell, 1959, p. 23"). If asked to convert to the author-number system, you need only change your in-text citations to numbers (for example, "Smith (16)" or "Campbell and Jones (14)").

At the same time, you must make minor variations in the "Works Cited" list, which now will be labeled "References" or "List of References." If your in-text citations are numbers, then you must number the list of references to correspond. Otherwise, alphabetize the list by the last name of the author. Also, you will usually capitalize only the first word of titles or books and articles (for example, "The biology of the algae"). But some fields, such as chemistry and physics, omit completely the title of a periodical article. Also, you will usually abbreviate and seldom underline the name of the periodical (for example, "Amer. J. Bot."; see 246–85 for listings of journals and their standard abbreviations). But you should note that fields in the social sciences, such as psychology, spell in full the name of periodicals and underline them.

Sketched below are basic rules for handling conventions of format by discipline according to the name and year system, the number system, and the footnote system. In general, use the name and year system with papers in the social sciences, biological and earth sciences, education, linguistics, and business. Use the number system with applied sciences, such as chemistry, computer science, math, or physics. Use the traditional footnote system with papers in the fine arts (art, theater, music) and humanities (excluding language and literature but including history, philosophy, and religion).

Consult the following chart for your area of study, then follow those guidelines as closely as possible.

GUIDE TO DOCUMENTATION SYSTEMS

NAME AND YEAR SYSTEM

One of the dominant influences upon the popularity of this system of documentation is the APA style manual. Officially entitled *Publication Manual of the American Psychological Association,* it sets standards for writers in many fields that wish to emphasize the publication date of a work and thus stress its timeliness. In general, the APA style requires an alphabetized list of references at the end of the paper and in-text citations to name and year of each source cited within the paper. Note the following:

1. Place the year immediately after the authority's name:

```
Smith (1983) ascribes no species-specific behavior to man.

However, Adams (1982) presents data that tend to be contra-

dictory.
```

2. If you do not mention the authority's name in your sentence, insert the name, year, and even page numbers in parentheses:

> Hopkins (1979) found some supporting evidence for a portion
> of the Marr data (Marr and Brown, 1979, pp. 23—32) through
> point bi-serial correlation techniques.

3. In the case of a direct quotation or a paraphrase to a specific page, include the author, year, *and* page number(s), as in these examples below:
   a. Quote or paraphrase in the middle of the sentence:

> He stated, "These data of psychological development suggest
> that retarded adolescents are atypical in maturational
> growth" (Jones, 1983, p. 215), but he failed to clarify which
> data were examined.

   b. A quotation or paraphrase that falls at the end of a sentence:

> Jones (1983) found that "these data of psychological develop-
> ment suggest that retarded adolescents are atypical in matu-
> rational growth" (p. 215).

   c. A long quotation set off from the text in a block (and therefore without quotation marks):

> Albert (1983) found the following:
> > Whenever these pathogenic organisms attack the human
> > body and begin to multiply, the infection is set in
> > motion. The host responds to this parasitic invasion
> > with efforts to cleanse itself of the invading agents.
> > When rejection efforts of the host become visible (fe-
> > ver, sneezing, congestion), the disease status exists.
> > (pp. 314—315)
>
> NOTE: APA style requires the "p." and "pp." for page numbers, and the
> page reference is not set out to the right margin as with MLA style.

3. For two authors, employ both names: "(Torgerson and Andrews, 1979)." For three authors, name them all in the first entry, as "(Torgerson, Andrews, and Dunlap, 1979)," but thereafter use "(Torgerson et al., 1979)." For four or more authors, employ "(Fredericks et al., 1979)" in the first and all subsequent instances.

4. Use small letters (a, b, c) to identify two or more works published in the same year by the same author, for example, "Thompson (1966a)" and "Thompson (1966b)."
5. If necessary, specify additional information; for example, "Thompson (1967, III)," "(Wallace, 1948, 1967)," and "White and Thurston (1979, pp. 211–14)":

> Horton (1966; cf. Thomas, 1962, p. 89) suggests an intercor-
> relation of these testing devices. But after multiple–group
> analysis, Welston (1979, p. 211) reached an opposite conclu-
> sion.

6. Alphabetize the list of references at the end of your paper. List chronologically two or more works by the same author (for example, Fitzgerald's 1983 publication would follow his 1979 publication). Main parts for a periodical entry are: name(s) of the author(s); date within parentheses; title of the article without quotation marks and with only the first word capitalized; name of the journal underlined and with all major words capitalized; volume number underlined; and inclusive page numbers. Main parts for a book entry are: name(s) of author(s); date within parentheses; title of the book underlined and with only first word capitalized (except for proper names); place; publisher. Note the APA style of these psychology entries:

> Anderson, J. R., and Bower, G. H. (1972). Recognition and
> retrieval processes in free recall. Psychological Review,
> 79, 97–123.
> Hall, Calvin S. (1973). A primer of Freudian psychology.
> Phoenix: NAL.

Similarly, other fields prefer moving the date forward in the entries to a position immediately following the author, as with these biology entries:

> Baldwin, K. M. 1979. Cardiac gap junction configuration
> after an uncoupling treatment as a function of time.
> J. Cell. Biol. 82: 66–75.
> Berlyn, G. P., and J. P. Mikshe. 1976. Botanical micro-
> technique and cytochemistry. Iowa State Univ. Press,
> Ames.

Consult the following discussions for further explanations of form and style for your specific discipline.

Social Sciences

Psychology Sociology Political Science Geography

The various disciplines of the social sciences employ the name and year system. Again, variations exist by discipline, but in general the stipulations of the APA *Publication Manual* have gained wide acceptance. However, emphasis upon the date of a work compels some disciplines to place the date immediately below the author's name.

PSYCHOLOGY

In-text Citation

Use name and year system with commas separating items and with the use of "p." or "pp." for page numbers (for example, "Shaffer, 1978" or "Shaffer, 1978, pp. 10–19"). See 221–23 for additional guidelines on the author-year system.

List of References

Alphabetize the list and label it "References." For books, list author, date, title underlined with only first word of title capitalized, place, and publisher. For journals, list author, date, title of the article without quotation marks and with only first word capitalized, title of the journal underlined and with major words capitalized, the volume underlined and followed by a comma, and the inclusive page numbers *without* "p." or "pp." unless volume is omitted, as with a magazine.

(Psychology)*

References

Ahlquist, J. W. (1980). <u>Communication deviance in hypothetical schizotypes</u>. Unpublished master's thesis, University
of Wisconsin.

Anderson, J. R., and Bower, G. H. (1972). Recognition and
retrieval processes in free recall. <u>Psychological Review</u>,
<u>79</u>, 97–123.

Gaito, John (Ed.). (1966). <u>Macromolecules and behavior</u>.
New York: Appleton–Century–Crofts.

---

*The form of these psychology entries conforms to *Publication Manual of the American Psychological Association*, 3rd ed. (Washington, D.C.: American Psychological Association, 1983).

McClelland, D. C. (1981). Is personality consistent? In A. I. Rubin, J. Aronoff, A. M. Barclay, & R. A. Zucker (Eds.). <u>Further explorations in personality</u>. New York: Wiley.

Miller, G. A. (1969, December). On turning psychology over to the unwashed. <u>Psychology Today</u>, pp. 53–54.

Winett, Richard A. (1970). Attribution of attitude and behavior change and its relevance to behavior therapy. <u>The Psychological Record</u>, <u>20</u>, 17–32.

Winter, D. G. (1979). <u>Navy leadership and management competencies: Convergence among tests, interviews and performance ratings</u>. Boston: McBer.

SOCIOLOGY / POLITICAL SCIENCE / GEOGRAPHY

In-text Citation

Use name and year system as shown on 221–23.

List of References

Label the list as "References." Keep the location of the year at a position immediately following the author's name. For books, list author, year, the title underlined with major words capitalized, the place of publication, and the publisher. For journals, list author, year, title of the article without quotation marks and with only the first word capitalized, followed by the name of the journal underlined and with major words capitalized, the volume number followed by a colon, and the inclusive page numbers without "p." or "pp."

Sociology/Political Science/Geography[*]

References

Adamny, David W., and George E. Agree. 1975. <u>Political Money</u>. Baltimore: Johns Hopkins University Press.

Baron, James N., and William Bielby. 1980. Bring the firms back in: Stratification, segmentation and the organization of work. <u>American Sociological Review</u> 45: 737–765.

---

[*]The form of these entries is based, in general, on the form and style of numerous journals in these three fields, especially upon *Annals of the American Association of Geographers, American Journal of Sociology,* and the *American Political Science Review.*

Beck, E. M., Patrick Horan, and Charles Tolbert. 1978.
Stratification in a dual economy: A sectoral model of
earns determination. American Sociological Review 43:
704–720.

Blalock, Hubert M. 1967. Causal inferences, closed popula-
tions, and measures of association. American Political
Science Review 61: 130–136.

Congressional Quarterly. 1978. Electing Congress. Washington, D.C.: Congressional Quarterly Inc.

Epstein, Edwin M. 1980. Business and labor under the Federal Election Campaign Act of 1971. In Michael J. Malbin
(ed.). Parties, Interest Groups, and Campaign Finance
Laws, pp. 107–151. Washington, D.C.: American Enterprise
Institute for Public Policy Research.

Wheare, K.C. 1966. Modern Constitutions. 2nd ed. New
York: Oxford University Press.

Biological and Earth Sciences

Agriculture   Anthropology   Archaeology   Astronomy
Biology   Botany   Geology   Zoology

The disciplines of this major grouping employ the name and year system.
Again, stylistic variations in form and style exist among the fields of study, but
all require the author's name followed by the year, within both the text and the
reference entries.

AGRICULTURE

In-text Citation

See general discussion of name and year system, 221–23.

List of References

In general, the form follows that of Sociology, immediately above, except
that title of the journals are abbreviated and *not* underlined, and indentation is five
spaces.

Agriculture[*]

[*]The form of these entries conforms, in general, to that found in numerous agriculture journals,
especially the journal *Animal Science*.

References

Corring, T., A. Aumaitre, and G. Durand. 1978. Development
    of digestive enzymes in the piglet from birth to 8
    weeks. Nutr. Metab. 22:231.

Cranwell, P. D. 1974. Gastric acid secretion in newly born
    piglets. Res. Vet. Sci. 16:105.

Cranwell, P. D. 1976. Gastric secretion in the young pig.
    Proc. Nutr. Soc. 35:28A (Abstr.).

Kmenta, J. 1971. Elements of econometrics. New York: Mac-
    millan.

ANTHROPOLOGY / ARCHAEOLOGY

In-text Citation

See general discussion on 226.

List of References

Label it as "References Cited" and set both name and date to the left, as shown below:

Anthropology/Archaeology[*]

References Cited

Austin, James H.
    1978   Chase, Chance, and Creativity: The Lucky Art of Nov-
        elty. New York: Columbia University Press.
Bastien, Joseph W.
    1978   Mountain of the Condor: Metaphor and Ritual in an
        Andean Ayllu. American Ethnological Society Monograph
        64. St. Paul: West Publishing Co.
Binford, Louis R.
    1962   Archaeology as Anthropology. American Antiquity
        28: 217–225.

[*]The form of these entries is based upon the stylistic format of the journal *American Anthropologist*.

```
Dunnell, Robert C.
   1978  Style and Function: A Fundamental Dichotomy.  Ameri-
      can Antiquity 43:192-202.
Dye, Daniel S.
   1949  A Grammar of Chinese Lattice.  2nd ed.  Harvard-
      Yenching Monograph Series VI.  Cambridge: Harvard Uni-
      versity Press.
```

ASTRONOMY

See format of geology, 229–30.

BIOLOGY / BOTANY / ZOOLOGY

In-text Citation

Use the name and year system (see 221–23 for additional examples and explanations), as in this example:

```
     This fact would ensure their continued presence in the
cell as a screening mechanism (McClure, 1976).  Many of the
other plants that have these air blisters are also shade
plants (Kirk and Tilney-Bassett, 1967), indicating that such
structures may be safeguards against loss of the shading
cover and subsequent photo-oxidation of the photosynthetic
pigments (Downs et al., 1980).  However, Pilney (1982)
```

List of References

Alphabetize the list and label it "Literature Cited." For books, list author, year, title of the book *without* underlining, publisher, place, and the total number of pages in the book (optional). For journals use name, date, title of the article with *no* quotation marks and with only the first word capitalized, followed by the abbreviated title of the journal *not* underlined, the volume number marked for boldface (wavy line), followed by a colon, and the page number(s).

Biology/Botany/Zoology*

---

*The form of these entries conforms to the *CBE Style Manual,* 4th ed. (Washington, D.C.: American Institute of Biological Sciences, 1978).

Literature Cited

Baldwin, K. M. 1979. Cardiac gap junction configuration
     after an uncoupling treatment as a function of time.
     J. Cell. Biol. 82: 66–75.

Berlyn, G. P., and J. P. Mikshe. 1976. Botanical microtech-
     nique and cytochemistry. Iowa State Univ. Press, Ames.

Gardner, J. D., and R. T. Jensen. 1981. Regulation of pan-
     creatic enzyme secretion in vitro. In Physiology of the
     Gastrointestinal Tract. L. R. Johnson, editor. Raven
     Press, New York. 831–871.

Hodson, P. H., and J. W. Foster. 1966. Dipicolinic acid
     synthesis in Penicillium citreoviride. J. Bacteriol.
     91: 562–69.

Klein, R. M., and D. T. Klein. 1970. Research methods in
     plant science. Natural History Press, Garden City, New
     York. 796 p.

Olive, L. S. 1962. The genus Protostelium. Amer. J. Bot.
     49: 297–303.

GEOLOGY

In-text Citation

As with the biological sciences, above, use name and year:

In view of Niue's position as a former volcanic island rising
from a submarine plateau (Schofield 1959), it might be further speculated that it has a late-stage, silicic, peralka-
line phase (Baker 1974). Such melts readily lose significant
amounts of uranium and other elements on crystallization (Ro-
sholt et al. 1971; Haffty and Nobel 1972; Dayvault 1980),
which are available to contemporary or later hydrothermal
systems (Wallace et al. 1980).

List of References

Alphabetize the list of references. For books list author, date, title *not* underlined and with only the first word capitalized, followed by a colon, then the place, publisher, and total number of pages. For journals, list author, date, title *without* quotation marks and with only first word capitalized, followed by a colon, then the title of the journal *not* underlined, followed by the volume and specific page references.

Geology[*]

Literature Cited

Donath, F. A., 1963, Strength variation and deformational behavior in anisotropic rock, p. 281–297 in Judd, Wm. R., Editor, State of stress in the earth's crust: New York, American Elsevier Publishing Co., Inc., 732 p.

Friedlander, G., Kennedy, J. W., and Miller, J. M., 1964, Nuclear and radiochemistry: New York, John Wiley and Sons, 585 p.

Heard, H. C., Turner, F. J., and Weiss, L. E., 1965, Studies of heterogeneous strain in experimentally deformed calcite, marble, and phyllite: Univ. Calif. Pub. Geol. Sci., v. 46, p. 81–152.

Hill, M. L., and Troxel, B. W., 1966, Tectonics of Death Valley region, California: Geol. Soc. America Bull., v. 77, p. 435–438.

Mattson, Peter H., 1979, Subduction, buoyant braking, flipping, and strike–slip faulting in the northern Caribbean: J. of Geology, v. 87, p. 293–304.

Thorpe, R. S., 1974, Aspects of magmatism and plate tectonics in the precambrian of England and Wales: Geol. J., v. 9, p. 115–136.

[*]The form of these geology entries conforms to *Suggestions to Authors of the Reports of the United States Geological Survey*, 6th ed. (Washington, D. C.: Dept. of the Interior, 1978).

Business and Economics

In-text Citation

Use the basic form of name and year system as explained on 221–23.

List of References

Titles of articles are placed within quotation marks and all major words are capitalized in titles of books, articles, and journals. Label the list "References." Note also the consistent use of month as well as year in these entries, following the publication information.

Business/Economics[*]

References

Anderson, James E. "Cross-Section Tests of the Heckscher-
     Ohlin Theorem: Comment," <u>American Economic Review</u>, Decem-
     ber 1981, <u>71</u>, 1037–39.

Carter, A. <u>Structural Change in the American Economy</u>. Cam-
     bridge: Harvard University Press, 1970.

Deardorff, Alan V. "Weak Links in the Chain of Comparative
     Advantage,"<u>Journal of International Economics</u>, May 1979,
     <u>9</u>, 197–209.

————————. "The General Validity of the Law of Comparative
     Advantage," <u>Journal of Political Economy</u>, October 1980,
     <u>88</u>, 941–57.

Dooley, Michael, and Peter Isard. "The Portfolio-Balance
     Model of Exchange Rates," International Finance Discussion
     Paper No. 141, Federal Reserve Board, May 1979.

Doti, James. "An Economic Theory of Shopping Behavior," Cen-
     ter for Economic Research Report No. 3, Chapman College,
     January 1978.

---

[*]The format of these business entries is based in general upon the style and format of several business and economic journals; *American Economic Review, Economics, Applied Economics, Economics Journal, Journal of Business,* and *Accounting Review,* to name a few.

Mincer, Jacob. "Labor Force Participation of Married Women:
    A Study of Labor Supply," in Aspect of Labor Economics,
    National Bureau of Economic Research, Princeton Univer-
    sity, 1962. 63-97.

Richardson, H. W. Input / Output and Regional Economics.
    New York: Weidenfield and Nicolson, 1972.

Education

In-text Citation

See general discussion on 221–23 and follow Name and Year system.

List of References

Label the list as "References." The form for books follows MLA style.
The form for periodicals follows generally that of APA style except that volume
numbers are *not* underlined and the date follows the name of the journal, not the
author's name.

Education[*]

                            References

Cross, L. H., and Frary, R. B. An empirical test of Lord's
    theoretical results regarding formula scoring of multiple-
    choice tests. Journal of Educational Measurement, 1977,
    14, 313-321.

Edelwich, J., and Brodsky, A. Burn-Out. New York: Human
    Services Press, 1980.

Grise, P. J. Florida's minimum competency testing program
    for handicapped students. Exceptional Children, 1980, 47,
    186-191.

Landsman, L. Is teaching hazardous to your health? Today's
    Education, 1978, 67 (2), 48-50.

Maslach, D. Burned-Out. Human Behavior, 1976, 5 (9), 16-22.

--------. Job burnout: How people cope. Public Welfare,
    1978(a), 36, 56-58.

[*]The form of these entries is based in general upon the style and format of several education
journals, such as *Journal of Educational Research*, *The Elementary School Journal*, and *Educational
and Psychological Measurement*.

————————. The client role in staff burn-out. <u>Journal of</u>
<u>Social Issues</u>, 1978, 34 (4), 111-124.

Home Economics

Follow the stipulations of APA style as explained and demonstrated on
224-25.

Linguistics

In-text Citation

Use the basic name and year system. In-text citations for linguistic studies
include almost always a specific page reference to the work along with the date,
separated by a colon, for example, "Jones 1983: 12–18" or "Gifford's recent
reference (1982: 162)." Therefore, follow basic standards for the name and year
system, adding page numbers regularly.

List of References

As shown below, label the list as "References." Place the year immediately after the author's name. Also, a period rather than a colon separates volume
and page(s). There is *no* underlining.

Linguistics[*]

References

Bach, Emmon, and Robin Cooper. 1978. The NP-S analysis of
relative clauses and compositional semantics. Linguistics
and Philosophy 2.145-50.

Bresnan, Joan. 1970. On complementizers: Toward a syntactic
theory of complement types. Foundations of Language
6.297-321.

Chomsky, Noam. 1965. Aspects of the theory of syntax. Cambridge, MA: MIT Press.

————————. 1975. Reflections on language. New York: Pantheon.

Keenan, Edward, and Bernard Comrie. 1977. Noun Phrase Accessibility and universal grammar. LI 8.63-99.

[*]The form of these entries conforms in general to that advocated by the Linguistic Society of
America, *LSA Bulletin*, No. 71 (December 1976), 43–45, and to the form and style practiced by the
journal *Language*.

————. ————. 1979. Noun Phrase Accessibility revis-
ited. Lg. 44.244–66.

Ross, John R. 1967. Constraints on variables in syntax.
MIT dissertation.

Physical Education

Follow the stipulations of APA style as explained and demonstrated on 224–25.

NUMBER SYSTEM

The number system is used in the applied sciences (chemistry, computer science, mathematics, and physics) and in the medical sciences (medicine, nursing, and general health). In simple terms, this system requires an in-text *number*, rather than page number or year, with a list of "Works Cited" that corresponds by number to the textual citations. Follow these basic stipulations:

After completing your "List of References," you should assign a number to each entry. Then, to designate your source of information, you should employ the appropriate number within your text. Furthermore, note the following:

1. Place the entry, enclosed within parentheses (or brackets), immediately after the authority's name:

    In particular the recent paper by Hershel, Hobbs, and

    Thomason (1) raises many interesting questions related to

    photosynthesis, some of which were anwered by Skelton (2),

    (3).

However, several fields use a raised superscript number: "Thomason[1]" or "Skelton.[2-3]" See Chemistry, 236.

2. If the sentence construction does not require the use of the authority's name, employ one of the following three methods:
   a. Insert both name and number within parentheses:

    Additional observations include alterations in carbohydrate

    metabolism (Evans, 3), changes in ascorbic acid incorporation

    into the cell (Dodd and Williams, 11) and adjoining membranes

    (Holt and Zimmer, 7).

b. Insert both name and number within parentheses and enclose the number within brackets (few journals, however, use this method):

```
The subject of the cytochrome oxidase system in cell metabo-
lism has received a great deal of attention (Singleton [4]).
```

c. Insert the number only, enclosing it within parentheses (or brackets):

```
It is known (1) that the DNA concentration of a nucleus dou-
bles during interphase.
```

3. If necessary, add specific data to the entry (for example, "3, Proposition 8" or "6, p. 76"):

```
The results of the respiration experiment published by Jones
(3, p. 412) had been predicted earlier by Smith (5).
```

Arrange your references in alphabetical order and number them consecutively (in which case, of course, the numbers will not appear in consecutive order in your text), *or* forego an alphabetical arrangement and number the references consecutively as they appear in the text, interrupting that order in your text when entering an earlier reference. An entry for the number system is usually similar to that for the name-and-year system except that it is preceded by a numeral on the line and a period, as with the computer science entries:

```
1. Aho, A. V.; Hopcroft, J. E.; and Ullman, J. D.  The Design
   and Analysis of Computer Algorithms.  Addison-Wesley,
   Reading, Mass., 1974.
2. Holt, R. C.  "Some deadlock properties of computer sys-
   tems."  Computer Surv.  4, 3 (Sept. 1972), 179-96.
```

Applied Sciences

Chemistry   Computer Science   Mathematics   Physics

The disciplines of the applied sciences, as well as the medical sciences (see below), employ the number system. Variations exist for each field in both textual citations and the form of entries in the list of references; therefore, you should study carefully the stipulations for individual fields below:

CHEMISTRY

In-text Citations

Use raised superscript numerals as references occur (like this [12]) and number your references in consecutive order, *not* alphabetical order:

The stereochemical features of arene molecules chemisorbed on metal surfaces cannot be assessed precisely.[3] However, composite statistics from theoretical calculations[4] and chemical studies[5-7] indicate that benzene is often chemisorbed

List of References

Label the list "References." The basic forms of chemical entries are demonstrated below. For books, you should note that titles are *not* underlined but placed within quotation marks and that the publisher precedes the city of publication. For journals, note that the title of the article is omitted, the journal is abbreviated and underlined, the date is marked for boldface (wavy line), the volume is underlined and followed by the page number(s).

Chemistry[*]

References

(1) Cowley, A. H.; Kilduff, J. E.; Wilburn, J. C. J. Am. Chem. Soc. 1981, 103, 1575.

(2) Rosencwaig, A. "Photoacoustics and Photoacoustic Spectroscopy"; Wiley-Interscience: New York, 1980; p. 309.

(3) Bowen, J. M.; Crone, T. A.; Head, V. L.; McMorrow, H. A.; Kennedy, P. K.; Purdie, N. J. Forensic Sci. 1981, 26(4), 664-70.

(4) Clarke, E. G. C. "Isolation and Identification of Drugs"; The Pharmaceutical Press: London, 1978; Vol. 1.

(5) Cotton, F. A. J. Am. Chem. Soc. 1968, 90, 6230.

(6) (a) Sievert, A. C.; Muetterties, E. L. Inorg. Chem. 1981, 20, 489. (b) Albright, T. A., unpublished data.
In this instance, the in-text superscript numeral may refer to [6] or to [6a] or to [6b]

Note: an acceptable alternative to the style above would place all lines to the right of the number:

[*]The form of these chemistry entries conforms to the *Handbook for Authors* (Washington, D.C.: American Chemical Society, 1978).

(3) Bowen, J. M. . . . .

   Forensic Sci. . . .

(4) Clarke, E. G. C. . . . . .

   Drugs"; The . . . .

(5) Cotton, F. A. . . . .

   90, 6230.

COMPUTER SCIENCE

In-text Citations

Use raised superscript numerals (as above for chemistry, like this[12]), and then number your "Works Cited" in consecutive order, not alphabetical order.

Works Cited

Uniformity in the form of entries, although not yet standard with all editors, suggests certain standards. For books, the titles *are* underlined, publisher precedes city of publication, and specific page(s) of books need not be listed. For journals, the title of the article is provided within quotation marks and with first word only of the title capitalized; title of the journal is underlined; volume number is underlined; issue number is provided whenever available, preceding the date and page number(s).

Computer Science

Works Cited

1. Aho, A. V.; Hopcroft, J. E.; and Ullman, J. D. The Design and Analysis of Computer Algorithms. Addison-Wesley, Reading, Mass., 1974.

2. Gligor, V. D., and Shattuck, S. H. "On deadlock detection in distributed systems." IEEE Trans. Softw. Eng. SE-6, 5 (Sept. 1980), 435-40.

3. Sklansky, J.; Wassel, G. N. Pattern Classifiers and Trainable Machines. Springer-Verlag, New York, 1981.

4. Holt, R. C. "Some deadlock properties of computer systems." Computer Surv. 4, 3 (Sept. 1972), 179-96.

MATHEMATICS

In-text Citation

First alphabetize and then number the list of references. All in-text citations are then made to the number, which you should place in your text within brackets and marked for boldface (wavy line), as in the following example:

In addition to the obvious implications it is already known from [5] that every D–regular Lindelof space is D–normal. Further results on D–normal spaces will appear in [8], which is in preparation. The results obtained here and in [2], [3], and [5] encourage further research.

List of References

For books the titles are underlined, publisher precedes city of publication, and specific page(s) of books need not be listed. For journals, title of the article is underlined, journal title is *not* underlined, volume is marked for boldface (wavy line), followed by year of publication with parentheses, followed by complete pagination of the article.

Mathematics[*]

References

1. M. Artin, On the joins of Hensel rings, Advances in Math. 7 (1971), 282–86.

2. R. Artzy, Linear geometry, Addison–Wesley, Reading, Mass., 1965.

3. I. M. Isaacs and D. S. Passman, Groups with representations of bounded degree, Canad. J. Math. 16 (1964), 299–309.

4. –––––––, Characterization of groups in terms of the degrees of their characters, Pacific J. Math. 15 (1965), 877–903.

5. O. Solbrig, Evolution and systematics. Macmillan, New York, 1966.

---

[*]The form of these entries conforms to *A Manual for Authors of Mathematical Papers*, 4th ed. (Providence: American Mathematical Society, 1973).

PHYSICS

In-text Citation

Use raised superscript numerals (like this[12]), and then number your list of references in consecutive order, not in alphabetical order.

List of References

For books, titles are underlined, publisher precedes place of publication, and specific page reference *should* be provided. For journals the title of the article is omitted entirely, the title of the journal is abbreviated and *not* underlined, the volume is marked for boldface (wavy line), and the year follows the page number(s).

Physics[*]

References

[1]T. Poorter and H. Tolner, Infrared Phys. **19**, 317 (1979).

[2]C. D. Motchenbacher and F. C. Fitchen, Low-Noise Electronic Design (Wiley, New York, 1973), p. 16.

[3]L. Monchick, S. Chem. Phys. **71**, 576 (1979).

[4]F. Riesz and Bela Nagy, Functional Analysis (Ungar, New York, 1955), Secs. 121 and 123.

[5]C. M. Hurd, Contemp. Phys. **23**, 469 (1982).

Medical Sciences

Health   Medicine   Nursing

Like the applied sciences, the medical sciences, as a general rule, employ the number system. Variations among journals do exist, but the style and format demonstrated below is standard.

In-text Citation

You should number the citations as they occur in your text. Employ the number system explained and demonstrated on 234–35.

List of References

Label the list "References." Do not alphabetize the list; rather, number it to correspond to sources as you cited them in your text. For books, list author, title underlined and with all major words capitalized, the place, publisher, and

---

[*]The form of these entries conforms to *Style Manual for Guidance in the Preparation of Journals Published by the American Institute of Physics,* rev. ed. (New York: American Institute of Physics, 1970).

year. For journals, list author, title without quotation marks and with only the
first word capitalized, the name of the journal abbreviated *without* periods and
underlined, the volume followed by a colon and page number(s), and the
year.

Health/Medicine/Nursing[*]

References

1. Crane, C. W., and A. Neuberger. The digestion and absorp-
   tion of protein by normal man. Biochem 74:313–323, 1960.

2. Angell, M. Juggling the personal and professional life.
   J Am Med Wom Assoc 37:64–68, 1982.

3. Antonovsky, A. Health, Stress, and Coping. San Fran-
   cisco, Jossey–Bass, 1979.

4. Ayman, D. The personality type of patients with arterio-
   lar essential hypertension. Am J Med Sci 186:213–233,
   1933.

5. Nash, Paul. Authority and Freedom in Education. New
   York, Wiley, 1966.

6. Rinke, C. The economic and academic status of women phy-
   sicians. JAMA 245:2305–2306, 1981.

7. Green, M. I., and R. J. Haggery (eds.). Ambulatory Pedi-
   atrics. Philadelphia, W. B. Saunders, 1968.

FOOTNOTE SYSTEM

Two major areas of study still use traditional footnotes: humanities (but not
language and literature) and the fine arts (such as music, art, dance). With this
method, you must employ superscript numerals within the text, (like this[15]) and
documentary footnotes. No "Works Cited" will be necessary at the end of the
paper. The discussion and examples below assume that notes will appear as
footnotes; however, some instructors accept endnotes, that is, all notes appear
together at the end of the paper, not at the bottom of individual pages. For ease of
typing, you might ask your instructor if he or she will accept endnotes rather than
footnotes.

---

[*]The form of these entries represents a standard as demonstrated by numerous medical journals, such as *JAMA*, *Nutrition Reviews*, and others.

Rules of Format

In-text Citation

Use Arabic numerals typed slightly above the line (like this[12]). Place this superscript numeral at the end of your quotation or paraphrase, with the number following without a space immediately after the final word or mark of punctuation, as in this sample:

> Colonel Warner soon rejoined his troops despite severe pain. He wrote in September of 1864: "I was obliged to ride at all times on a walk and to mount my horse from some steps or be helped on. My cains with which I walked when on foot were strapped to my saddle."[6] Such heroic dedication did not go unnoticed, for the Washington Chronicle cited Warner as "an example worthy of imitation."[7] At Gettysburg Warner's troops did not engage in heavy fighting and suffered only limited casualties of two dead and five wounded.[8]

List of References

The references will appear as footnotes at the bottom of the page to correspond with the superscript numeral in the text (see immediately above). Some papers will require footnotes on almost every page. Follow these conventions:

1. Single space footnotes, but double space between notes.
2. Indent the note five spaces, use a raised superscript numeral with no space between it and the first word of the note.
3. Number the notes consecutively throughout the entire paper.
4. Collect at the bottom of each page all footnotes for citations made on that page.
5. Separate the footnotes from your text by triple spacing or, if you prefer, a twelve-space bar line from the left margin.
6. Basic form of the notes should conform to the following:

For a book:

[1]W. V. Quine, Word and Object (Cambridge, MA: MIT Press, 1966), p. 8.

For a journal article:

[2]G. S. Boolos, "On Second-Order Logic," Journal of Philosophy, 72 (1975), pp. 590–510.

Follow these basic forms, but study the sample lists below for additional examples for the disciplines of history, religion, art, and others.

7. Subsequent references after a first full reference should be shortened to author's name and page number. When an author has two works mentioned, you must employ a shortened version of the title, "Jones, *Masks*, p. 25." In general, avoid latinate abbreviations such as *loc. cit.* or *op. cit.;* however, whenever a note refers to the source in the immediately preceding note, you may use *Ibid.* with the page number as follows:

> [3]S. C. Kleene, <u>Introduction to Metamathematics</u> (Princeton, N.J.: Van Nostrand, 1964), p. 24.
>
> [4]<u>Ibid</u>., p. 27.
>
> [5]Abraham J. Heschel, <u>Man Is Not Alone: A Philosophy of Religion</u> (New York: Farrar, Straus, and Young, 1951), p. 221.
>
> [6]Keene, p. 24.
>
> [7]<u>Ibid</u>., p. 27.

Footnotes as Endnotes

Your professor will often permit placement of all notes at the end of the paper, a practice that simplifies greatly the typing process. If you place all notes at the end of your paper, follow these conventions:

1. Begin notes on a new page at the end of your text.
2. Entitle the page "Notes" or "References," centered and placed two inches from the top of the page. This page is unnumbered, but number all other pages of endnotes.
3. Indent the first line of each note five spaces, type the note number slightly above the line, begin the note, and use the left margin for succeeding lines.
4. Double-space the notes and double-space between the notes. Triple-space between the heading and the first note.

Note the following sample:

Notes

> [1]W. V. Quine, <u>Word and Object</u> (Cambridge, MA: MIT Press, 1966), p. 8.
>
> [2]G. S. Boolos, "On Second-Order Logic," <u>Journal of Philosophy</u>, 72 (1975), pp. 509-510.
>
> [3]S. C. Kleene, <u>Introduction to Metamathematics</u> (Princeton, N.J.: Van Nostrand, 1964), p. 24.

⁴Ibid., p. 27.

⁵Abraham J. Heschel, <u>Man Is Not Alone: A Philosophy of Religion</u> (New York: Farrar, Straus, and Young, 1951), p. 221.

⁶Kleene, p. 24.

⁷Ibid., p. 27

⁸Heschel, p. 222.

Humanities

History   Philosophy   Religion and Theology

For the fields of the humanities listed above you should employ the footnote system. Languages and literature, although considered humanities, follow a different format as established by the Modern Language Association, the MLA style, which is discussed above in the major portion of this text 194–219.

In-text Citation

Use the form of raised superscript numbers as explained on 241.

List of References

Place the references at the bottom of each page on which a citation occurs. See explanation above, 241–42, and duplicate the form and style of the following examples:

Lower portion of a religious paper

In some cases, the attempts of anthropologists to explain certain religious phenomena have only resulted in several

---

¹E. E. Evans-Pritchard, <u>Nuer Religion</u> (Oxford: Clarendon Press, 1956), p. 84.

²Claude Lévi-Strauss, <u>The Savage Mind</u> (Chicago: University of Chicago Press, 1966), chap. 9.

³Ibid., p. 213.

⁴E. E. Evans-Pritchard, <u>Theories of Primitive Religion</u> (Oxford: Clarendon Press, 1965), chap. 2.

⁵Ibid., p. 45.

⁶Evans-Pritchard, <u>Nuer</u>, p. 85.

⁷Evans-Pritchard, <u>Primitive Religion</u>, p. 46.

Lower portion of a history paper

Such heroic dedication did not go unnoticed, for the <u>Washington Chronicle</u> cited Warner as "an example worthy of imitation."[7]

[4]G. E. Thomas, "Puritans, Indians, and the Concept of Race," <u>New England Quarterly</u>, 48 (1975), 3–27.

[5]Thomas Jefferson, <u>Notes on the State of Virginia</u> (1784), ed. William Peden (Chapel Hill, N.C., Univ. of Virginia Press, 1955), p. 59.

[6]Papers of Gen. A. J. Warner (P–973, Service Record and Short Autobiography), Western Reserve Historical Society.

[7]Ibid., clipping from the <u>Washington Chronicle</u> with Service Record and Short Autobiography (P–973).

Lower portion of one page of a philosophy paper

Indeed, both Russell and Brandt, whom several authorities have cited for their contributions, advocate the reform of philosophical positions.

[8]Norman Daniels, "Wide Reflective Equilibrium and Theory Acceptance in Ethics," <u>The Journal of Philosophy</u>, 76 (1979), 264.

[9]<u>Ibid</u>.

[10]Jeremy Bentham, <u>An Introduction to the Principles of Morals and Legislation</u>, ed. J. H. Burns and H. L. A. Hart (London: Althone Press, 1970), I, 10–11.

[11]Daniels, "Reflective Equilibrium," 265.

[12]See Tom Beauchamp and Alexander Rosenberg, <u>Hume and the Problem of Causation</u> (New York: Oxford, 1981), ch. VI for a discussion of whether Hume ever held such a view.

Fine Arts

Art   Dance   Music   Theater

Follow the stipulations for the footnote system as described on 240–242.

In-text Citation

Employ the method of raised superscript numerals (like this[14]) within the text so that these numerals match the numbered footnotes at the bottom of each page. For additional information, see 241.

List of References

As with the humanities, above, the references are placed as footnotes at the bottom of each page to correspond to the textual superscript numeral. Conform to conventions as demonstrated above, 241–42, and in the samples below:

Lower portion of a music paper

In the Roman music printing of that particular combination of

typefaces only Libro de canti a tre di Carpentras of 1537

[13]Suzanne G. Cusick, "Valerio Dorico: Music Printer in Sixteenth Century Rome," Studies in Musicology, 43 (1981), p. 214.

[14]Alfred Einstein, The Italian Madrigal, 3 vols. (Princeton, 1949), I, 360.

[15]Cusick, p. 214.

[16]There are three copies of the papal brief in the archives of the German College, now situated on Via S. Nicola da Tolentino. The document is printed in Thomas D. Culley, Jesuits and Music, I (Rome and St. Louis, 1970), 358–59.

Lower portion of one page of an art paper

conception of a moral stance that would be appropriate to

male and to female models only dramatizes once more the cul-

[17]Erwin Panofsky, Renaissance and Renascences in Western Art, ed. Grego Paulsson, 2nd ed. (New York, 1969), pp. 42–113.

[18]Denys Hay, ed., The Age of the Renaissance (New York, 1967), p. 286.

[19]Panofsky, p. 43.

[20]Hay, p. 287.

[21]Ibid., p. 288.

[22]John M. Wallace, "'Examples Are Best Precepts': Readers and Meanings in Seventeenth-Century Poetry," Critical Inquiry, I (December, 1974), pp. 273–90. This article relates the art of the period to the rhetorical theory.

Appendix
List of General Reference Books and Journals

APPLIED AND PHYSICAL SCIENCES

GENERAL

Books

Applied Science and Technology Index. New York: H. W. Wilson, 1958-date. Before 1958, see Industrial Arts Index.

ASLIB Book List: A Monthly List of Recommended Scientific and Technical Books, With Annotations. London: ASLIB, 1935- Monthly.

Bibliographic Guide to Technology: 1980. Boston: G. K. Hill, 1981.

Bolton, Henry C. Catalogue of Scientific and Technical Periodicals, 1665–1895. 2nd ed. 1987; rpt. New York: Johnson Reprint, 1974.

Caldwell, Lynton K. Science, Technology, and Public Policy: A Selected and Annotated Bibliography. 2 vols. Bloomington, IN: Indiana University, Dept. of Govt. 1968–1969.

Ching-Chih, Chen. Scientific and Technical Information Sources. Cambridge, MA: The MIT Press, 1977.

Considine, Douglas M., ed. Van Nostrand's Scientific Encyclopedia. Princeton, NJ: Van Nostrand Reinhold, 1976.

Current Contents. Philadelphia, PA: Institute for Scientific Information, 1961- . Weekly.

Daintith, John, ed. Dictionary of Physical Sciences. New York: Pica Press; distr. New York: Universe Books, 1977.

Darrow, Ken, and Rick Pam. Appropriate Technology Sourcebook. Rev. ed. 2 vols. Stanford, Calif.: Volunteers in Asia, 1981.

Deason, Hilary J., ed. The AAAS Science Book List. 3d ed. Baltimore: George W. King Printing, 1970.

Dorian, Angelo F. Dorian's Dictionary of Science and Technology. 2nd rev. ed. New York: Elsevier-North Holland, 1979.

Feldman, Robert J., et al. Cowles Encyclopedia of Science, Industry and Technology. 2nd revised ed. New York: Cowles, 1969.

Ferguson, Eugene S., comp. Bibliography of the History of Technology. Cambridge, MA: The MIT Press, 1968.

Gerrish, Howard H. Technical Dictionary. Text ed. South Holland, IL: Goodheart-Wilcox, 1976.

Grogan, Denis. Science and Technology: An Introduction to Literature. 3d ed. Hamden, CT: Shoe String, 1976.

Herner, Saul. A Brief Guide to Sources of Scientific and Technical Information Washington: Information Resources Press, 1980.

Index to Book Reviews in the Sciences. Philadelphia, Pa.: Institute for Scientific Information. Monthly and Semiannual Cumulations, 1980.

Index to Scientific Reviews. Philadelphia, Pa.: Institute for Scientific Information. Semiannually with Annual Cumulations, 1974-date.

Industrial Arts Index. New York: H. W. Wilson, 1913–1957. Superseded by Applied Science and Technology Index.

Lansford, Effie, and Theodore J. Kopkind. A Basic Collection for Scientific and Technical Libraries. New York: Special Libraries Association, 1971.

Lasworth, Earl J. Reference Sources in Science and Technology. Metuchen, NJ: Scarecrow, 1972.

Malinowsky, H. R., and Jeanne M. Richardson. Science and Engineering Literature. 3d ed. Littleton, CO: Libraries Unlimited, Inc., 1980.

McGraw-Hill Dictionary of Scientific and Technical Terms. Ed. Daniel N. Lapedes. New York: McGraw-Hill, 1978.

McGraw-Hill Encyclopedia of Science and Technology. 4th ed. New York: McGraw-Hill, 1977.

McGraw-Hill Yearbook of Science and Technology. New York: McGraw-Hill, annually.

Mitcham, Carl, and Robert McKay. *Bibliography of the Philosophy of Technology*. Chicago: University of Chicago Press, 1973.

Owen, Dolores, and Marguerite Hanchey. *Abstracts and Indexes in Science and Technology: A Descriptive Guide*. Metuchen, NJ: Scarecrow, 1974.

Parker, C. C., and R. V. Turley. *Information Sources in Science and Technology*. Boston: Butterworths, 1975.

Powell, Russell H., ed. *Handbooks and Tables in Science and Technology: A Bibliography and Index With Selected Annotations*. Phoenix, AZ: Oryx, 1979.

Rechenbach, C. W., and E. R. Garnett. *A Bibliography of Scientific, Technical, and Specialized Dictionairies, Polyglot, Bilingual, Unilingual*. Washington: Catholic University of America Press, 1969.

Rider, Kenneth J. *History of Science and Technology: A Select Bibliography for Students*. 2nd ed. New York: International Publications Service, 1970.

Scientific and Technical Books and Serials in Print: 1982. Ann Arbor: Bowker, 1982.

Susskind, Charles. *Understanding Technology*. Baltimore: Johns Hopkins, 1973.

Swanson, Gerald, ed. *Technology Guide Book: 1974*. Boston: G. K. Hall, 1974.

Technical Book Review Index. New York: Special Libraries Association, 1935–date.

Ulman, Joseph N. and Jay R. Gould. *Technical Reporting*. 3d ed. New York: Holt, Rinehart, and Winston, 1972.

Uvarov, E. B., and D. R. Chapman, eds. *The Penguin Dictionary of Science*. 4th rev. ed. New York: Schocken Books, 1972.

CHEMICAL ENGINEERING
Books

Baines, A. *Research in the Chemical Industry: The Environment, Objectives and Strategy*. Englewood, N.J.: Burgess-International Ideas, 1969.

Brenchley, David L., and David C. Turley, eds. *Industrial Source Sampling*. New ed. Woburn, MA: Ann Arbor Science, 1973.

Chemical Engineering Research in the United Kingdom. (Published by the Institute of Chemical Engineering in England). New York: State Mutual Books, 1981.

Clason, W. E. *Elsevier's Dictionary of Chemical Engineering*. 2 vols. New York: Elsevier-North Holland, 1969.

Cosidine, Douglas M. *Chemical and Process Technology Encyclopedia*. New York: McGraw-Hill, 1974.

Ernst, Richard. *Dictionary of Chemistry, Including Chemical Engineering and Fundamentals of Applied Sciences*. 2 vols. New York: International Pub. Ser., 1969.

Institution of Chemical Engineers, Annual Research Meeting, 7th, 1980. Collected Papers. (Published by the Institution of Chemical Engineers in England). New York: State Mutual Books, 1981.

Kent, James A. *Riegel's Handbook of Industrial Chemistry*. 7th ed. New York: Van Nos Reinhold, 1974.

Peck, Theodore P., ed. *Chemical Industries Information Sources*. Detroit: Gale, 1979.

Pecsok, Robert L., ed. *Chemical Technology Handbook*. Washington, D.C.: American Chemical Society, 1975.

Perry, Robert H., and C. H. Chilton, *Chemical Engineers' Handbook*. 5th ed. New York: McGraw-Hill, 1973.

Weekman, Vern W., Jr., ed. *Annual Reviews of Industrial and Engineering Chemistry*. Washington, D.C.: American Chemical Society, 1972–date.

Journals

American Institute of Chemical Engineers Journal (AICES)

Applied Chemical News (Appl. Chem. News)

Chemical and Engineering News (Chem. and Eng. News)

Chemical Economy and Engineering Review (Chem. Econ. and Eng. Rev.)

Chemical Engineering (Chem. Eng.)

Chemical Engineering Communications (Chem. Eng. Comm.)

Chemical Engineering Education (Chem. Eng. Ed.)

Chemical Engineering Progress (Chem. Eng. Prog.)

Chemical Progress (Chem. Prog.)

Chemical Processing (Chem. Proc.)

Chemical Week (Chem. Week)

Chemicals Today (Chem. Today)

Chemtech

Industrial and Engineering Chemistry Fundamentals (Ind. Eng. Chem. Fund.)

Industrial and Engineering Chemistry Process Design and Development (Ind. Eng. Chem. Design and Dev.)

International Chemical Engineering (Int. Chem. Eng.)

Petro/Chem Engineer (Petro/Chem Eng.)

CHEMISTRY

Books

Abd-El-Wahed, Anwar, comp. *Technical Dictionary: Chemical Technology*. New York: Adler's, 1976.

American Chemical Society. *Handbook for Authors*. Washington, D.C.: American Chemical Society, 1978.

American Chemical Society. *Searching the Chemical Literature*. Washington, D.C.: American Chemical Society, 1977.

Antony, Arthur. *Guide to Basic Information Sources in Chemistry*. New York: Wiley, 1979.

Bennett, Harry, ed. *Concise Chemical and Technical Dictionary*. 3d ed. New York: Chemical Pub., 1974.

Bottle, R. T., ed. *Use of Chemical Literature*. 3d ed. London: Butterworths, 1979.

Burman, C. R. *How to Find Out In Chemistry*. 2nd ed. Elmsford, New York: Pergamon, 1966.

Chemical Abstracts: Key to the World's Chemical Literature. Easton, PA: American Chemical Society, 1907– . Weekly.

Chemical Titles. Easton, PA: American Chemical Society, 1960– . Biweekly.

Chen, Philip S. *A New Handbook of Chemistry*. Camarillo, CA: Chemical Elements, 1975.

Clark, George L. *Encyclopedia of Chemistry*. 2nd ed. New York: Van Nostrand Reinhold, 1966.

Dean, John A., ed. *Lange's Handbook of Chemistry*. 12th ed. New York: McGraw-Hill, 1979.

Gardner, William, and Edward I. Cooke. *Chemical Synonyms and Trade Names: A Dictionary and Commercial Handbook*. 8th ed. New York: International Pub. Ser., 1978.

Gordon, Arnold J., and Richard A. Ford. *The Chemist's Companion: A Handbook of Practical Data, Techniques, and References*. New York: Wiley, 1972.

Grant, Julius. *Hackh's Chemical Dictionary*. 4th ed. New York: McGraw-Hill, 1973.

Hampel, Clifford A, and Gessner G. Hawley. *Glossary of Chemical Terms*. New York: Van Nostrand Reinhold, 1976.

Hampel, Clifford A., and Gessner G. Hawley, eds. *The Encyclopedia of Chemistry*. 3d ed. New York: Reinhold, 1973.

Hawley, Gessner G. *The Condensed Chemical Dictionary*. 9th ed. New York: Van Nostrand Reinhold, 1977.

Literature Resources for Chemical Process Industries. Washington, D.C.: American Chemical Society, 1954.

Maizell, Robert E. *How to Find Chemical Information: A Guide for Practicing Chemists, Teachers, and Students*. New York: Wiley-Interscience, 1979.

Mellon, Melvin Guy. *Chemical Publications: Their Nature and Use*. 4th ed. New York: McGraw-Hill, 1965.

Selected Titles in Chemistry. 4th ed. Washington, D.C.: American Chemical Society, 1968.

Singer, T. E., and Julian F. Smith. *Literature of Chemical Technology*. Washington, D.C.: American Chemical Society, 1968.

Weast, Robert C. *Handbook of Chemistry and Physics*. 62nd ed. Cleveland: CRC Press, 1981.

Windholz, Martha, ed. *Merck Index*. 9th ed. Rahway, NJ: Merck, 1976.

Journals

Accounts of Chemical Research (Acc. of Chem. Res.)

Analytical Chemistry (Analyt. Chem.)

American Chemical Society Journal (Amer. Chem. Soc. J.)

Chemical Abstracts (Chem Abstracts)

Chemical Bulletin (Chem. Bull.)

Chemical Industries Center Newsletter (Chem. Indust. Center Newsl.)

Chemical Reviews (Chem. Rev.)

Chemical Technology (Chem. Tech.)

Chemical Times and Trends (Chem. Times and Trends)

Chemist

Chemistry International (Chem. Interna.)

Chemtech

Clinical Chemistry (Clinical Chem.)

Current Clinical Chemistry (Current Clinical Chem.)

Farm Chemicals (Farm Chem.)

Industrial and Engineering Chemistry (Indust. and Eng. Chem.)

Inorganic Chemistry (Inorg. Chem.)

Journal of Chemical and Engineering (J. Chem. and Eng.)

Journal of Chemical Documentation (J. Chem. Doc.)

Journal of Chemical Physics (J. Chem. Phys.)

Journal of Chemical Education (J. Chem. Educ.)

Journal of Chemical Information and Computer Sciences (J. Chem. Inf. and Compt. Sciences)

Journal of Organic Chemistry (J. Org. Chem.)

Journal of Physical Chemistry (J. Phys. Chem.)

Journal of the Chemical Society (J. Chem. Soc.)

Journal of the American Chemical Society (J. Amer. Chem. Soc.)
Octagon
Pure and Applied Chemistry (Pure and Applied Chem.)
Sciquest
Vortex

ELECTRONICS

Books

Amos, S. W. *Dictionary of Electronics*. Woburn, MA: Butterworth, 1981.

Annotated Bibliography of Electronic Data Processing. Gainesville: University of Florida Press, 1968.

Buchsbaum, Walter H. *Buchsbaum's Complete Handbook of Practical Electronics Reference Data*. 2nd ed. Englewood Cliffs, NJ: Prentice-Hall, 1978.

Chaney & Putnam, eds. *Electronic Properties Research Literature Retrieval Guide*. 4 vols. New York: IFI Plenum, 1979.

Electronic Properties of Materials: A Guide to Literature. 3 vols. New York: Plenum, 1967–1971.

Gerrish, Howard H. *Electricity-Electronics Dictionary*. South Holland, IL: Goodheart, 1970.

Graf, Rudolf F. *Modern Dictionary of Electronics*. 5th ed. Indianapolis: Howard Sams, 1977.

Goedecke, W. *Dictionary of Electrical Engineering, Telecommunications, and Electronics*. 3 vols. New York: Ungar, 1974.

Herrick, Clyde N. *Electronics Handbook*. Santa Monica, CA: Goodyear, 1975.

Hohn, Eduard. *Dictionary of Electrotechnology*. New York: Methuen, 1980.

Howard W. Sams Editorial Staff. *Handbook of Electronic Tables and Formulas*. 5th ed. Indianapolis: Howard Sams, 1979.

Mandl, Matthew. *Handbook of Modern Electronic Data*. Englewood Cliffs, NJ: Reston, 1973.

Markus, John. *Electronics Style Manual*. New York: McGraw-Hill, 1978.

Moore, C. K., and K. J. Spencer. *Electronics: A Bibliographical Guide*. Vol. 2. New York: IFI Plenum, n.d.

Morrill, Chester, Jr. *Computers and Data Processing Information Sources*. Detroit: Gale, 1969.

Randle, Gretchen R., ed. *Electronic Industries Information Sources*. Detroit: Gale, 1968.

Shiers, George. *Bibliography of the History of Electronics*. Metuchen, NJ: Scarecrow, 1972.

Young, E. C. *The New Penguin Dictionary of Electronics*. New York: Penguin, 1979.

Journals

Bell Laboratories Record
Bell System Technical Journal
Budget Electronics
Circuit News
Consumer Electronics Product News
Electrical Communication
Electrical Design News Magazine
Electrical Engineer
Electrical Review
Electrical World
Electronic Design
Electronic Engineering
Electronic News
Electronic Technician/Trader
Electronics
Electronics and Power
Electronics Letters
Elementary Electronics
IEEE Journal of Quantum Electronics
International Journal of Electronics; Theoretical and Experimental
Journal of Electronic Materials
Popular Electronics
The Radio and Electronics Engineer
Radio-Electronics

ENGINEERING

Books

Anderson, J. C., et al. *Data and Formulae for Engineering Students*. 2nd ed. Elmsford, N.Y.: Pergamon, 1969.

Classed Subject Catalog of the Engineering Societies Library. 10th Supplement. Boston: G. K. Hall, 1974.

Clauser, H. R., ed. *Encyclopedia of Engineering Materials and Processes*. New York: Reinhold, 1963.

Engineering Index Annual. New York: Engineering Index, annually.

Engineering Index, Inc. *Engineering Index Thesaurus*. New York: MacMillan Info., 1972.

Ernst, ed. *Dictionary of Engineering and Technology*. New York: Oxford Univ. Press, 1981.

Eshbach, O. W., and Mott Sounders. *Handbook of Engineering Fundamentals*. 4th ed. New York: Wiley, 1975.

Gartmann, H. DeLaval. *Engineering Handbook*. 3d ed. New York: McGraw-Hill, 1970.

Guest, G. Martin. *Brief History of Engineering*. Philadelphia, PA: International Ideas, 1974.

Jones, Franklin D., and Paul B. Schubert. *Engineering Encyclopedia*. 3d ed. New York: Industrial Press, 1963.

Kyed, James M., and James H. Matatazzo. *Scientific, Engineering and Medical Societies Publications in Print 1978–1979*. 3d ed. Ann Arbor: Bowker, 1979.

Malinowsky, H. Robert, and Jeanne M. Richardson. *Science and Engineering Literature: A Guide to Reference Sources*. 3d ed. Littleton, CO: Libraries Unlimited, 1980.

Mildren, K. W., ed. *Use of Engineering Literature*. Woburn, MA: Butterworth, 1976.

Mount, Ellis, ed. *Guide to Basic Information Sources in Engineering*. New York: Halsted, 1976.

Oppermann, Alfred. *Dictionary of Modern Engineering*. 3d ed. 2 vols. New York: International Publications Service, 1972–1974.

Parsons, S. A. *How to Find Out About Engineering*. Elmsford, NY: Permagon, 1972.

Perry, Robert H. *Engineering Manual: A Practical Reference of Design*. New York: McGraw-Hill, 1976.

Roland, Hall C. *The Armchair Engineer*. Beaverton, OR: Dilithium, 1981.

Schenck, Hilbert. *Theories of Engineering Experimentation*. 3d ed. New York: McGraw-Hill, 1978.

Sounders, Mott. *Engineer's Companion*. New York: Wiley, 1966.

Journals

American Institute of Plant Engineers Journal
Assembly Engineering
Chief Engineer
Consulting Engineer
Cost Engineering
Engineer
Engineering
Engineering and Science
Engineering and Science Review
Engineering Design
Engineering Digest
Engineering Education
Engineering Industries Journal
Engineering Journal
Engineering News
Industrial Engineering
International Journal of Engineering Sciences
International Operating Engineer
Letters in Applied and Energy Sciences
Manufacturing Engineering
Materials Engineering
Modern Plant Operation and Maintenance
Ocean Resources Engineering

Product Engineering
Production Engineering
Professional Engineer
Sea Technology
Technology Review

GEOLOGY

Books

American Geological Institute. *Dictionary of Geological Terms*. Rev ed. Garden City, NJ: Doubleday, 1976.

Bates, Robert L., and Julia A. Jackson, eds. *Glossary of Geology*. Falls Church, VA: American Geological Institute, 1980.

Bibliography and Index of Geology. Boulder, CO: Geological Society of America in cooperation with the American Geological Institute, monthly with annual indexes.

Bibliography of North American Geology. 49 vols. Washington, D.C.: U.S. Geological Survey; distr. Washington: GPO, 1923–1971.

Challinor, John. *A Dictionary of Geology*. 5th ed. New York: Oxford University Press, 1978.

Coates, Donald R. *Environmental Geology*. New York: Wiley, 1981.

Kaplan, Stuart R. *Guide to Information Sources in Mining, Minerals, and Geosciences*. New York: Wiley, 1965.

Lapedes, Daniel N., ed. *McGraw-Hill Encyclopedia of the Geological Sciences*. New York: McGraw-Hill, 1978.

Mason, Shirley L. *Source Book in Geology, Fourteen Hundred to Nineteen Hundred*. Ed. by Kirtley F. Mather. Cambridge, MA: Harvard Univ. Press, 1970.

New Publications of the Geological Survey. Washington: U.S. Geological Survey; distr. Washington: GPO, 1971–date, monthly with annual cumulations.

U.S. Geological Survey Library. *Catalog of the U.S. Geological Survey Library*. Boston: G. K. Hall, 1964. Supplement.

Ward, Dederick, and Marjorie Wheeler. *Geologic Reference Sources: A Subject and Regional Bibliography to Publications and Maps in the Geological Sciences*. Metuchen, NJ: Scarecrow, 1972.

Whitten and Brooks Dictionary of Geology. New York: Penguin, 1973.

Whitten, D. G. A. *Penguin Dictionary of Geology*. Baltimore, MD: Penguin, 1976.

Zylka, T. *Geological Dictionary*. New York: State Mutual Books, 1980.

Journals

American Journal of Science
American Mineralogist
Chemical Geology
Comments of Earth Sciences: Geophysics
Earth Science
Earth Science Reviews
Economic Geology
Geological Magazine
Geological Society of America Bulletin
Geology; a venture in earth science reporting
International Geology Review
Journal of Geological Education
Journal of Geology
Journal of Geophysical Research
Petroleum Geology
The Quarterly Journal of Engineering Geology
U.S. Geological Survey. Journal of Research

MATHEMATICS

Books

Aaboe, Asger. *Episodes from the Early History of Mathematics.* Washington, D.C.: Mathematical Assoc., 1975.

Aleksandrov, A. D., et al., eds. *Mathematics: Its Content, Methods, and Meaning.* 2nd ed. 3 vols. Cambridge, MA: MIT Press, 1969.

American Mathematical Society. *Index to Translations Selected by the AMS.* Providence, RI: Amer. Math. Soc., 1966.

American Mathematical Society. *Mathematical Reviews Cumulative Index: 1973–1979.* Providence, RI: Amer. Math. Soc., 1981.

Bell, J. L., and A. B. Slomson. *Models and Ultraproducts: An Introduction.* New York: Elsevier-North Holland, 1972.

Carr, George S. *Formulas and Theorems in Pure Mathematics.* New York: Chelsea Pub., 1970.

Dick, Elie M. *Current Information Sources in Mathematics: An Annotated Guide to Books and Periodicals, 1960–1971.* Littleton, CO: Libraries Unlimited, 1973.

Darling, A. R., ed. *Use of Mathematical Literature.* Boston: Butterworths, 1977.

Eves, Howard. *Introduction to the History of Mathematics.* 4th ed. New York: Holt, Rinehart, and Winston, 1976.

Gaffney, M. P., and L. A. Steen, eds. *Annotated Bibliography of Expository Writing in the Mathematical Sciences.* Washington, D.C.: Mathematics Assoc., 1976.

Gellert, W., et al., eds. *The VNR Concise Encyclopedia of Mathematics.* Florence, KY: Reinhold, 1977.

International Catalogue of Scientific Literature 1901–1914. Section A: Mathematics. Metuchen, NJ: Scarecrow, 1974.

Korn, Granino A., and Theresa M. Korn. *Mathematical Handbook for Scientists and Engineers.* 2nd ed. New York: McGraw-Hill, 1968.

May, K. O. *Bibliography and Research Manual of the History of Mathematics.* Toronto: University of Toronto Press, 1973.

Millington, William, and T. Alaric Millington. *Dictionary of Mathematics.* New York: Barnes and Noble, 1971.

National Council of Teachers of Mathematics. *Cumulative Index: The Mathematics Teachers, 1908–1965.* Reston, VA: NCTM, 1967.

Parke, Nathan G. *Guide to the Literature of Mathematics and Physics.* Rev. ed. New York: Dover, 1958.

Pemberton, J. E. *How to Find Out in Mathematics.* 2nd ed. Elmsford, N.Y.: Pergamon, 1970.

Schaaf, William L. *High School Mathematics Library.* Rev. ed. Reston, VA: NCTM, 1976.

Schaefer, Barbara K. *Using Mathematical Literature: A Practical Guide.* New York: Marcel Dekker, 1979.

Shapiro, Max S. *Mathematics Encyclopedia: A Made Simple Book.* Garden City, NY: Doubleday, 1977.

Sneddon, I. N., ed. *Encyclopedic Dictionary of Mathematics for Engineers.* Elmsford, NY: Pergamon, 1976.

Steen, Lynn, and J. A. Seebach, eds. *Fifty-Year Index of the Mathematics Magazine.* Washington, D.C.: Math. Assoc., 1979.

The Universal Encyclopedia of Mathematics. New York: Simon and Schuster, 1964.

Universal Encyclopedia of Mathematics. New York: Simon and Schuster, 1969.

Journals

Advances in Mathematics (Adv. in Math.)
American Journal of Mathematics (Am. J. Math.)
American Mathematical Monthly (Am. Math. Monthly)
American Mathematical Society, Bulletin (Bull. Am. Math. Soc.)
American Mathematical Society, Memoirs (Memoirs Am. Math. Soc.)
American Mathematical Society, Proceedings (Proc. Am. Math. Soc.)
American Mathematical Society, Transactions (Trans. Am. Math. Soc.)

American Statistical Association Journal (Am. Stat. Assn. J.)
Annals of Mathematics (Ann. of Math.)
Applied Mathematics and Optimization (Appl. Math. & Optim.)
Arithmetic Teacher
Canadian Journal of Mathematics (Canad. J. Math.)
Canadian Mathematical Bulletin (Canadian Math. Bull.)
Discrete Mathematics (Discrete Math.)
Duke Mathematical Journal (Duke Math. J.)
Fibonacci Quarterly (Fibonacci Q.)
Institute of Mathematics and Its Application, Journal (J. Inst. Math. & Its Appl.)
International Journal of Computer Mathematics (Inter. J. Compt. Math.)
Investigation in Mathematics Education (Invest. Math. Ed.)
Journal of Algebra (J. Algebra)
Journal for Research in Mathematics Education (J. Res. Math. Ed.)
Journal of Geometry (J. Geom.)
Journal of Undergraduate Mathematics (J. Undergrad. Math.)
Mathematical Gazette (Math. Gaz.)
Mathematical Intelligencer (Math. Intell.)
Mathematical Log (Math. Log)
Mathematical Programming Study (Math. Progr. Study)
Mathematical Reviews (Math. Rev.)
Mathematical Scientist (Math. Sci.)
Mathematics Magazine (Math. Mag.)
Mathematics of Computation (Math. of Computation)
Mathematics Student (Math. Student)
Mathematics Teacher (Math. Teacher)
Pacific Journal of Mathematics (Pacific J. Math.)
Quarterly Journal of Mathematics (Q. J. Math.)
Quarterly of Applied Mathematics (Q. Appl. Math.)
SIAM Review
Scripta Mathematica
Studies in Applied Mathematics (Stud. Appl. Math.)
Two-Year College Mathematics Journal (Two-Year College Math. J.)

PHOTOGRAPHY

Books

Barger, M. Susan. Bibliography of Photographic Processes in Use Before 1880: Their Materials, Processing, and Conservation. Rochester, N.Y.: Tech. and Ed. Center of the Graphic Arts, RIT., 1980.

Boni, Albert. Photographic Literature. 2 vols. New York: Morgan and Morgan, 1962–1972.

Bunnell, Peter C., and Robert A. Sobieszek. Literature of Photography. 62 books. New York: Arno, 1973.

Camerart Photo Trade Dictionary 1979. 17th ed. New York: International Pub. Ser., 1979.

Flowers, Damon B. The Photographic Index for 1980. Vol IV. Detroit: Photo Research, 1981.

Gaunt and Penzold. Focal Encyclopedia of Photography. New York: Focal Press, 1980.

Harwood, Mary. Photography Language: A Running Press Glossary. Philadelphia, PA: Running Press, 1978.

Jones, Bernard E., ed. Cassell's Cyclopedia of Photography. The Literature of Photography Series. 1911; rpt. New York: Arno, 1973.

Kirillou, N. I. Problems in Photographic Research and Technology. New York: Pitman, 1967.

Magoon, Charles E. Photos at the Archives. New York: Macmillan, 1981.

Page, A. A Dictionary of Photographic Terms. New York: Heinman, 1966.

Petzold, Paul. Focal Book of Practical Photography. New York: Focal Press, 1980.

Spencer, D. A. Focal Dictionary of Photographic Technologies. New York: Focal Press, 1973.

Struebel, Leslie, and Hollis N. Todd. Dictionary of Contemporary Photography. Dobbs Ferry, N.Y.: Morgan and Morgan, 1976.

Swelund, Charles. Photography: A Handbook of History, Materials, and Processes. New York: Holt, Rinehart, and Winston, 1974.

Journals

Afterimage
Animator
Aperture
British Journal of Photography
Camera
History of Photography
Industrial Photography
Journal of Photographic Science
Leica Photography
Modern Photography
Photo Life; Canada's Photography Monthly
Photograph
Photographer
Photographic Science and Engineering
Photographic Society of America Journal
Popular Photography
Professional Photographer
Studio Photography
Technical Photography
Visual

PHYSICS

Books

Annual Review of Nuclear Science. Palo Alto, CA: 1952–date.

Besancom, Robert M., ed. *Encyclopedia of Physics.* 2nd ed. New York: Reinhold, 1974.

Coblans, Herbert, ed. *Use of Physics Literature.* Woburn, MA: Butterworths, 1975.

Current Papers in Physics. London: Institution of Electrical Engineers, 1966–date. Bimonthly.

Current Physics Index. New York: American Institute of Physics, 1975–date. Quarterly.

Fluegge, E., ed. *Encyclopedia of Physics.* 54 vols. New York: Springer-Verlag, 1956–date.

Gray, Dwight E., ed. *American Institute of Physics Handbook.* 3d ed. New York: McGraw-Hill, 1972.

Hyman, Charles J., and Ralph Idlin, eds. *Dictionary of Physics and Allied Sciences.* New York: Unger, 1978.

Isaacs, A., and H. J. Gray, eds. *A New Dictionary of Physics.* 2nd ed. New York: Longman, 1975.

Kuhn, Thomas S., et al. *Sources of History of Quantum Physics.* Philadelphia, PA: American Philosophical Society, 1967.

Lapedes, Daniel, ed. *McGraw-Hill Dictionary of Physics and Mathematics.* New York: McGraw-Hill, 1978.

Lerner, Rita G., and George L. Trigg, eds. *Encyclopedia of Physics.* Reading, MA: Addison-Wesley, 1980.

Mayer, Herbert. *Physik Duenner Schichten-Physics of Thin Films: Complete Bibliography.* 2 vols. New York: International Publications Service, 1972.

Physics Abstracts. London: Institution of Electrical Engineers, 1898–date. Bimonthly.

Pitt, Valerie H., ed. *Penguin Dictionary of Physics.* New York: Penguin Books, 1977.

Solid State Physics Literature Guides. New York: Plenum, 1972–date.

Thewlis, J., ed. *Concise Dictionary of Physics: And Related Subjects.* 2nd ed. Elmsford, NY: Pergamon, 1979.

Whitford, Robert H. *Physics Literature: A Reference Manual.* 2nd ed. New York: Scarecrow Press, 1968.

Yates, Bryan. *How To Find Out About Physics: A Guide to Sources of Information Arranged by the Decimal Classification.* New York: Pergamon, 1965.

Journals

Advances in Physics (Advances in Phys.)
American Journal of Physics (Am. J. Phys.)
American Physical Society, Bulletin (Bull. Am. Phys. Soc.)
Annals of Physics (Ann. of Phys.)
Applied Physics (Appl. Phys.)
Canadian Journal of Physics (Canad. J. Phys.)
Chemical Physics (Chem. Phys.)
Contemporary Physics (Contem. Phys.)
Foundations of Physics (Found. Phys.)
Journal of Applied Physics (J. Appl. Phys.)
Journal of Chemical Physics (J. Chem. Phys.)
Journal of Computational Physics (J. Computational Phys.)
Journal of Mathematical Physics (J. Math. Phys.)
Journal of Physics (J. Phys.)
Journal of Physics and Chemistry of Solids (J. Phys. & Chem. Solids)
Journal of Statistical Physics (J. Statis. Phys.)
Journal of the Mechanics and Physics of Solids (J. Mech. & Phys. Solids)
Medical Physics (Med. Phys.)
Nuclear Physics (Nuclear Phys.)
Physical Review (Phys. Rev.)
Physical Review Letters (Phys. Rev. Letters)
Physics Bulletin (Phys. Bull.)
Physics Education (Phys. Educ.)
Physics in Technology (Phys. in Tech.)
Physics Letters (Phys. Letters)
Physics Today (Phys. Today)
Reviews of Modern Physics (Rev. Mod. Phys.)
Transport Theory and Statistical Physics (Transport Theory & Stat. Phys.)

ART

Books

Adeline, Jules. *Adeline Art Dictionary.* New York: Ungar, 1966. Supplement.

American Art Dictionary 1980. 48th ed. Ed. by Jacques Cattell Press. Washington, D.C.: Bowker, 1980.

Art Books, 1950–1979. 1st ed. New York: Bowker, 1979.

Art Index. New York: H. W. Wilson, 1929–date.

Baigell, Matthew. *Dictionary of American Art.* New York: Harper & Row, 1979.

Bibliographic Guide to Art and Architecture, 1976. Boston, MA: G. K. Hall, 1977.

Britannica Encyclopedia of American Art. Ed. by Milton Rugoff. Chicago: Encyclopedia Britannica, 1973.

Buckley, Mary, and David Baum. *Color Theory: A Guide to Information Sources.* Detroit: Gale, 1975.

Bunch, Clarence, ed. *Art Education: A Guide to Information Sources.* Detroit: Gale, 1977.

Chamberlin, Mary W. *Guide to Art Reference Books.* Chicago: American Library Assoc., 1959.

Chanticleer Press. *Encyclopedia of American Art.* New York: Dutton, 1981.

Columbia University. *Catalog of the Avery Memorial Architectural Library.* 19 vols. Boston: G. K. Hall. 1968.

Cummings, Paul. *Dictionary of Contemporary American Artists.* 3d ed. New York: St. Martin's Press, 1977.

De La Croix, Horst, and Richard G. Tansey. *Art Through the Ages.* 2 vols. 7th ed. New York: Harcourt Brace Jovanovich, 1980.

Ehresmann, Donald L. *Fine Arts: A Bibliographic Guide to Basic Reference Works, Histories, and Handbooks.* Littleton, CO: Libraries Unlimited, 1975.

Encyclopedia of World Art. 15 vols. New York: McGraw-Hill, 1959–1968.

Goldman, Bernard. *Reading and Writing in the Arts: A Handbook.* Rev. ed. Detroit: Wayne State Univ. Press, 1978.

Hall, R. J. *Dictionary of Subjects and Symbols in Art.* 2nd rev. ed. New York: Harper & Row, 1979.

Huddleston, Eugene L., and Douglas A. Noverr, eds. *The Relationship of Painting and Literature: A Guide to Information Sources.* Detroit: Gale, 1978.

Jacobs, Jay. *Color Encyclopedia of World Art.* New York: Crown, 1975.

Jones, Lois S. *Art Research Methods and Resources: A Guide to Finding Art Information.* Dubuque, IA: Kendall-Hunt, 1978.

Karpel, Bernard, ed. *Arts in America: A Bibliography.* 4 vols. Washington, D.C.: Smithsonian, 1979–1980.

Mayer, Ralph. *A Dictionary of Art Terms and Techniques.* New York: Harper & Row, 1981.

Muehsam, Gerd. *Guide to Basic Information Sources in the Visual Arts.* Santa Barbara, CA: ABC-Clio.; Oxford, England: Jeffrey Norton Pub., 1978.

Murray, Peter, and Linda Murray. *A Dictionary of Art and Artists.* Rev. ed. New York: Penguin, 1972.

Myers, Bernard S., and Shirley D. Myers. *Dictionary of 20th Century Art.* New York: McGraw-Hill, 1974.

Osborne, Harold, ed. *Oxford Companion to Art.* New York: Oxford University Press, 1970.

Research Libraries of the New York Public Library and the Library of Congress. *Bibliographic Guide to Art and Architecture: 1980.* Boston: G. K. Hall, 1981.

Ryerson Library-Art Institute of Chicago. *Index to Art Periodicals.* 11 vols. Boston: G. K. Hall, 1962 (Supplement, 1975).

Samuels, Peggy and Harold Samuels. *The Illustrated Bibliographical Encyclopedia of Artists of the American West.* Garden City, NY: Doubleday, 1976.

Smith, Lyn W., and Nancy D. Moure. *Index to Reproductions of American Paintings.* Metuchen, NJ: Scarecrow, 1977.

Smith, Ralph C. *A Bibliographical Index of American Artists.* 1930; rpt. Detroit: Gale, 1976.

Sokol, David M. *American Architecture and Art: A Guide to Information Sources.* Detroit: Gale, 1976.

Sturgis, Russell, and Henry E. Krehbiel. *Annotated Bibliography of Fine Art.* 1897; rpt. Boston: Longwood, 1976.

Visual Dictionary of Art. Greenwich, CT: New York Graphic Society, 1974.

Walker, John Albert. *Glossary of Art, Architecture and Design Since 1945.* 2d rev. ed. London: Bingley; Hamden, CT: Linnet Books, 1977.

Who's Who in American Art 1980. 14th ed. Ed. by Jacques Cattell Press. Washington, D.C.: Bowker, 1980.

Journals

American Art Journal
American Art Review
American Artist
Apollo
Archives of American Art Journal
Art and Artists
Art and Man
Art Bulletin
Art Direction
Art Education
Art in America
Art International
Art Journal
Art Language
Art Letter
Art News
Art Week
Art Workers News
Artforum
Artlook
Artmagazine
Arts and Activities
Arts Magazine
Burlington Magazine
Communication Arts Magazine
Connoisseur
Craft Horizons
Design
Design News

Design Quarterly
Feminist Art Journal
Flash Art
Form
Glass Art Magazine
Graphic Arts Monthly
Illustrator Magazine
Industrial Design
Interior Design
Journal of Aesthetics and Art Criticism
Leonardo
National Sculpture Review
New Art Examiner
New York Arts Journal
Pictures on Exhibit
Print
Print Collectors Newsletter
School Arts Magazine
Studies in Art Education
Studio International
Visual Dialog
Women Artists Newsletter
Worldwide Art Catalogue Bulletin

BIOLOGICAL SCIENCES

Books

Abercrombie, Michael, C. J. Hickman, and M. L. Johnson. *Dictionary of Biology*. 6th ed. Baltimore: Penguin Books, 1973.

Altman, Philip L., and Dorthy S. Dittmer, eds. *Biology Data Book*. 2nd ed. 3 vols. Madison, WI: FASEB, 1972–1974.

Biological Abstracts. Philadelphia: Biological Abstracts, 1926–date.

Biological and Agricultural Index. New York: H. W. Wilson, 1947–date.

Blackwelder, Richard E. *Guide to the Taxonomic Literature of Vertebrates*. Ames, IA: Iowa State Univ. Press, 1972.

Blake, S. F. *Geological Guide to Floras of the World*. Totowa, NJ: Allanheld, 1961.

Blanchard, J. Richard, and Lois Farrell. *Guide to Sources for Agricultural and Biological Research*. Berkeley, CA: Univ. of California Press, 1981.

Bottle, R. T., and H. V. Wyatt, eds. *Use of Biological Literature*. 2nd ed. Woburn, MA: Butterworths, 1972.

Brooks, Stewart M. *Basic Science and the Human Body: Anatomy and Physiology*. St. Louis, MO: Mosby, 1975.

Brown, R. W. *Composition of Scientific Words*. Rev. ed. Washington, D.C.: Smithsonian, 1954; rpt. 1978.

Carter, John L., and Ruth C. Carter. *Bibliography and Index of North American Carboniferous Brachiopods 1898–1968*. Boulder, CO: Geological Society, 1970.

Considine, Douglas M., ed. *Van Nostrand's Scientific Encyclopedia*. New York: Reinhold, 1976.

Cowgill, R. W. *Experiments in Biochemical Research Technique*. Huntington, NY: Krieger, 1957.

Denenberg, V. H. *Statistics and Experimental Design for Behavioral and Biological Researchers: An Introduction*. New York: Halsted Press, 1976.

Durrenberger, R. W. *Dictionary of Environmental Sciences*. Palo Alto, CA: National Press Books, 1973.

Encyclopedia of the Life Sciences. Garden City, NY: Doubleday, 1965–1966.

Gabbiani, Giulio, et al. *Reflections on Biologic Research*. St. Louis, MO: Green, 1967.

Gray, Peter, ed. *Encyclopedia of the Biological Sciences*. 2nd ed. New York: Reinhold, 1970.

Gray, Peter, *Student Directory of Biology*. New York: Reinhold, 1973.

Holman, H. H. *Biological Research Method: A Practical Guide*. New York: Hafner, 1969.

International Catalogue of Scientific Literature, 1904–1914. New York: Johnson Reprint, n.d.

Jenkins, F. B. *Science Reference Sources*. 5th ed. Cambridge, MA: MIT Press, 1969.

Johnson, Robert. *Investigative Biology*. Winston-Salem, NC: Hunter, 1980.

Kirk, Thomas G., Jr. *Library Research Guide to Biology: Illustrated Search Strategy and Sources*. Ann Arbor, MI: Pierian Press, 1978.

Lapedes, D. N., ed. *McGraw-Hill Dictionary of the Life Sciences*. New York: McGraw-Hill, 1976.

Martin, E. A., ed. *Dictionary of Life Sciences*. New York: Pica Press; distr. New York: Universe Books, 1977.

Mills, Harlow B., et al. *A Century of Biological Research*. Frank N. Egerton. 3rd ed. Reprint of 1958 ed. New York: Arno, 1978.

Orr, J. B., et al. *What Science Stands For*. New York: Arno, 1937.

Siler, William, and Donald A. Lindberg, eds. *Computers in Life Science Research*. New York: Plenum, 1975.

Smith, Roger C., and W. Malcolm Reid. *Guide to the Literature of the Life Sciences*. 8th ed. Minneapolis, MN: Burgess, 1972.

Steen, Edwin B. *Dictionary of Biology*. 2nd ed. Totowa, NJ: Barnes & Noble, 1975.

Steere, William C., ed. *Biological Abstracts: BIOSIS-The First Fifty Years*. New York: Plenum, 1976.

Swift, Lloyd H. *Botanical Bibliographies: A Guide to Bibliographical Materials Applicable to Botany*. Monticello, NY: Lubrecht & Cramer, 1974.

Swift, Lloyd H. *Botanical Classifications: A Comparison Angiosperm Classification*. Hamden, CT: Shoe String, 1974.

Willis, J. C. *A Dictionary of the Flowering Plants and Ferns*. 8th ed. New York: Cambridge Univ. Press, 1973.

Woodford, F. P., ed. *Scientific Writing for Graduate Students*. New York: Rockefeller Univ. Press, 1968.

Journals

Advancement in Science
Advances in Botanical Research (Advances Botan. Res.)
Advancing Frontiers of Plant Sciences
American Biology Teacher
American Journal of Anatomy (Am. J. Anat.)
American Journal of Botany (Am. J. Botany)
American Journal of Physiology (Am. J. Physiol.)
American Midland Naturalist (Am. Midland Naturalist)
American Naturalist (Am. Naturalist)
American Scientist (Am. Scientist)
American Zoologist (Am. Zool.)
Anatomical Record
Animal Behavior
Annals of the Missouri Botanical Garden (Ann. Mo. Botan. Garden)
Applied Microbiology (Appl. Microbiol.)
Archives of Biochemistry and Biophysics (Arch. Biochem. & Biophys.)
Audubon Field Notes
Audubon Magazine
Bacteriological Reviews (Bacteriol. Rev.)
Behavior Genetics
Biochemical and Biophysical Research Commission (Biochem. & Biophys. Research Comm.)
Biochemical Genetics (Biochem. Genetics)
Biochemistry (Biochem.)
Biochemistry Journal (Biochem. J.)
Biological Bulletin (Biol. Bull.)
Biology Digest (Biol. Dig.)
Bioscience
Botanical Review (Botan. Rev.)
Bulletin of Aquatic Biology (Bull. Aquatic Biol.)
Bulletin of Experimental Biology and Medicine (Bull. Exptl. Biol. & Med.)
Bulletin of Mathematical Biology (Bull. Math. Biol.)

Bulletin of the Atomic Scientists (Bull. Atomic Scientists)
Canadian Journal of Botany (Canadian J. Botany)
Canadian Journal of Microbiology (Canadian J. Microbiol.)
Canadian Journal of Zoology (Canadian J. Zool.)
Cell Differentiation
Current Contents
Developmental Biology (Develop. Biol.)
DOKLADY-Biochemistry Section
DOKLADY-Biological Sciences Section
DOKLADY-Botanical Sciences Section
Ecology
Evolution
Experimental Cell Research (Exptl. Cell Research)
Federation Proceedings (Federation Proc.)
General Science Quarterly (Gen. Sci. Quart.)
Genetics
Geological Society of America-Bulletin (Geol. Soc. Am. Bull.)
Heredity
Herpetologica
Human Biology (Human Biol.)
Human Genetics
Hydrobiologica
International Abstracts of Biological Sciences (Intern. Abstr. Biol. Sci.)
International Bureau for Plant Taxonomy (Intern. Bur. Plant Taxonomy)
Journal of Animal Behavior (J. Animal Behavior)
Journal of Animal Ecology (J. Animal Ecology)
Journal of Applied Physiology (J. Appl Phys.)
Journal of Bacteriology (J. Bacteriol.)
Journal of Biological Chemistry (J. Biol. Chem.)
Journal of Biological Education (J. Biol. Educ.)
Journal of Clinical Investigation (J. Clin. Invest.)
Journal of Ecology (J. Ecol.)
Journal of Experimental Biology (J. Exptl. Biol.)
Journal of Experimental Botany (J. Exptl. Botany)
Journal of Experimental Medicine (J. Exptl. Med.)
Journal of Experimental Zoology (J. Exptl. Zool.)
Journal of General Microbiology (J. Gen. Microbiol.)
Journal of Geology (J. Geol.)
Journal of Heredity (J. Heredity)
Journal of Herpetology (J. Herpetology)
Journal of Immunology (J. Immunology)

Journal of Lipid Research (J. Lipid Res.)
Journal of Mammology (J. Mammol.)
Journal of Molecular Biology (J. Molecular Biol.)
Journal of Morphology (J. Morphol.)
Journal of Natural History (J. Nat. History)
Journal of Paleontology (J. Paleontol.)
Journal of Physiology (J. Physiol.)
Journal of Protozoology (J. Protozool.)
Journal of Wildlife Management (J. Wildl. Mgmt.)
Linnean Society of London Journal (Linnean Soc. London J.)
Microbial Ecology
Microbiological Reviews (Microbiol. Rev.)
Mutation Research (Mutation Res.)
National Academy of Sciences-Proceedings (Proc. Nat. Acad. Sci.)
National Wildlife (Nat. Wildl.)
Naturalist
Nature
New York Academy of Sciences, Annals of (Ann. NY Acad. Sci.)
Palaeobotanist
Physiology of Science (Physiol. Sci.)
Physiological Reviews (Physiol. Rev.)
Physiological Zoology (Physiol. Zool.)
Physiology and Behavior (Physiol. & Beh.)
Plant Physiology (Plant Physiol.)
Plant World
Proceedings of the National Academy of Science (Proc. Nat. Acad. Sci.)
Quarterly Review of Biology (Quart. Rev. Biol.)
Radiation Research (Radiation Res.)
Review of Applied Mycology (Rev. Appl. Mycology)
Science
Science Education (Sci. Ed.)
Scientific American (Sci. Am.)
Scientific American Monthly (Sci. Am. Monthly)
Scientific Monthly (Sci. Monthly)
Social Biology (Soc. Biol.)
Soil Conservation (Soil Conserv.)
Stain Technology
Systematic Zoology (System. Zool.)
Theoretical Population Biology

BUSINESS

Books

Accountants' Index. New York: American Institute of Certified Public Accountants, 1921–date.

Ammer, Christine, and Dean S. Ammer. *Dictionary of Business and Economics*. New York: Free Press, 1977.

Battista, O. A., ed. *Business-One Thousand Directory*. Fort Worth, TX: Research Services, 1982.

Beardsley, Richard, ed. *The Videolog in Business*. 1980–81 ed. New York: J. Norton, 1981.

Bibliographic Guide to Business and Economics. 2 vols. Boston: G. K. Hall, 1976.

Brownstone, David M., et al. *The VNR Dictionary of Business and Finance*. New York: Von Nostrand Reinhold, 1980.

Brownstone, David M., and Gorton Carruth. *Where to Find Business Information*. New York: Wiley, 1979.

Business and Economics Books and Serials in Print. New York: Bowker, 1981.

Business Periodical Index. New York: H. W. Wilson, 1958–date.

Clark, Donald T., and Bert A. Gottfried. *University Dictionary of Business and Finance*. New York: Apollo, 1974.

Daniells, Lorna. *Business Information Sources*. Berkeley, CA: Univ. of California Press, 1976.

Davids, L. E. *Instant Business Directory*. New York: Watts, 1971.

Encyclopedia of Accounting Systems. 3 vols. Prentice-Hall Editorial Staff. Ed. by Jerome Pescow. Englewood Cliffs, NJ: Prentice-Hall, 1975.

Figueroa, Oscar, and Charles Winkler. *A Business Information Guidebook*. New York: American Mgmt., 1980.

Georgi, Charlotte. *The Arts and the World of Business: A Selected Bibliography*. Los Angeles, CA: UCLA Mgmt., 1976.

Gilmour, R. *Business Systems Handbook: Analysis, Designs, and Documentation Standards*. Englewood Cliffs, NJ: Prentice-Hall, 1979.

Giordano, Albert G. *Concise Dictionary of Business Terminology*. Englewood Cliffs, NJ: Prentice-Hall, 1981.

Grant, Mary M., and Norma Cote, eds. *Directory of Business and Financial Services*. 7th ed. New York: Special Libraries Assn., 1976.

Johannsen, Hano, and G. Terry Page. *The International Dictionary of Business*. Englewood Cliffs, NJ: Prentice-Hall, 1981.

Lovett, Robert W., ed. *American Economic and Business History: Information Sources*. Detroit: Gale, 1971.

Moore, Norman D. *Dictionary of Business, Finance, and Investment*. Dayton, OH: Investor's Systems, 1975.

Munn, Glenn G. *Encyclopedia of Banking and Finance*. Ed. Ferdinand L. Garcia. 7th ed. Boston: Bankers, 1973.

Nemmers, Erwin Esser. *Dictionary of Economics and Business*. 4th ed. Totowa, NJ: Rowan and Littlefield, 1978.

Research Libraries of the New York Public Library and the Library of Congress. *Bibliographic Guide to Business and Economics: 1980*. Boston: G. K. Hall, 1981.

Rosenberg, Jerry M. *Dictionary of Business and Management*. New York: Wiley, 1978.

Seidler, Lee J., and D. R. Carmichael. *Accountants' Handbook*. 6th ed. New York: Ronald Press, 1981.

Systems Research Institute Staff. *Directory of Administration and Management*. Los Angeles: Systems Research, 1981.

Van Fleet, David D. *An Historical Bibliography of Administration, Business, and Management*. Monticello, IL: Vance Biblios., 1978.

Verbal Information Systems: A Comprehensive Guide to Writing Manuals. Cleveland, OH: Assn. of Systems Mgmt., 1974.

Wasserman, Paul, et al., eds. *Encyclopedia of Business Information Sources*. 4th rev. ed. Detroit: Gale, 1980.

Journals

Academy of Management Journal
Accountants' Digest
Accounting and Business Research
Accounting Journal
Accounting, Organizations and Society
Accounting Review
Administrative Management
Advanced Management Journal
Advertising Age
American Banker
American Import and Export Bulletin
Appraisal Journal
Association Management
Banker
Banker's Magazine
Banking
Barron's National Business and Financial Weekly
Better Investing
Business and Society Review
Business Conditions Digest
Business History Review
Business Horizons
Business International
Business Quarterly
Business Today
Business Week
CA Magazine
Canada Commerce

Changing Times
Columbia Journal of World Business
Commerce
Commerce America
Commercial and Financial Chronicle
Consumers' Research Bulletin
Cost and Management
CPA Journal
Distribution Worldwide
Director
Dollars & Sense
Dun's
Economic Review
Executive
Federal Reserve Bulletin
Finance
Financial Executive
Financial Management
Financial Post
Financial World
Forbes
Fortune
From Nine to Five
Futures
Harvard Business Review
Income Opportunities
Industrial Management
Industrial Marketing
Institutional Investor
Internal Auditor
International Financial Statistics
International Management
International New Product Newsletter
International Trade Forum
Journal of Accountancy
Journal of Accounting Research
Journal of Advertising
Journal of Advertising Research
Journal of Business
Journal of Business Education
Journal of Business Research
Journal of Commercial Bank Lending
Journal of Finance
Journal of General Management
Journal of Insurance
Journal of Management Studies
Journal of Marketing
Journal of Marketing Research
Journal of Money, Credit & Banking
Journal of Retailing
Journal of Systems Management
Kiplinger Washington Letter
Labor Market and Employment Security
Lloyd's Bank Review
Magazine of Wall Street
Management Accounting
Management Quarterly
Management Research

Management Review
Marketing
Modern Office Procedures
National Tax Journal
Nation's Business
New York University Bulletin
Office Executive
Operational Research Quarterly
Operations Research
Personnel
Personnel Administrator
Personnel and Guidance Journal
Personnel Journal
Personnel Management
Purchasing World
Research Management
Social Security Bulletin
Survey of Current Business
Tax Adviser
Value Line
Visual Merchandising
Wall Street Journal

COMPUTER TECHNOLOGY

Books

Belzer, Jack. *Encyclopedia of Computer Science and Technology*. 14 vols. New York: Dekker, 1980.

Belzer, Jack. *Index to Encyclopedia of Computer Science and Technology*. New York: Dekker, 1981.

Carter, Ciel. *Guide to Reference Sources in the Computer Sciences*. New York: Macmillan, 1974.

Chandor, Anthony. *A Dictionary of Computers*. Baltimore: Penguin Books, 1970.

Davis, Gordon B. *Computers and Information Processing*. New York: McGraw-Hill, 1977.

Hall, James Logan. *On-Line Bibliographic Data Bases: 1979 Directory*. London: Aslib, 1979.

Hines, T. *Computer Filing of Index, Bibliographic and Catalog Entries*. Williamsport, PA: Bodart, 1966.

Hsiao, T. C., ed. *Computer Dissertations Nineteen Fifty to Nineteen Seventy Five*. Latham, NY: Science and Technology Press, 1980.

Jordain, Philip B. *Condensed Computer Encyclopedia*. New York: McGraw-Hill, 1969.

Lytel, Allan, and Lawrence Buckmaster. *ABC's of Computers*. Indianapolis, IN: Sams, 1974.

Morrill, Chester, Jr. *Computers and Data Processing Information Sources*. Detroit: Gale, 1969.

Pitchard, Alan. *A Guide to Computer Literature: An Introductory Survey of the Sources of Information*. 2nd ed. Hampden, CT: Shoe String Press, 1972.

Prenis, John. *Computer Terms: A Running Press Glossary*. Philadelphia, PA: Running Press, 1977.

Quinn, Karen Takle. *Guide to Literature on Computers*. Washington, D.C.: American Society for Engineering Education, 1970.

Ralston, Anthony, ed. *Encyclopedia of Computer Science*. New York: Van Nostrand Reinhold, 1976.

Sippl, Charles J., and Charles P. Sippl. *Computer Dictionary and Handbook*. 2nd ed. Indianapolis, IN: Sams, 1972.

Solomon, Martin B., Jr., and Nora G. Lovan. *Annotated Bibliography of Films in Automation, Data Processing, and Computer Science*. Lexington, KY: Univ. Press of Kentucky, 1967.

Spencer, Donald. *Computer Dictionary for Everyone*. New York: Scribner, 1981.

Stark, Peter. *Computer Programming Handbook*. Blue Ridge Summit, PA: TAB Books, 1975.

van Cleemput, W. M. *Computer Aided Design of Digital Systems: A Bibliography*. Woodland Hills, CA: Computer Science Press, 1976.

Weik, Martin H. *Standard Dictionary of Computers and Information Processing*. Rev. 2nd ed. Rochelle Park, NJ: Hayden, 1977.

Williams, Martha E., and Sandra H. Rouse. *Computer-Readable Bibliographic Data Bases: A Directory and Data Sourcebook*. Washington, D.C.: American Society for Information Science, 1976–date.

Youden, W. W., ed. *Computer Literature Bibliography, 1946–1967*. 2 vols in 1. Reprint of 1967 ed. New York: Arno, 1970.

Journals

ACM Communications
Acta Informatica
Apple
Artificial Intelligence
Association for Computing Machinery, Journal.
Automatic Control and Computer
Automatica
Automation and Remote Control
BYTE; the small systems journal
Computer

Computer Age
Computer Decisions and Computer Design
Computer Digest
Computer Graphics
Computer Graphics and Image Processing
Computer Journal
Computer Methods in Applied Mechanics and Engineering
Computer Music Journal
Computer Products
Computer Review
Computers and Chemical Engineering
Computers and Chemistry
Computers and Education
Computers and Electrical Engineering
Computers and Fluids
Computers and Geosciences
Computers and Graphics
Computers and Mathematics with Applications
Computers and Operations Research
Computers and People
Computers and Structures
Computers and the Humanities
Computerware
Computerworld
Computing; archives for electronic computing
Computing Reviews
Control Engineering
Creative Computing
Data Base
Data Communications
Data Management
Data Processing
Data Processing Digest
Data Processing in Education
Data Processor
Datamation
Digital Design
Digital Processes
EDP Analyzer
EDP Performance Review
IBM Systems Journal
IEEE Transactions on Automatic Control
IEEE Transactions on Computers
IEEE Transactions on Information Theory
IEEE Transactions on Systems, Man, and Cybernetics
Information and Control
Information and Letters
Information Sciences
Information Systems
Intelligent Machines Journal
Interactive Computing
International Journal of Computer and Information Sciences
International Journal of Man-Machine Studies
Journal of Computer and System Sciences
Journal of Computer-Based Information

Officemation Reports
Oncomputing
Operating Systems Review
People's Computers
Personal Computing
Popular Computing
SIAM Journal on Computing
Simulation
Small Systems World
Software-Practice and Experience
Systems-Computers-Controls
Word Processing News
Word Processing Report
Word Processing Systems

EDUCATION

Books

Altbach, Philip G., et al. *International Bibliography of Comparative Education.* New York: Praeger, 1981.

Avy, Donald, et al. *Introduction to Research in Education.* 2nd ed. New York: Holt, Rinehart, Winston, 1979.

Baatz, Charles A., ed. *Philosophy of Education: A Guide to Information Sources.* Detroit: Gale, 1980.

Banks, Olive. *The Sociology of Education: A Bibliography.* Totowa, NJ: Rowman, 1978.

Berliner, David C., ed. *Review of Research in Education, Seven.* Itasca, IL: Peacock Pub., 1979.

Bernard van Leer Foundation, ed. *Compensatory Early Childhood Education: A Selective Working Bibliography.* New York: International Publications Service, 1971.

Berry, Dorthea M. *A Bibliographic Guide to Educational Research.* 2nd ed. Metuchen, NJ: Scarecrow, 1980.

Blishen, Edward. *Encyclopedia of Education.* New York: Philosophical Library, 1970.

Brickman, William W. *Bibliographical Essays on Curriculum and Instruction.* Folcroft, PA: Folcroft, 1976.

Brickman, William W. *Bibliographical Essays on Educational Reference Works.* Reprint of 1975 ed. Folcroft, PA: Folcroft, 1978.

Burke, Arvid J., and Mary A. Burke. *Documentation in Education.* New York: Teachers College Press, Columbia Univ., 1967.

Camp, William L., and Bryan L. Schwark. *Guide to Periodicals in Education and Its Academic Disciplines.* 2nd ed. Metuchen, NJ: Scarecrow, 1975.

Cohen, Louis and Lawrence Manion. *Research Methods in Education*. Totowa, NJ: Biblio Dist., 1980.

Current Index to Journals in Education. New York: Macmillan, 1969–date.

Deighton, L. C. *Encyclopedia of Education*. 10 vols. New York: Macmillan, 1971.

Dewey, John. *Dictionary of Education*. Ed. by Ralph B. Winn. 1959; rpt. Westport, CT: Greenwood, 1972.

Ebel, Robert L. *Encyclopedia of Educational Research*. 4th ed. London: Macmillan, 1969.

Education Abstracts. Vol. 1–16. Paris: UNESCO. Monthly, 1949–1964.

Education Index. Vol. 1–date, Bronx, NY: Wilson, 1929–date.

Educational Resources Information Center. *Current Index to Journals in Education*. New York: Macmillan, 1969–date.

Educational Resources Information Center. *Early Childhood Education: An ERIC Bibliography*. New York: Macmillan Info., 1973.

Educational Resources Information Center. *Educational Documents Abstracts*. New York: Macmillan, 1968–date.

Educational Resources Information Center. *Educational Documents Index*. New York: Macmillan, 1966–date.

Educational Resources Information Center. *Educational Finance: An ERIC Bibliography*. New York: Macmillan, 1972.

Educational Technology Reviews. 12 vols. Englewood Cliffs, NJ: Educational Technology, 1973.

Gay, L. R. *Educational Research*. 2nd ed. Columbus, OH: Merrill, 1981.

Good, Carter V. *Essentials of Educational Research: Methodology and Design*. Englewood Cliffs, NJ: Prentice-Hall, 1972.

Guide to American Educational Directories. 5th ed. Coral Springs, FL: Klein, 1980.

Hall, G. Stanley, and John M. Mansfield. *Hints Toward a Select and Descriptive Bibliography of Education*. Reprint of 1886 ed. Detroit: Gale, 1973.

Kennedy, James R., Jr. *Library Research Guide to Education*. Ann Arbor, MI: Pierian, 1979.

Manheim, Theodore, et al. *Sources in Educational Research*. Detroit: Wayne State Univ. Press, 1969.

Manheim, Theodore, Gloria L. Dardarian, and Diane A. Satterthwaite. *Sources in Educational Research: A Selected and Annotated Bibliography*. Vol. 1: Parts I–X. Detroit: Wayne State Univ. Press, 1969.

Monroe, Paul, ed. *Cyclopedia of Education, 5 vols*. Reprint of 1911 ed. Detroit: Gale, 1968.

Monroe, Will S. *Bibliography of Education*. Reprint of 1897 ed. Detroit: Gale, 1968.

Page, G. Terry, and J. B. Thomas. *International Dictionary of Education*. Cambridge, MA: MIT Press, 1980.

Park, Joe. *Rise of American Education: An Annotated Bibliography*. Evanston, IL: Northwestern University Press, 1965.

Powell, John P. *Philosophy of Education: A Select Bibliography*. 2nd ed. Atlantic Highlands, NJ: Humanities, 1971.

Quay, Richard H. *In Pursuit of Equality of Educational Opportunity: A Selective Bibliography and Guide to the Research Literature*. New York: Garland, 1978.

Ralston, Valerie H. *Education: A Guide to Selected Sources*. Storrs, CT: University of Connecticut Library, 1977.

Research Libraries of the New York Public Library and Columbia University, Teachers College Library. *Bibliographic Guide to Education: 1980*. Boston: G. K. Hall, 1981.

Resources in Education Annual Cumulation. 3 vols. Phoenix, AZ: Oryx, 1980.

Rowntree, Derek. *Dictionary of Education*. New York: Harper and Row, 1981.

Sax, Gilbert. *Foundations of Educational Research*. 2nd ed. Englewood Cliffs, NJ: Prentice-Hall, 1979.

Winick, Mariann P. *The Progressive Education Movement: An Annotated Bibliography*. New York: Garland, 1976.

Woodbury, Marda L. *A Guide to Sources of Educational Information*. 2nd ed. Arlington, VA: Information Resources, 1981.

Journals

Adult Education
Adult Leadership
American Education
American Educational Research Journal
American School Board Journal
American Teacher
CEA Critic
Canadian Journal of Education
Change
Childhood Education
Chronicle of Higher Education
College and University
College Board Review
College English
College Student Journal
Comparative Education
Comparative Education Review

ENGLISH LANGUAGE AND LITERATURE

GENERAL

Books

Altick, Richard D., and Andrew Wright. *Selective Bibliography for the Study of English and American Literature*. 5th ed. New York: Macmillan, 1974.

Baldensperger, Fernand, and Werner P. Friederich. *Bibliography of Comparative Literature*. 3rd ed. 1950; rpt. New York: Russell & Russell, 1960.

Holman, C. Hugh. *Handbook to Literature*. 4th ed. Indianapolis, IN: Bobbs-Merrill, 1980.

Kennedy, Arthur G., and Donald B. Sands. *A Concise Bibliography for Students of English*. Rev. William E. Colburn. Stanford: Stanford Univ. Press, 1972.

Magill, Frank N., ed. *Masterplots*. 12 vols. New York: Salem Press, 1976. Annual Review.

Moulton, Charles Wells. *Library of Literary Criticism of English and American Authors*. 8 vols. 1901–1905; rpt. Magnolia, MA: Peter Smith, 1935–1940.

AMERICAN LITERATURE

Books

Blanck, Jacob, comp. *Bibliography of American Literature*. 6 vols. New Haven: Yale University Press, 1955–73.

Clark, Harry Hayden, comp. *American Literature: Poe Through Garland*. New York: AHM, 1971.

Davis, Richard Beale, comp. *American Literature Through Bryant*. New York: AHM, 1969.

Evans, Charles. *American Bibliography*. 14 vols. Magnolia, MA: Peter Smith, 1967.

Gerstenberger, Donna, and George Hendrick. *American Novel: 1789 to 1968*. 2 vols. Chicago: Swallow, 1961 & 1970.

Gohdes, Clarence. *Bibliographical Guide to the Study of Literature of the USA*. 4th ed. Durham, NC: Duke Univ. Press, 1976.

Hart, James D., ed. *The Oxford Companion to American Literature*. 4th ed. New York: Oxford Univ. Press, 1965.

Havlice, Patricia Pate. *Index to American Author Bibliographies*. Metuchen, NJ: Scarecrow, 1971.

Jones, Howard Mumford, and Richard M. Ludwig. *Guide to American Literature and Its Backgrounds Since 1890.* 4th ed. Cambridge, MA: Harvard Univ. Press, 1972.

Kunitz, Stanley J., and Howard Haycraft, eds. *American Authors, 1600–1900.* 7th ed. New York: H. W. Wilson, 1969.

Leary, Lewis. *Articles on American Literature: 1900–1950.* Durham, NC: Duke Univ. Press, 1954.

———. *Articles on American Literature: 1950–1967.* Durham, NC: Duke Univ. Press, 1970.

———, and John Auchard. *Articles on American Literature: 1968–1975.* Durham, NC: Duke Univ. Press, 1979.

Nilon, Charles H. *Bibliography of Bibliographies in American Literature.* New York: Bowker, 1970.

Nyren, Dorothy, ed. *Modern American Literature.* 3rd ed. New York: Ungar, 1964.

Richard, Robert F., ed. *Concise Dictionary of American Literature.* 1955; rpt. Westport, CT: Greenwood, 1977.

Spillner, Robert E., et al., eds. *Literary History of the United States.* 4th ed. 3 vols. New York: Macmillan, 1974.

Stern, Milton R., and Seymour L. Gross. *American Literature Survey.* 4 vols. New York: Penguin, 1977.

Tate, Allen. *Sixty American Poets.* Folcroft, PA: Folcroft, 1945.

Trent, W. P., et al. *Cambridge History of American Literature.* 3 vols. New York: Macmillan, 1943.

Ward, A. C. *American Literature, Eighteen Hundred Eighty to Nineteen Thirty.* 1932; rpt. Totowa, NJ: Cooper Square, 1975.

Journals

American Literary Realism: 1870–1910
American Literature
American Notes & Queries
American Quarterly
American Scholar
CEA Critic
College English
Contemporary Literature
Criticism: A Quarterly for Literature and the Arts
Early American Literature
ESQ: Journal of American Renaissance
Essays in Criticism
Essays in Literature
Explicator
Journal of American Studies
Journal of Modern Literature

MLA Abstracts
Modern Drama
Modern Fiction Studies
New England Quarterly
Nineteenth Century Fiction
PMLA
Resources for American Literary Study
Southern Literary Journal
Studies in American Humor
Twentieth Century Literature
Western American Literature

BLACK LITERATURE

Books

Clack, ed. *Black Literature Resources.* New York: Dekker, 1975.

Davis, Arthur. *From the Dark Tower: Afro-American Writers from 1900 to 1960.* Washington, D.C.: Howard Univ. Press, 1974.

Deodene, Frank, and William P. French. *Black American Fiction Since 1952: A Preliminary Checklist.* Chatham, NY: Chatham Bookseller, 1970.

Fairbanks, Carol, and Eugene A. Engeldinger. *Black American Fiction: A Bibliography.* Metuchen, NJ: Scarecrow, 1978.

Hallie Q. Memorial Library. *Index to Periodical Articles by and About Negroes.* Boston: G. K. Hall, 1971.

Hughes, Langston, and Arna Bontempts, eds. *Poetry of the Negro, 1746–1970.* New York: Doubleday, 1970.

Inge, Thomas M., et al., ed. *Black American Writers: Bibliographic Essays.* 2 vols. New York: St. Martin's Press, 1978.

Kallenbach, Jessamine S. *Index to Black American Literary Anthologies.* Boston: G. K. Hall, 1979.

Kornweibel, Theodore. *No Crystal Stair: Black Life and the Messenger, 1917–1928.* Westport, CT: Greenwood, 1975.

Lindfors, Bernth, ed. *Black African Literature in English: A Guide to Information Sources.* Detroit: Gale, 1979.

Mitchell, Loften. *Voices of the Black Theatre.* New York: T. J. White, 1975.

Rush, Theressa Gunnels, et al. *Black American Writers Past and Present: A Biographical and Bibliographical Dictionary.* Metuchen, NJ: Scarecrow, 1975.

Spalding, Henry D. *Encyclopedia of Black Folklore and Humor.* Middle Village, NY: Jonathan David, 1979.

Turner, Darwin T., comp. *Afro-American Writers.* Northbrook, IL: AHM, 1970.

Welsch, Erwin K. *Negro in the United States: A Research Guide*. Bloomington, IN: Indiana Univ. Press, 1965.

Whitlow, Roger. *Black American Literature: A Critical History*. Totowa, NJ: Littlefield, 1974.

Work, Monroe Nathan. *A Bibliography of the Negro in Africa and America*. New York: Octagon, 1966.

Journals

Bibliographic Survey: The Negro in Print
Black American Literature Forum
Black Scholar
Black World
Crisis
Ebony
Journal of African Studies
Journal of Black Studies
Journal of Negro History
Negro Heritage
Negro History Bulletin
Research in African Studies

BRITISH LITERATURE

Books

Arnold, James F., and J. W. Robinson. *English Theoretical Literature 1559–1900: A Bibliography Incorporating Lowe's Bibliographical Account*. Elmsford, NY: British Book Center, 1971.

Baker, Ernest A. *History of the English Novel*. 11 vols. 1967; rpt. New York: Barnes and Noble, 1975.

Cambridge History of English Literature. 15 vols. New York: Cambridge Univ. Press, 1961.

Courthope, William J. *A History of English Poetry*. 6 vols. 1895–1910; rpt. New York: Russell & Russell, 1962.

Harvey, Paul, and Dorthy Eagle, eds. *The Oxford Companion to English Literature*. 4th ed. New York: Oxford Univ. Press, 1967.

Kunitz, Stanley J., and Howard Haycraft. *British Authors Before 1800: A Biographical Dictionary*. New York: H. W. Wilson, 1952.

Kunitz, Stanley J., and Howard Haycraft. *British Authors of the Nineteenth Century*. New York: H. W. Wilson, 1936.

Mellown, Elgin W. *A Descriptive Catalogue of the Bibliographies of Twentieth Century British Poets, Novelists, and Dramatists*. 2nd rev. & enl. ed. Troy, NY: Whitston, 1978.

Ray, Gordon N. *Bibliographical Resources for the Study of Nineteenth Century English Fiction*. Folcroft, PA: Folcroft, 1964.

Temple, Ruth Z., and Martin A. Tucker. *Twentieth Century British Literature: A Reference Guide and Bibliography*. New York: Ungar, 1966.

Watson, George. *Cambridge Bibliography of English Literature*. 5 vols. New York: Cambridge Univ. Press, 1965.

Years Work in English Studies. New York: Humanities, annually.

Journals

Abstracts of English Studies
Comparative Literature
ELH
Eighteenth Century Studies
English Literary Renaissance
English Studies
Essays in Criticism
Essays in Literature
Explicator
Journal of Commonwealth Literature
Journal of English and Germanic Philology
Modern Philology
Philological Quarterly
PMLA
Renaissance News
Review of English Literature
Review of English Studies
Romance Philology
Seventeenth Century News
Shakespeare Quarterly
Studies in English Literature: 1500–1900
Studies in Philology
Studies in Romanticism
Victorian Poetry
Victorian Studies

DRAMA

Books

Anderson, Michael, et al. *Crowell's Handbook of Contemporary Drama*. New York: Crowell, 1971.

Baker, Blanch M. *Dramatic Bibliography*. 1933; rpt. New York: Arno, 1968.

Baker, Blanch M. *Theatre and Allied Arts*. 1953; rpt. New York: Arno, n.d.

Breed, Paul F., and Florence M. Sniderman. *Dramatic Criticism Index*. Detroit: Gale, 1972.

Chicorel, Marietta, ed. *Chicorel Theater Index to Drama Books and Periodicals*. Vol. 21. New York: Chicorel Library, 1975.

Coleman, Arthur, and Gary R. Tyler. *Drama Criticism*. 2 vols. Denver, CO: Swallow, 1970.

Cumulated Dramatic Index, 1909–1949. 2 vols. Westwood, MA: Faxon, 1965.

Eddleman, Floyd E., ed. *American Drama Criticism: Interpretations, 1890–1977*. 2nd ed. Hamden, CT: Shoe String, 1979.

Palmer, Helen H. *European Drama Criticism, 1900–1975*. 2nd ed. Hamden, CT: Shoe String, 1977.

Play Index. 5 vols. New York: H. W. Wilson, 1953, 1963, 1968, 1973, 1978.

Journals

Comparative Drama
Creative Drama
Drama
Drama Review
Education Theatre Journal
Modern Drama
New York Guide and Theatre Magazine
New York Theatre Critics Reviews
Performing Arts Journal
Shakespeare Quarterly
Theatre
Theatre Arts
Theatre Arts Monthly
Theatre Quarterly
Tulane Drama Review
Variety

LANGUAGE

Books

A Dictionary of American English on Historical Principals. Ed. by Sir William Craigie and J. R. Hulbert. 4 vols. Chicago: Univ. of Chicago Press, 1938–1944.

Bailey, Richard W., and Dolores M. Burton. *English Stylistics: A Bibliography*. Cambridge, MA: The MIT Press, 1968.

Kennedy, Arthur G., and Donald B. Sands. *A Concise Bibliography for Students of English*. 5th ed. Stanford, CA: Stanford Univ. Press, 1972.

Oxford English Dictionary. Ed. by James A. H. Murray, et al. 13 vols. New York: Oxford Univ. Press, 1933.

Journals

American Notes & Queries
American Quarterly
American Scholar
American Speech
College Composition and Communication
College English
ETC: A Review of General Semantics
English
English Language Notes
English Studies
General Linguistics
International Journal of American Linguistics
Journal of Linguistics
Language
Modern Language Abstracts
Modern Language Forum
Modern Language Journal
Modern Language Notes
Modern Language Quarterly
Modern Language Review
Modern Philology
Oral English
Philological Quarterly
Studies in Philology

MYTH AND FOLKLORE

Books

Daigle, Richard J., and Frederick R. Lapides, eds. *The Mentor Dictionary of Mythology and the Bible*. New York: New American Library, 1973.

Eastman, Mary Huse. *Index to Fairy Tales, Myths, and Legends*. 2nd ed. Westwood, MA: Faxon, 1926. Supplements 1937, 1952.

Ireland, Norma O. *Index to Fairy Tales, 1949–1972, Including Folklore, Legends, and Myths in Collections*. Westwood, MA: Faxon, 1973.

MacCulloch, John A., et al., eds. *Mythology of All Races*. 13 vols. 1932; rpt. New York: Cooper Square, n.d.

Thompson, Stith. *Motif Index of Folk Literature*. Rev. and enl. ed. 6 vols. Bloomington, IN: Indiana Univ. Press, 1955–1958.

Journals

Abstracts of Folklore Studies
American Folklife
American Folklife Society Newsletter
Appalachian Notes
Center for Southern Folklore Magazine
Folklore
Folklore Institute Journal
Journal of American Folklore
Mythic Society Quarterly Journal
Parabola
Southern Folklore Quarterly

NOVEL

Books

Adelman, Irving, and Rita Dworkin. *The Contemporary Novel: A Checklist of Critical Literature on the British and American Novel Since 1945*. Metuchen, NJ: Scarecrow, 1972.

Chase, Richard. *American Novel and Its Tradition*. Baltimore: Johns Hopkins, 1980.

Drescher, Horst W., and Bernd Kahrmann. *The Contemporary English Novel: An Annotated Bibliography of Secondary Sources.* New York: Intl. Pub. Service, 1973.

Holman, C. Hugh. *American Novel Through Henry James.* 2nd ed. Arlington Heights, IL: Harlan Davidson, 1979.

Nevius, Blake. *American Novel: Sinclair Lewis to the Present.* Arlington Heights, IL: Harlan Davidson, 1970.

Palmer, Helen, and Jane Dyson. *English Novel Explication: Criticisms to 1972.* Hamden, CT: Shoe String, 1973.

Watt, Ian. *British Novel: Scott through Hardy.* Arlington Heights, IL: Harlan Davidson, 1973.

Wiley, Paul L. *British Novel: Conrad to the Present.* Arlington Heights, IL: Harlan Davidson, 1973.

Woodress, James. *American Fiction 1900–1950: A Guide to Information Sources.* Detroit: Gale, 1974.

Wright, Lyle H. *American Fiction: A Contribution Towards a Bibliography.* 3 vols. San Marino, CA: Huntington Library, 1969, 1979.

Journals

Abstracts of English Studies
American Literature
American Literary Realism: 1870–1910
Critique: Studies in Modern Fiction
Essays in Literature
Explicator
Journal of Canadian Fiction
Journal of Commonwealth Fiction
Journal of Modern Literature
Modern Fiction Studies
New England Quarterly
Nineteenth Century Fiction
Novel
PMLA
Southern Literary Journal
Studies in the Novel
Studies in Twentieth Century Literature
Twentieth Century Literature
Victorian Studies
Western American Literature

POETRY

Books

Dyson, A. E., ed. *English Poetry: Select Bibliographical Guides.* New York: Oxford Univ. Press, 1971.

Frizzell-Smith, Dorothy B., and Eva L. Andrews. *Subject Index to Poetry for Children and Young People, 1957–1975.* Chicago: American Library Assoc., 1977.

Kuntz, Joseph M. *Poetry Explication: A Checklist of Interpretations since 1925 of British and American Poems Past and Present.* Rev ed. Denver: Swallow, 1962.

Smith, William J., ed. *Granger's Index to Poetry.* 6th ed. New York: Columbia Univ. Press, 1973.

Journals

American Literature
American Notes & Queries
American Poet
American Poetry & Poetics
American Poetry Review
American Quarterly
Berkeley Poetry Review
Cincinnati Poetry Review
College English
Contemporary Poetry
ELH
Early American Literature
English
English Language Notes
English Studies
Epos
Explicator
Green River Review
Journal of American Studies
Modern Poetry Studies
New England Quarterly
Parnassus: Poetry in Review
PMLA
Poetics
Poetry
Poetry Review
Poetry Society of America, Bulletin
Shakespeare Quarterly
Southern Poetry Review
Studies in Romanticism
Victorian Poetry
Victorian Studies

SHORT STORY

Books

Cook, Dorothy E., and Isabel S. Monro. *Short Story Index.* New York: H. W. Wilson, 1953. Supplements.

Short Story Index: Collections Indexed 1900–1978. New York: H. W. Wilson, 1979.

Walker, Warren S., ed. *Twentieth-Century Short Story Explication.* 3rd ed. Hamden, CT: Shoe String, 1977.

Journals
American Literature
American Notes & Queries
College English
Contemporary Literature
Critique: Studies in Modern Fiction
Journal of American Studies
Journal of Canadian Fiction
Explicator
Modern Fiction Studies
Nineteenth Century Fiction
Southern Literary Journal
Studies in American Humor
Studies in Short Fiction
Studies in Twentieth Century Literature
Western American Literature

WORLD LITERATURE

Books
Adelman, Irving, and Rita Dworkin. *The Contemporary Novel: A Checklist of Critical Literature on the British and American Novel Since 1945*. Metuchen, NJ: Scarecrow, 1972.

Bede, Jean-Albert, and William Edgerton, eds. *Columbia Dictionary of Modern European Literature*. 2nd ed. New York: Columbia Univ. Press, 1980.

Harvey, Paul, ed. *The Oxford Companion to Classical Literature*. 2nd ed. New York: Oxford Univ. Press, 1937.

Harvey, Paul, and J. E. Heseltine, eds. *The Oxford Companion to French Literature*. Oxford: Clarendon Press, 1959.

Horstein, Lillian H., ed. *Readers Companion to World Literature*. Rev. ed. New York: New American Library, 1973.

Morgan, Bayard Q. *A Critical Bibliography of German Literature in English Translation, 1481–1927*. 2nd ed. Metuchen, NJ: Scarecrow, 1965.

Shipley, Joseph T., ed. *Directory of World Literary Terms*. Boston: Writer, n.d.

Journals
Classical Journal
French Review
French Studies
Germanic Review
Journal of English and Germanic Philology
Journal of Medieval and Renaissance Studies
Journal of Spanish Studies
Medievalia et Humanistica
Slavonic and East European Review
Studies in Twentieth Century Literature
World Literature Today

Yale French Studies
Yale Italian Studies

FOREIGN LANGUAGES

GENERAL

Books
Collison, Robert L. *Dictionaries of English and Foreign Languages*. 2nd ed. New York: Hafner, 1971.

MLA International Bibliography. New York: Modern Language Assoc., 1921–date.

Von Ostermann, Georg F. *Manual of Foreign Languages*. 4th ed. New York: Boardman, 1952.

Year's Work in Modern Language Studies. New York: International Publications Service, annually.

Journals
Books Abroad
Modern Language Quarterly
Modern Language Review
Modern Philology
Philological Quarterly
PMLA
Romance Notes
Romance Philology
Studies in Philology
Symposium

FRENCH

Books
Alden, Douglas W., ed. *French Twenty Bibliography: Critical and Biographical References for the Study of French Literature Since 1885*. New York: French Institute, 1981.

Alden, Douglas W., and Richard A. Brooks, eds. *Critical Bibliography of French Literature: Twentieth Century*. Vol. 6 in 3 parts. Syracuse, NY: Syracuse Univ. Press, 1979.

Bassan, Fernande, et al. *An Annotated Bibliography of French Language and Literature*. New York: Garland, 1975.

Bloch, Oscar, and W. Wartburg. *Dictionnaire étymologique de la langue française*. New York: French and European Publ., 1975.

Bonnefoy, Claude, et al. *Dictionnaire de littérature française contemporaine*. New York: French and English Publ., 1977.

Brooks, Richard A., ed. *Critical Bibliography of French Literature: The Eighteenth Century Supplement*. Vol. 4a. Syracuse, NY: Syracuse Univ. Press, 1968.

Cassell's French Dictionary. Ed. Denis Girard, et al. New York: Macmillan, 1977.

Cioranescu, Alexandre. *Bibliographie de la littérature française du dix-huitième siècle*. 3 vols. New York: Adler's, n.d.

Dubois, Marguerite, and Marie Dubois. *Dictionnaire de locutions français-anglais: Dictionary of Idioms French-English*. New ed. Paris: Larousse, 1973.

Dulong, Gaston. *Bibliographie linguistique du Canada français*. Portland, OR: International Scholarly Book Service, 1966.

Golden, H. H., and S. O. Simches. *Modern French Literature and Language*. Millwood, NY: Kraus Reprint, 1953.

Grand Larousse encyclopédique. 24 vols. Elmsford, NY: Maxwell Science Intl., 1973. Supplements.

Griffin, Lloyd, et al. *Modern French Literature and Language: A Bibliography of Homage Studies*. Ann Arbor, MI: University Microfilms, 1976.

Harvard University Library. *French Literature: Classification Schedule, Author and Title Listing, Chronological Listing*. 2 vols. Cambridge, MA: Harvard Univ. Press, 1973.

Harvey, Paul, and Janet E. Heseltine, eds. *Oxford Companion to French Literature*. Oxford: Clarendon Press, 1959.

Johnson, H. H. *A Short Introduction to the Study of French Literature*. Folcroft, PA: Folcroft, 1973.

Johnson, Nancy A. *Current Topics in Language: Introductory Readings*. Englewood Cliffs, NJ: Winthrop, 1976.

Kempton, Richard. *French Literature: An Annotated Guide to Selected Bibliographies*. New York: Modern Language Assoc., 1981.

Kettridge, Julius O. *Dictionary of Technical Terms*. (Fr.-Eng., Eng.-Fr.) 2 vols. New York: French and European Publ., n.d.

Lanson and Tuffrau. *Manual illustré d'histoire de la littérature française*. New York: French and European Publ., n.d.

Larousse classique. Paris: Larousse, 1977.

Littre, Emile. *Dictionnaire de la langue française*. New York: French and English Publ., n.d.

Mahaffey, Denis, ed. *Concise Bibliography of French Literature*. New York: Bowker, 1976.

Mankin, Paul, and Alex Szogyi. *Anthologie d'humor français*. Glenview, IL: Scott, Foresman, 1971.

Mansion, J. E., ed. *Harrap's Standard French and English Dictionary*. New York: Scribner's, 1972.

Ploetz, Richard A. *Manual of French Literature*. Reprint of 1878 ed. Philadelphia, PA: Richard West, 1973.

Popkin, Debra, and Michael Popkin, ed. *Modern French Literature*. 2 vols. New York: Ungar, 1977.

Thieme, Hugo R. *Bibliographie de la littérature française de 1800 a 1930*. 1933; rpt. New York: International Publications Service, 1971.

Wells, Benjamin. *Modern French Literature*. Folcroft, PA: Folcroft, 1973.

Journals

L'Express
French Notes
French Notes and Queries
French Review
French Studies
Hommes et Mondes
Information Littéraire
Mercure de France
Le Monde (Newspaper)
Le Moyen Age
Neophilologus
Nouvelle Revue Française
Les Nouvelles Littéraires (Newspaper)
Réalités
Revue des Deux Mondes
Revue d'Esthétique
Revue d'Histoire Littéraire
Revue de Littérature Comparée
Revue de Paris
Revue des Sciences Humaines
Romania
Studi Francesi
Les Temps Modernes
Yale French Studies

GERMAN

Books

Betterige, Harold T., ed. *Cassell's German Dictionary: German-English, English-German*. Rev. ed. New York: Macmillan, 1978.

Binger, Norman. *Bibliography of German Plays on Microcards*. Hamden, CT: Shoe String, 1970.

Burns, Friedrich, ed. *Lese der Deutschen Lyrik: Von Klopstock bis Rilke*. New York: Irvington, 1961.

Dornseiff, Franz. *Der Deutsche Wortschatz nach Sachruppen*. 7th ed. New York: Degruyter, 1970.

Duden, R., ed. *Der Grosse Duden.* 10 vols. New York: Adler's, 1971.

Erdelyi, Gabor, and Agnes F. Peterson. *German Periodical Publications.* Stanford, CA: Hoover Institution Press, 1967.

Faulhaver, Uwe K., and Penrith B. Goff. *A Reference Guide to German Literature.* New York: Garland, 1979.

Geils, Peter, and Willi Gorzny, eds. *Bibliography of German Language Publications Seventeen Hundred to Nineteen Hundred Ten.* 160 vols. Ridgewood, NJ: K. G. Saur, 1979–1982.

German Books in Print, Nineteen Eighty to Eighty One: ISBN Register. Ridgewood, NJ: G. K. Saur, 1980.

Grimm, Jacob, and Wilhelm Grimm. *Deutsches Woerterbuch.* 32 vols. New York: Adler's, 1973.

Groeg, Otto J., ed. *Who's Who in Germany: A Biographical Dictionary.* 2 vols. 7th ed. New York: International Publications Service, 1978.

Hankamer, Paul. *Deutsche Literaturgeschichte.* 1930; rpt. New York: AMS, 1970.

Jones, Trevor, ed. *The Oxford Harrap Standard German-English Dictionary.* 3 vols. Oxford University Press, 1978.

Keller, Howard H. *A German Word Family Dictionary: Together With English Equivalents.* Berkeley, CA: University of California Press, 1978.

Kohlschmidt, Werner, and Werner Mohr, eds. *Reallexikon der deutschen Literaturgeschichte.* 2nd ed., 3 vols. New York: DeGruyter, 1958–1977.

Kopp, W. LaMarr. *German Literature in the United States, 1945–1960.* Chapel Hill, NC: Univ. of North Carolina Press, 1968.

Magill, C. B. *German Literature.* New York: Oxford Univ. Press, 1974.

Morgan, Bayard Q. *Critical Bibliography of German Literature in English Translation, 1481–1927.* 1938; rpt. Metuchen, NJ: Scarecrow, 1965.

Nollen, John S. *A Chronology of Practical Bibliography of Modern German Literature.* 1903; rpt. West Newfield, ME: Longwood, 1976.

Oberschelp, Reinhard. *Bibliography of German Language Publications Nineteen Hundred Eleven to Nineteen Hundred Sixty-Five.* Ridgewood, NJ: G. K. Saur, 1976–1980.

Rose, Ernst. *A History of German Literature.* New York: New York University Press, 1960.

Smith, Murray F. *Selected Bibliography of German Literature in English Translation, 1956–1960.* Metuchen, NJ: Scarecrow, 1972.

Springer, Otto, ed. *Langescheidt's New Muret-Sanders German-English Encyclopedia Dictionary.* 2 vols. New York: Hippocrene, 1963–1974.

Vexler, Robert I. *Germany: A Chronology and Fact Book.* Dobbs Ferry, NY: Oceana, 1973.

Wahrig, G. *German-English Dictionary.* New York: State Mutual Books, 1980.

Wer Ist Wer? 20th ed. New York: International Publications Service, 1973.

Journals

German Documentation Literature
German International
German Life and Letters
German News
German Quarterly
German Tribune
Germanic Review
Germanistik
Germany
Kulturbrief
Kunst und Literatur
Kurbiskern
Literat
Ran
Scala International
Spiegel
Stein
Welt und Wort
Wiesbadener Leben

LATIN

Books

Cassell's New Compact Latin Dictionary. New York: Dell, 1981.

Cole, A. T., and D. O. Ross, eds. *Studies in Latin Language and Literature.* New York: Cambridge Univ. Press, 1972.

Dolan, Walter, intro. *The Classical World Bibliography of Roman Drama and Poetry and Ancient Fiction.* New York: Garland, n.d.

Faider, Paul. *Repertoire des index et lexiques d'auteurs latins.* 1926; rpt. New York: Burt Franklin, 1971.

Glare, P. G., ed. *Oxford Latin Dictionary.* New York: Oxford Univ. Press, 1968–1980.

Graesse, Johann G. *Orbis Latinis: Lexikon lateinischer geographischer Mamen des Mittelalters und der Neuzeit.* 3 vols. New York: International Publications Service, 1970.

Hammond, Mason. *Latin: A Historical and Linguistic Handbook.* Cambridge, MA: Harvard Univ. Press, 1976.

MacDonald, Gerald, ed. *Antonio de Nebrija: Vocabulario de romance en latin.* Philadelphia, PA: Temple Univ. Press, 1973.

Mackail, John W. *Latin Literature*. New York: Ungar, 1966.

Mantinband, James H. *Dictionary of Latin Literature*. Totowa, NJ: Littlefield, Adams & Co., 1964.

McGuire, Martin R., and Hermigild Dressler. *Introduction to Medieval Latin Studies: A Syllabus and Bibliographical Guide*. 2nd ed. Washington, D.C.: Catholic University Press, 1977.

Traupman, John C., ed. *New College Latin and English Dictionary*. New York: Bantam, 1970.

Wagenvoort, Hendrik. *Studies in Roman Literature, Culture and Religion*. Commager, Steele, eds. New York: Garland, 1978.

Journals
American Classical Review
American Journal of Philology
AREPO
Arethusa
Arion
Athenaeum
Classical Bulletin
Classical Journal
Classical Outlook
Classical Philology
Classical Quarterly
Classical Review
Classical World
Greek, Roman and Byzantine Studies
Hellenism
Modern Greek Studies Association Bulletin
Nestor
Philological Quarterly
Phoenix
Quarterly Check-List of Classical Studies
Ramus

RUSSIAN

Books
Alford, M. H., and V. L. Alford. *Russian-English Scientific and Technical Dictionary*. 2 vols. Elmsford, NY: Pergamon, 1970.

Gilbert, Martin. *Russian History Atlas*. New York: Macmillan, 1972.

Harkins, William E. *Dictionary of Russian Literature*. 1956; rpt. Westport, CT: Greenwood, 1971.

Horecky, Paul L., ed. *Basic Russian Publications: A Bibliographic Guide to Western-Language Publications*. Chicago: Univ. of Chicago Press, 1965.

Horecky, Paul L. *Basic Russian Publications: A Selected and Annotated Bibliography on Russian and the Soviet Union*. Chicago: University of Chicago Press, 1962.

Institute for the Study of the U.S.S.R., et al. *Who Was Who in the U.S.S.R.* Metuchen, NJ: Scarecrow, 1972.

Junger, Harri, ed. *Literature of the Soviet Peoples: A Historical and Biographical Survey*. New York: Ungar, 1971.

Line, Maurice B., et al. *Bibliography of Russian Literature in English Translation to 1945*. 1963; rpt. Totowa, NJ: Rowman, 1972.

Maichel, Karol. *Guide to Russian Reference Books*. 5 vols. Stanford, CA: Hoover Institution Press, 1962–1967.

Mersh. *Modern Encyclopedia of Russian and Soviet Literature: Mersh*. Vol. 3. Gulf Breeze, FL: Academic International, 1979.

Muller, V. K., ed. *English-Russian Dictionary*. Rev. ed. New York: Dutton, 1973.

Smirnitsky, A. I., ed. *Russian-English Dictionary*. 3rd ed. New York: Saphrograph, n.d.

Worth, Dean S. *A Bibliography of Russian Word-Formation*. Columbus, OH: Slavica, 1977.

Zenkovsky, Serge A., and David L. Armbruster, eds. *Guide to Bibliographies of Russian Literature*. Nashville, TN: Vanderbilt University Press, 1970.

SPANISH

Books
Aquino-Bermudez, et al. *Mi diccionario ilustrado: edición bilingue*. New York: Lothrop, 1972.

Bourland, Caroline B. *The Short Story in Spain in the Seventeenth Century, with a Bibliography of Novels from 1576 to 1700*. Folcroft, PA: Folcroft, 1927.

Bryant, Shasta M. *The Spanish Ballad in English*. Lexington, KY: Univ. Press of Kentucky, 1973.

Cardenas, Anthony, et al. *Bibliography of Old Spanish Texts*. 2nd., rev. enl. ed. Madison, WI: Hispanic Seminary, 1977.

Celorio, Marta, and Annette C. Barlow. *Handbook of Spanish Idioms*. New ed. New York: Regents, 1974.

Chatham, James R., and Carmen C. McClendon. *Dissertations in Hispanic Languages and Literatures: An Index of Dissertations Completed in the United States and Canada*. Lexington, KY: Univ. Press of Kentucky, 1981.

Hauser, Gaylord, and Ragnar Berg. *Dictionary of Foods*. Greenwich, CT: Lust, Benedict, 1971.

Johnson, Arnold, and Martin Peterson. *Encyclopedia of Food Technology*. Westport, CT: AVI, 1974.

Joseph, Marjory L., and William D. Joseph. *Research Fundamentals in Home Economics*. Redondo Beach, CA: Plycon Press, 1979.

Lowenstein, Eleanor. *Bibliography of American Cookery Books, 1742–1860*. Worcester, MA: American Antiquarian, 1972.

Masnick, George, and Mary Jo Bane. *The Nation's Families: 1960–1990*. Boston: Auburn House, 1980.

Montagne, Prosper. *The New Larousse Gastronomique Encyclopedia of Food, Wine, and Cooking*. Ed. by Charlotte Turgeon. New York: Crown, 1977.

Rudolph, G.A. *The Kansas State University Receipt Book and Household Manual*. Manhattan, KS: Kansas State University, 1968.

Simon, Andre L. *Bibliotheca Gastronomica: A Catalog of Books and Documents on Gastronomy*. 1953; rpt. New Castle, DE: Oak Knoll, 1978.

Simon, Andre L., and Robin Howe. *Dictionary of Gastronomy*. 2nd ed. New York: Overlook, 1979.

Vicaire, Georges. *Bibliographie Gastronomique*. 1890; rpt. New Castle, DE: Oak Knoll, 1978.

Ward, Artemus. *Encyclopedia of Food*. 1923; rpt. Ann Arbor, MI: Finch Press, 1974.

Journals

Ahea Newsletter
Better Homes and Gardens
Canadian Home Economics Journal
Changing Times
Consumer Reports
Cookbook Digest
Cuisine et vins de France
Domestic Science
Executive Housekeeper
Family Economics Review
Food and Cookery Review
Good Housekeeping
Home Economics Research Abstracts
Home Economics Research Journal
Homemaker
Journal of Food Science
Journal of Home Economics
Journal of Marriage and the Family
Journal of Nutrition
McCall's
Mademoiselle
Tips and Topics in Home Economics

Vogue
What's New in Home Economics
Woman's Day

MUSIC

Books

Apel, Willi. *Harvard Dictionary of Music*. 2nd rev. ed. Cambridge, MA: Harvard Univ. Press, 1969.

Bahle, Bruce, ed. *The International Cyclopedia of Music and Musicians*. 10th ed. New York: Dodd, Mead, 1975.

Baker, Theodore. *Baker's Biographical Dictionary of Musicians*. 6th ed. Ed. by Nicolas Slonimsky. New York: Schirmer, 1978.

Bibliographic Guide to Music: 1976. Boston: G. K. Hall, 1976

Blom, Eric. *General Index to Modern Musical Literature in the English Language Including Periodicals for the Years 1915–1926*. 1927; rpt. New York: Da Capo, 1970.

Boston Public Library. *Dictionary Catalog of the Music Collection, Boston Public Library*. 20 vols. Boston: G. K. Hall, 1972. 1st Supplement. 4 vols., 1977.

Chaplin, John. *Cyclopedia of Music and Musicians*. 3 vols. New York: Gordon, 1974.

Charles, Sydney R. *Handbook of Music and Music Literature*. New York: Free Press, 1972.

Clough, Francis F., and G. J. Cuming. *The World's Encyclopedia of Recorded Music*. 3 vols. Rpt. of 1966 ed. Westport, CT: Greenwood, n.d.

Curcio, Louise. *Musicians Handbook*. New York: J. Patelson Music, 1968.

Davies, J. H. *Musicia: Sources of Intermotion in Music*. 2nd ed. Elmsford, NY: Pergamon, 1969.

Duckles, Vincent. *Music Reference and Research Materials*. 2nd ed. New York: Free Press, 1974.

Feather, Leonard. *Encyclopedia of Jazz in the Seventies*. New York: Horizon, 1976.

————. *Encyclopedia of Jazz in the Sixties*. New York: Horizon, 1967.

Fuller-Maitland, John A. *A Consort of Music*. New York: Arno, 1973.

Grant, W. Parks, *Handbook of Music Terms*. Metuchen, NJ: Scarecrow, 1967.

Lowenberg, Alfred. *Annals of Opera, 1597–1940*. 2 vols. 3rd. rev. ed. Totowa, NJ: Rowman and Littlefield, 1978.

Mixter, K. E. *General Bibliography for Music Research*. 2nd ed. Detroit: Information Coordinators, 1975.

Oxford History of Music. Ed. by William H. Hodow, 8 vols. 1929–38; rpt. Totowa, NJ: Cooper Square, 1973.

Research Libraries of the New York Public Library and the Library of Congress. *Bibliographic Guide to Music: 1980.* Boston, MA: G. K. Hall, 1981.

Roxon, Lillian. *Rock Encyclopedia.* New York: Grosset and Dunlap, 1971.

Sainsbury, John S. *Dictionary of Musicians from the Earliest Time.* 1825; rpt. Saint Clair Shores, MI: Scholarly, 1976.

Scholes, Percy A. *Oxford Companion to Music.* 10th ed. John O. Ward, ed. New York: Oxford University Press, 1970.

Shapiro, Nat. *Popular Music: An Annotated Index of American Popular Songs.* 6 vols. New York: Adrian, 1973.

Stambler, Irwin. *Encyclopedia of Pop, Rock, and Soul.* New York: St. Martin's, 1977.

Strunk, Oliver, ed. *Source Readings in Music History.* 5 vols. New York: Norton, 1950.

Thompson, Kenneth. *St. Martin's Dictionary of Twentieth-Century Composers, 1910–1971.* New York: St. Martin's, 1973.

Thompson, Oscar, ed. *International Cyclopedia of Music and Musicians.* 10th rev. ed. New York: Dodd, Mead, 1975.

Vinton, John, ed. *The Dictionary of Contemporary Music.* New York: Dutton, 1974.

Westrop, J. A., and F. L. Harrison, eds. *New College Encyclopedia of Music.* New York: Norton, 1981.

Who's Who in Music and Musicians' International Directory. Saint Clair Shores, MI: Scholarly, 1935.

Young, Percy M. A. *Critical Dictionary of Composers and Their Music.* 1954; rpt. Westport, CT: Hyperion Press, 1981.

Journals
ACTA Musicologia
American Music Teacher
Brass and Percussion
British Catalogue of Music
Choral Journal
Clavier
Current Musicology
Educational Music Magazine
Journal of the American Musicological Society
Journal of Band Research
Journal of Music Theory
Journal of Music Therapy
Journal of Renaissance and Baroque Music
Journal of Research in Music Education
Modern Music
Music and Letters
Music Index

Music Journal
Music Journal Biographical Cards
Music Review
Musica Disciplina
Musical America
Musical Quarterly
Musical Record
Musical Times
Musician
Notes
Opera Journal
Piano Quarterly
Sonorum Speculum

PHILOSOPHY

Books

Angeles, Peter A. *Dictionary of Philosophy.* New York: Harper and Row, 1981.

Baldwin, James M., et al. *Dictionary of Philosophy and Psychology.* New York: Gordon, 1977.

Borchardt, D. H. *How to Find Out in Philosophy and Psychology.* Elmsford, NY: Pergamon, 1968.

Brugger, Walter. *Philosophical Dictionary.* Kenneth Baker, trans. and ed. Spokane, WA: Gonzaga Univ. Press, 1972.

Copleston, Frederick. *A History of Philosophy.* 9 vols. Garden City, NY: Doubleday, 1977.

Davidson, R. F. *Philosophies Men Live By.* 2nd ed. New York: Holt, Rinehart and Winston, 1974.

DeGeorge, Richard T. *The Philosopher's Guide.* Lawrence, KS: Regents, 1980.

Donlon, Walter, intro. *The Classical World Bibliography of Philosophy, Religion, and Rhetoric.* New York: Garland, n.d.

Edwards, Paul, ed. *The Encyclopedia of Philosophy.* 4 vols. New York: Free Press, 1973.

Flew, Antony. *Dictionary of Philosophy.* New York: St. Martin's, 1980.

Guerry, Herbert, ed. *A Bibliography of Philosophical Bibliographies.* Westport, CT: Greenwood, 1977.

Harvard University Library. *Philosophy and Psychology: Classification Schedule, Author and Title Listing.* 2 vols. Cambridge, MA: Harvard University Press, 1973.

Jordak, Francis E. *A Bibliographical Survey for a Foundation in Philosophy.* Lanham, MD: University of America Press, 1978.

Koren, H. J. *Research in Philosophy.* Atlantic Highlands, NJ: Duquesne, 1966.

Lacey, A. R. *A Dictionary of Philosophy.* Boston, MA: Routledge and Yegar, 1977.

Lineback, Richard H., ed. *The Philosopher's Index: A Retrospective Index to Non-U.S. English Language Publications from 1940.* 3 vols. Bowling Green, OH: Philosophy Documentation Center, 1980.

Matczak, Sebastian A. *Philosophy: A Select, Classified Bibliography of Ethics, Economics, Law, Politics, Sociology.* Jamaica, NY: Learned Publishers, 1970.

————. *Research and Composition in Philosophy.* Atlantic Highlands, NJ: Humanities, 1971.

Nauman, St. Elmo, Jr. *Dictionary of American Philosophy.* Totowa, NJ: Littlefield, 1979.

Passmore, John. *A Hundred Years of Philosophy.* Baltimore: Penguin, 1978.

Peterfreund, Sheldon P., and Theodore C. Denise. *Contemporary Philosophy and Its Origins.* New York: Van Nos Reinhold, 1967.

Philosophers Index: 1979 Cumulative Edition. Bowling Green, OH: Philosophy Documentation Center, 1980.

Runes, Dagobert D., ed. *Dictionary of Philosophy.* rev., enl. ed. New York: Philosophical Library, 1981.

————. *Who's Who in Philosophy.* Vol. 1. 1942; rpt. Westport, CT: Greenwood, n.d.

Steenbergen, G. J., and Johan Groofen. *New Encyclopedia of Philosophy.* Ed. and trans. by Edmond Van Den Bossche. New York: Philosophical Library, 1972.

Journals
American Philosophical Quarterly
American Philosophical Society
Bibliography of Philosophy
Diogenes
Ethics
Humanist
International Journal of Ethics
Journal of Existentialism
Journal of the History of Ideas
Journal of Philosophy
Journal of Philosophy, Psychology, and Scientific Method
Journal of Symbolic Logic
Journal of the History of Philosophy
Journal of Thought
Man and World
Mind
Pacific Philosophy Forum
Personalist
Philosopher's Index
Philosophia Mathematica
Philosophical Quarterly
Philosophical Review
Philosophical Studies
Philosophy
Philosophy and Phenomenological Research

Philosophy and Rhetoric
Philosophy of Science
Philosophy of Social Studies
Philosophy Today
Review of Metaphysics
Self-Realization Magazine
Southern Journal of Philosophy
Southwestern Journal of Philosophy
Soviet Studies in Philosophy
Studies in Soviet Thought

PSYCHOLOGY

Books
Annual Reviews of Psychology. Palo Alto, CA: Annual Reviews, 1950–date.

Bachrach, Arthur J. *Psychological Research: An Introduction.* 4th ed. New York: Random House, 1981.

Badia, Pietro, et al., eds. *Research Problems in Psychology.* Reading, MA: Addison-Wesley, 1970.

Beigel, Hugo G. *Dictionary of Psychology and Related Fields.* New York: Ungar, 1974.

Borchardt, D. H. *How to Find Out in Philosophy and Psychology.* Elmsford, NY: Pergamon, 1968.

Chaplin, J. P. *Dictionary of Psychology.* New York: Dell, 1975.

Coelho, George V., et al., ed. *Coping and Adaptation: A Behavioral Science Bibliography.* New York: Basic Books, 1974.

Columbia University. *Cumulated Subject Index to Psychological Abstracts, 1927–1960.* 2 vols. Boston: G. K. Hall, 1966 Supplements.

Coon, Dennis L. *Introduction to Psychology Exploration and Application.* 2nd ed. St. Paul, MN: West, 1980.

Crabtree, J. Michael, and Kenneth E. Mayer, eds. *Bibliography of Aggressive Behavior: A Reader's Guide to the Research Literature.* New York: A. R. Liss, 1977.

Davidoff, Linda L. *Introduction to Psychology.* New York: McGraw-Hill, 1980.

Elliott, C. K. *Guide to the Documentation of Psychology.* Hamden, CT: Shoe String, 1971.

Eysenck, H. J., et al. *Encyclopedia of Psychology.* 2nd ed. 3 vols. New York: Seaburg, 1979.

Freeman, Ruth St. J., and H. A. Freeman. *Counseling: A Bibliography with Annotations.* New York: Scarecrow Press, 1964.

Goldenson, Robert M. *Encyclopedia of Human Behavior.* 2 vols. Garden City, NY: Doubleday, 1974.

Grinstein, Alexander. *The Index of Psychoanalytic Writings*. 14 vols. New York: International Universities, 1956–60; 1963–66; 1971.

Harriman, Philip L. *Handbook of Psychological Terms*. Totowa, NJ: Littlefield, Adams, 1977.

Harvard University Psychologists. *Harvard List of Books in Psychology*. 4th ed. Cambridge, MA: Harvard University Press, 1971.

Kiell, Norman, ed. *Psychiatry and Psychology in the Visual Arts and Aesthetics: A Bibliography*. Madison, WI: University of Wisconsin Press, 1965.

Louttit, Chauncey M. *Bibliography of Bibliographies on Psychology, 1900–1927*. 1928; rpt. New York: Burt Franklin, 1970.

Louttit, Chauncey M. *Handbook of Psychological Literature*. New York: Gordon, 1974.

Psychological Abstracts. Lancaster, PA: American Psychological Assn., 1927–date.

Psychological Index, 1894–1935. 42 vols. Princeton, NJ: Psychological Review Co., 1895–1936. (Superseded by *Psychological Abstracts*.)

Research Libraries of the New York Public Library and the Library of Congress. *Bibliographic Guide to Psychology: Nineteen Seventy-nine*. Boston: G. K. Hall, 1982.

Statt, David. *Dictionary of Psychology*. New York: Harper and Row, 1982.

Swanson, Gerald, ed. *Psychology Book Guide; 1974*. Boston: G. K. Hall, 1974.

Watson, Robert I. *The Great Psychologists*. New York: Harper and Row, 1978.

Wilkening, Howard E. *The Psychology Almanac: A Handbook for Students*. Monterey, CA: Brooks-Cole, 1973.

Journals

Acta Psychologica
American Journal of Clinical Hypnosis
American Journal of Community Psychology
American Journal of Mental Deficiency
American Journal of Psychiatry
American Journal of Psychoanalysis
American Journal of Psychology
American Journal of Psychotherapy
American Psychoanalytic Association Journal
American Psychologist
Annual Review of Psychology
Behavior Modification
Behavior Research Methods and Instrumentation
Behavioral Science
Biological Psychiatry
Biological Psychology
Child Development Abstracts and Bibliography
Cognitive Psychology
Community Mental Health Journal
Comprehensive Psychiatry
Contemporary Psychoanalysis
Contemporary Psychology
Educational and Psychological Measurement
Hospital and Community Psychiatry
Human Behavior
Human Development
Human Relations
Individual Psychologist
International Journal of Mental Health
International Journal of Psychology
International Journal of Social Psychiatry
Journal of Abnormal and Social Psychology
Journal of Applied Behavior Analysis
Journal of Applied Behavioral Science
Journal of Applied Psychology
Journal of Clinical Child Psychology
Journal of Clinical Psychology
Journal of Educational Psychology
Journal of Experimental Child Psychology
Journal of Experimental Psychology
Journal of Experimental Social Psychology
Journal of General Psychology
Journal of Health and Social Behavior
Journal of Humanistic Psychology
Journal of Individual Psychology
Journal of Personality and Social Psychology
Journal of Psychology
Journal of Social Psychology
Journal of the Experimental Analysis of Behavior
Journal of Verbal Learning and Verbal Behavior
Memory and Cognition
Menninger Clinic Bulletin
Mental Retardation
New Behavior
New Psychiatry
Perception and Psychophysics
Perceptual and Motor Skills
Personnel Psychology
Perspectives on Psychiatric Care
Psychiatry
Psychological Bulletin
Psychological Monographs
Psychological Record
Psychological Reports
Psychological Review
Psychology
Psychology Today
School Psychology Digest
State and Mind

RELIGION

Books

Adams, Charles J., ed. *A Reader's Guide to the Great Religions*. 2nd ed. Riverside, NJ: Free Press, 1977.

Attwater, Donald, ed. *A Catholic Dictionary*. 3rd ed. New York: Macmillan, 1961.

Bach, Marcus. *Major Religions of the World: Their Origins, Basic Beliefs, and Development*. New York: Abingdon, 1977.

Beckh, Hermann. *From Buddha to Christ*. Spring Valley, NY: St. George Book Service, 1978.

Broderick, Robert. *Catholic Encyclopedia*. Appleton, WI: Nelson, 1981.

Buttrick, George A., et al. *The Interpreter's Bible*. 12 vols. New York: Abingdon, 1951–57.

Buttrick, George A., and Keith R. Crim. *The Interpreter's Dictionary of the Bible*. 5 vols. New York: Abingdon, 1976.

Capps, Donald, et al., eds. *Philosophy of Religion: A Guide to Information Sources*. Detroit: Gale, 1976.

The Catholic Periodical and Literature Index. Ed. Catherine M. Pilley. 18 vols. New York: Catholic Library Assoc., 1934–date.

Cross, F. L., and Elizabeth A. Livingstone. *The Oxford Dictionary of the Christian Church*. New York: Oxford University Press, 1974.

Ellison, John W., ed. *Nelson's Complete Concordance to the Revised Standard Version of the Bible*. New York: Nelson, 1978.

Ferm, Vergilius. *An Encyclopedia of Religion*. 1945; rpt. Westport, CT: Greenwood, 1976.

Frazer, James George. *The New Golden Bough*. Ed. by Theodore H. Gastner. rev. ed. New York: New American Library, 1975.

Gibb, H. A., and J. H. Kramers, eds. *Shorter Encyclopedia of Islam*. Ithaca, NY: Cornell University Press, 1957.

Hawes, G., and S. Knight. *Atlas of Man and Religion*. Elmsford, NY: British Book Center, 1976.

Hick, John, ed. *Philosophy of Religion*. 2nd ed. Englewood Cliffs, NJ: Prentice-Hall, 1973.

Hutchison, John A. *Paths of Faith*. 3rd ed. New York: McGraw-Hill, n.d.

Jacquet, Constant, H., Jr., ed. *Yearbook of American and Canadian Churches*. New York: Abingdon, 1980.

Joy, Charles R., ed. *Harper's Topical Concordance*. Rev. ed. New York: Harper and Row, 1976.

Kennedy, James. *Library Research Guide to Religion and Theology: Illustrated Search Strategy and Sources*. Ann Arbor, MI: Pierian, 1973.

Kuenen, Abraham. *National Religions and Universal Religions*. New York: AMS, 1978.

Landman, Isaac. *Universal Jewish Encyclopedia and Reader's Guide*. 11 vols. New York: Ktav, 1944.

Lives of the Saints. Ed. Thurston Attwater. 4 vols. Westminister, MD: Christian Classics, 1976.

Marx, Herbert L., ed. *Religions in America*. New York: Wilson, 1977.

May, Herbert G., and G. H. S. Hunt, eds. *Oxford Bible Atlas*. 2nd ed. New York: Oxford University Press, 1974.

Mazar, Benjamin, and Michael Avi-Yonah, eds. *Illustrated World of the Bible Library*. 5 vols. Hartford, CT: Davey, Daniel, & Co., 1961.

McKenzie, John L. *Dictionary of the Bible*. New York: Macmillan, 1965.

Mead, Frank Spencer. *Handbook of Denominations in the United States*. 7th ed. New York: Abingdon, 1980.

Melton, J. Gordon. *Encyclopedia of American Religions*. 2 vols. Wilmington, NC: McGrath, 1978.

Mensching, Gustav. *Structure and Pattern of Religion*. Mystic, CT: Verry, 1976.

Mitros, Joseph F. *Religions: A Select, Classified Bibliography*. Intro by Sebastian A. Matczak. Jamaica, NY: Learned Publications, 1973.

Morris, Raymond P. *A Theological Book List*. Cambridge, MA: Greeno, Hadden, 1971.

Novak, Michael. *Ascent of the Mountain Flight of the Dove: An Invitation to Religious Studies*. New York: Harper & Row, 1978.

Parrinder, Geoffrey. *A Dictionary of Non-Christian Religions*. Philadelphia: Westminster, 1973.

Parrinder, Geoffrey. *Introduction to Asian Religions*. New York: Oxford University Press, 1976.

Reese, William. *Dictionary of Philosophy and Religion, Eastern and Western*. Atlanta, GA: Humanics, 1981.

Regazzi, John J., and Theodore C. Hines. *A Guide to Indexed Periodicals in Religion*. Metucher, NJ: Scarecrow, 1975.

Religious Books and Serials in Print, 1980–81. New York: Bowker, 1980.

Rice, Edward. *Ten Religions of the East*. New York: Scholastic Book Service, 1978.

Smith, Huston, et al. *Great Religions of the World*. Story of Man Library. Washington, DC: National Geographic, 1978.

Strong, James, ed. *Strong's Exhaustive Concordance of the Bible*. Nashville: Abingdon, 1977.

Tylor, Edward. *Religion in Primitive Culture*. Gloucester, MA: Peter Smith, 1972.

Waarden, Jacques. *Classical Approaches to the Study of Religion: Aims, Methods, and Theories of Research; Pt. 2, Bibliography*. Hawthorne, NY: Mouton, 1974.

Wach, Joachim. *Types of Religious Experience*. Chicago: Univ. of Chicago Press, 1972.

Wiersbe, Warren W. *A Basic Library for Bible Students*. Grand Rapids, MI: Baker Book House, 1981.

Wright, George E., and Floyd V. Filson. *The Westminster Historical Atlas to the Bible*. Rev. ed. Philadelphia: Westminster, 1956.

Journals
America
American Academy of Religion Journal
American Judaism
Anglican Theological Review
Biblical Archaeologist
Biblical Research
Catholic Digest
Christian Century
Christian Herald
Christian Scholar
Christianity and Crisis
Christianity Today
Church History
Commentary
Commonweal
Dialog
Ecumenical Review
Ecumenist
Encounter
Expository Times
Foundations
Harvard Theological Review
Hibbert Journal
History of Religions
International Journal of Religious Education
International Review of Missions
Interpretation
Journal for the Scientific Study of Religion
Journal of Biblical Literature
Journal of Religion
Journal of Religious Thought
Motive
New Review of Books and Religion
Religion in Life
Religious and Theological Abstracts

Religious Education
Religious Studies
Religious Studies Review
Review of Religious Research
Risk
Studies in Religion
Theological Education
Theology Today
United Church Observer

SOCIAL SCIENCES

GENERAL

Books
Belson, W. A., and B. A. Thompson. *Bibliography on Methods of Social and Business Research*. New York: Halsted, 1973.

Clarke, Jack A., ed. *Research Materials in the Social Sciences*. 2nd ed. Madison: University of Wisconsin Press, 1967.

Ducharme, Raymond A., et al. *Bibliography for Teachers of Social Studies*. New York: Teachers College Press of Columbia University, 1968.

Ferman, Gerald S., and Jack Levin. *Social Science Research: A Handbook*. Cambridge, MA: Schenkman, 1977.

Gould, Julius, and W. J. Kolb. *UNESCO Dictionary of the Social Sciences*. 2nd ed. New York: Free Press, 1970.

Hoselitz, Bert F., ed. *A Reader's Guide to the Social Sciences*. Rev. ed. New York: Free Press, 1972.

International Index. New York: H. W. Wilson, 1907–65.

London Bibliography of the Social Sciences. London: London School of Economics, 1931–date.

Rothschild, Max, ed. *Jewish Social Studies Cumulative Index*. New York: Ktav, 1968.

Rzepecki, Arnold. *Book Review Index to Social Science Periodicals*. Ann Arbor, MI: Pierian, 1978–date.

Sills, David L., ed. *International Encyclopedia of the Social Sciences*. 8 vols. New York: Free Press, 1977.

Simon, Julian. *Basic Research Methods in Social Science*. 2nd ed. New York: Random House, 1978.

Social Sciences and Humanities Index. 27 vols. New York: H. W. Wilson, 1965–74.

Social Sciences Index. New York: H. W. Wilson, 1974–date.

U.S. Superintendent of Documents. *Monthly Catalog of United States Government Publications*. Washington, DC: GPO, 1895–date.

White, Carl M., et al. *Sources of Information in the Social Sciences*. 2nd ed. Chicago: American Library Association, 1973.

ECONOMICS

Books

Batson, Harold E. *Select Bibliography of Modern Economic Theory* 1870–1929. Clifton, NJ: Kelley, 1930.

Belson, W. A., and B. A. Thompson. *Bibliography on Methods of Social and Business Research*. New York: Halsted, 1973.

Berenson, Conrad, and Raymond Colton. *Research and Report Writing for Business and Economics*. New York: Random House, 1970.

Bibliographic Guide to Business and Economics: 1976. Boston: G. K. Hall, 1976.

Brown, Harry M. *Business Report Writing*. New York: Van Nos Reinhold, 1980.

Business and Economics Books and Serials in Print. New York: Bowker, 1981.

Cohen, J. *Special Bibliography in Monetary Economics and Finance*. New York: Gordon, 1976.

Dorfman, Robert, and Nancy S. Dorfman. *Economics of the Environment: Selected Readings*. 2nd ed. New York: Norton, 1977.

Emory, C. William. *Business Research Methods*. Rev. ed. Homewood, IL: Irwin, 1982.

Field, Barry C., and Cleve E. Willis. *Environmental Economics: A Guide to Information Sources*. Detroit: Gale, 1979.

Geiger, H. Kent. *National Development 1776–1966: A Selective and Annotated Guide to the Most Important Articles in English*. Metuchen, NJ: Scarecrow, 1969.

Greenwood, Douglas. *The McGraw-Hill Dictionary of Modern Economics: A Handbook of Terms and Organizations*. 2nd ed. New York: McGraw-Hill, 1973.

Harvard University. *Kress Library of Business and Economics Catalogue*. 4 vols. New York: Kelley, 1940–1967.

Houston, Samuel R., et al., eds. *Methods and Techniques in Business Research*. New York: MSS Information, 1973.

Hughes, Catherine, ed. *Economic Education: A Guide to Information Sources*. Detroit: Gale, 1977.

Joint Bank-Fund Library, Washington, DC *Economics and Finance: Index to Periodical Articles, Nineteen Forty-Seven to Nineteen Seventy-One*. 2nd Supplement. Boston: G. K. Hall, 1979.

Joint Bank-Fund Library, Washington, DC *Economics, Finance, and Development: Subject Headings Used in the Main Catalog of the Joint Bank-Fund Library*. Boston: G. K. Hall, 1979.

Kooy, Marcelle, ed. *Studies in Economics and Economic History*. Durham, NC: Duke University Press, 1972.

Matlock, Larry K., and Michael D. Silber. *Who's Who in Hard Money Economics, 1980–1981*. Mill Valley, CA: Matlock-Silber, 1981.

New York Public Library and Library of Congress. *Bibliographic Guide to Business and Economics*. Boston: G. K. Hall, 1979.

Novotny, Jan M. *Library of Public Finance and Economics*. 1953; rpt. New York: Burt Franklin, 1971.

Sloan, Harold S., and Arnold J. Zurcher, eds. *Dictionary of Economics*. 5th ed. New York: Barnes & Noble, 1970.

Swanson, Gerald, ed. *Business and Economics Book Guide*. 2 vols. Boston: G. K. Hall, 1974.

United Nations. *World Economic Survey, 1979–80*. New York: International Publications Service, 1980.

Verwey, Gerlof. *Economist's Handbook: A Manual of Statistical Sources*. 1934; rpt. Detroit: Gale, 1971.

Zaremba, Joseph, ed. *Mathematical Economics and Operations Research: A Guide to Information Sources*. Detroit: Gale, 1978.

Journals
ACES Bulletin
American Economic Review
American Economist
American Journal of Agricultural Economics
American Journal of Economics and Sociology
Applied Economics
Barron's
Business Economics
Cambridge Journal of Economics
Challenge
Economic and Business Digest
Economic and Business Review
Economic and Social Review
Economic Bulletin
Economic Development and Cultural Change
Economic History Review
Economic Indicators
Economic Inquiry

Economic Journal
Economic News
Economic Notes
Economic Record
Economic Studies
Economica
European Economic Review
Explorations in Economic Research
Federal Reserve Bulletin
International Development Review
International Economic Review
Journal of Developing Areas
Journal of Econometrics
Journal of Economic Abstracts
Journal of Economic Education
Journal of Economic History
Journal of Economic Issues
Journal of Economic Literature
Journal of Economic Theory
Journal of Industrial Economics
Journal of International Economics
Journal of Political Economy
Journal of Urban Economics
Land Economics
National Institute of Economic Review
Oxford Bulletin of Economics and Statistics
Problems of Economics
Quarterly Journal of Economics
Quarterly Review of Economics and Business
Review of Economic Studies
Review of Economics and Statistics
Southern Economic Journal
Wall Street Journal

GEOGRAPHY

Books

American Geographical Society Library. *Research Catalogue of the American Geographical Society*. 15 vols. Boston: G. K. Hall, 1962.

Brewer, J. Gordon. *The Literature of Geography: A Guide to Its Organization and Use*. Hamden, CT: Shoe String, 1978.

Directory of the AAG. Washington, DC: Association of American Geographers, 1978.

Freeman, T. W., et al., eds. *Geographers: Bibliographical Studies*. Vol. 3. Lawrence, MA: Merrimack Book Service, 1980.

Goode's World Atlas. Ed. Edward B. Espenshade. 15th ed. Chicago: Rand McNally, 1977.

Harris, Chauncy D., and Jerome D. Fellman. *International List of Geographical Serials*. 3rd ed. Chicago: Univ. of Chicago, Dept. of Geography, 1980.

Hoggart, Keith. *Geography and Local Administration: A Bibliography*. Monticello, IL: Vance Bibliographies, 1980.

Kish, George. *Bibliography of International Geographical Congresses, Eighteen Seventy-One to Nineteen Seventy-Six*. Boston: G. K. Hall, 1979.

-------, ed. *A Source Book in Geography*. Cambridge, MA: Harvard University Press, 1978.

Lock, Muriel. *Geography and Cartography: A Reference Handbook*. 3rd ed. Hamden, CT: Shoe String, 1976.

Monkhouse, F. J. *A Dictionary of the Natural Environment*. Ed. John Small. Rev. ed. New York: Halsted, 1977.

The Statesman's Yearbook. New York: St. Martin's, 1961–date.

The Times Atlas of the World. Rev. ed., produced by the *Times of London*. New York: Times Books, 1980.

United Nations. *Statistical Yearbook*. New York: United Nations, 1961–date.

United Nations Statistical Office. *Demographic Yearbook*. New York: International Publications Service, 1962–date.

Van Balen, John. *Geography and Earth Science Publications*. 2 vols. Ann Arbor, MI: Pierian, 1968–1975.

Wasserman, Paul, et al., eds. *Encyclopedia of Geographic Information Sources,* 3rd ed. Detroit: Gale, 1978.

Journals
American Cartographer
Annals of the Association of American Geographers
Cartographic Journal
Cartography
Current Geographical Publications
Economic Geography
Focus
Geoforum
Geographical Analysis
Geographical Journal
Geographical Magazine
Geographical Review
Geography
Journal of Geography
Journal of Historical Geography
Journal of Regional Science
National Geographical Literature and Maps
Professional Geographer
Surveying and Mapping

HISTORY

Books
Beers, Henry Putney. *Bibliographies in American History*. New York: H. W. Wilson, 1942; rpt. New York: Octagon, 1973.

Bengetson, Hermann. *Introduction to Ancient History*. Trans. R. I. Frank and Frank D. Gilliard. Berkeley: Univ. of California Press, 1976.

Bennett, James D., and Lowell H. Harrison. *Writing History Papers*. St. Louis, MO: Forum Press, 1979.

Bradford, T. C. *Bibliographers' Manual of American History*. 5 vols. New York: Gordon, n.d.

Brewer, E. *The Historic Notebook*. New York: Gordon, n.d.

Brewster, John W., and Joseph A. McLeod. *Index to Book Reviews in Historical Periodicals 1972*. Metuchen, NJ: Scarecrow, 1976.

Britannica Book of the Year. Ed. James Ertel. Chicago: Encyclopaedia Britannica, 1938–date.

Brooks, Philip C. *Research in Archives: The Use of Unpublished Primary Sources*. Chicago: Univ. of Chicago Press, 1969.

Combined Retrospective Indexes to Journals in History, 1838–1974. 11 vols. Arlington, VA: Carrollton, 1977.

Cooper, William R. *Archaic Dictionary*. 1876; rpt. Detroit: Gale, 1969.

Facts on File Master Indexes. New York: Facts on File, 1946–date.

Facts on File Yearbook. New York: Facts on File, 1941–date.

Higham, John. *Writing American History: Essays and Modern Scholarship*. Bloomington, IN: Indiana Univ. Press, 1970.

Higham, Robin. *Official Histories: Essays and Bibliographies from Around the World*. Manhattan, KS: Kansas State Univ., 1970.

International Bibliography of Historical Sciences. New York: H. W. Wilson, 1930–date.

Langer, William Leonard, comp. and ed. *An Encyclopedia of World History: Ancient, Medieval, and Modern*. 5th ed. Boston: Houghton Mifflin, 1972.

Laqueur, W., and G. L. Mosse. *The New History: Trends in Historical Research and Writing Since World War Two*. Santa Fe, NM: Gannon, 1970.

Martin, Michael, and Leonard Gelber. *Dictionary of American History*. Rev. ed. Totowa, NJ: Littlefield, 1978.

McCoy, F. N. *Researching and Writing in History: A Practical Handbook for Students*. Berkeley, CA: Univ. of California Press, 1974.

McDermott, John F., ed. *Research Opportunities in American Cultural History*. 1961; rpt. Westport, CT: Greenwood, 1977.

New York Public Library. *Dictionary Catalog of the History of the Americas Collection*. 28 vols. Boston: G. K. Hall, 1961.

Poulton, Helen J., and Marguerite S. Howland. *The Historian's Handbook*. Norman: Univ. of Oklahoma Press, 1977.

Radice, Betty. *Who's Who in the Ancient World*. Baltimore: Penguin, 1973.

Schlesinger, Arthur M., and Dixon R. Fox, eds. *A History of American Life*. 12 vols. New York: Macmillan, 1927–55.

Stoffle, Carla, and Simon Karter. *Materials and Methods for History Research*. New York: Neal-Schuman, 1979.

Vincent, John M. *Historical Research: An Outline of Theory and Practice*. 1911; rpt. New York: Burt Franklin, 1974.

Williamson, Derek. *Historical Bibliography*. Hamden, CT: Shoe String, 1967.

Winso, Justin, ed. *Narrative and Critical History of America*. 8 vols. 1889; rpt. New York: AMS, 1978.

Journals

American Heritage
American Historical Review
American History Illustrated
American Neptune
American West
Americana
Capitol Studies
Civil War History
Civil War Times Illustrated
Comparative Studies in Society and History
Diplomatic History
Economic History Review
English Historical Review
Historian
Historical Journal
History
History and Theory
History Today
Journal of American History
Journal of Contemporary History
Journal of Economic History
Journal of Medieval History
Journal of Modern History
Journal of Social History
Journal of Southern History
Journal of the History of Ideas
Journal of the West
Journal of Urban History
Local Historian
Man Kind
New Statesman
North American Review
Pacific Historical Review
Past and Present
Prologue
Railroad History
Real West
Renaissance News
Reviews in American History

Social History
Societas
Speculum
Western Historical Quarterly

POLITICAL SCIENCE

Books

Banks, Arthur S., ed. *Political Handbook of the World: Nineteen Eighty*. 6th ed. New York: McGraw-Hill, 1980.

Brock, Clifton. *The Literature of Political Science: A Guide for Students, Librarians, and Teachers*. New York: Bowker, 1969.

Brown, Marshall G., and Gordon Stein. *Freethought in the United States: A Descriptive Bibliography*. Westport, CT: Greenwood, 1978.

Garceau, Oliver, ed. *Political Research and Political Theory*. Cambridge, MA: Harvard University Press, 1968.

Griffith, Ernest S., ed. *Research in Political Science*. Port Washington, NY: Kennikat, 1969.

Harmon, Robert B. *Political Science: A Bibliographical Guide to the Literature*. Metuchen, NJ: Scarecrow, 1965. Supplements, 1968, 1972, 1974.

Harmon, Robert B. *Political Science Bibliographies*. 2 vols. Metuchen, NJ: Scarecrow, 1973–1976.

Holler, Frederick L. *The Information Sources of Political Science*. 3rd ed. Santa Barbara, CA: ABC-Clio, 1980.

Holt, Robert T., and John E. Turner, eds. *The Methodology of Comparative Political Research*. New York: Free Press, 1972.

International Bibliography of Political Science, 1977. Vol. 26. New York: International Publications Service, 1979.

McCulloch, John R. *Literature of Political Economy*. 1845; rpt. New York: Kelley, n.d.

McLaughlin, Andrew C., and Albert B. Hart, eds. *Cyclopedia of American Government*. 3 vols. 1914; rpt. Gloucester, MA: Peter Smith, 1949.

Roberts, G. K. *Dictionary of Political Analysis*. New York: St. Martin's, 1971.

Sperber, Hans, and Travis Trittschuh. *American Political Terms: An Historical Dictionary*. Detroit: Wayne State University Press, 1962.

The Statesman's Yearbook. New York: St. Martin's Press, 1961–date.

Vose, Clement E. *A Guide to Library Sources in Political Science: American Government*. Washington, DC: American Political Science Assoc., 1975.

Wilcox, Laird M., compiled by. *Bibliography on the American Left*. Kansas City, MO: American Research Service: 1981.

Wilcox, Laird M., compiled by. *Bibliography on the American Right*. Kansas City, MO: American Research Service, 1981.

Yearbook of the United Nations. Lake Success, NY: United Nations, 1947–date.

Journals

Administrative Science Quarterly
American Bar Association Journal
American Political Science Review
Annals of the American Academy of Political and Social Science
Atlantic Community Quarterly
Canadian Journal of Political Science
Center Magazine
China Quarterly
Columbia Law Review
Commentary
Comparative Political Studies
Comparative Politics
Comparative Studies in Society and History
Congressional Digest
Congressional Quarterly Almanac
Congressional Quarterly Weekly Report
Congressional Record
Cornell Law Review
Current History
Daedalus
Dissent
Foreign Affairs
Government and Opposition
International Affairs (Great Britain)
International Review of Administrative Sciences
International Social Science Journal
International Studies Quarterly
Journal of Applied Behavioral Science
Journal of Inter-American Studies
Journal of Inter-American Studies and World Affairs
Journal of Law and Economics
Journal of Political Economy
Journal of Politics
Journal of Public Law
Journal of Social Issues
Midwest Journal of Political Science
Orbis
Parliamentary Affairs
Political Science Quarterly
Political Science Review
Political Studies
Politics
Politics and Society
Polity
Public Administration Review

Public Interest
Public Opinion Quarterly
Review of Politics
Science & Society
State Government
State Government Administration
Studies in Soviet Thought
Urban Affairs Quarterly
Washington Monthly
Western Political Quarterly
World Affairs
World Politics
Yale Review

SOCIOLOGY

Books

Abramson, Harold J., and Nicholas Sofios. *Index to Sociology Readers, 1960–1965*. 2 vols. Metuchen, NJ: Scarecrow, 1973.

Barnes, Henry E., et al., eds. *Contemporary Social Theory*. 1940; rpt. New York: Russell, 1971.

Bart, Pauline B., and Linda Frankel. *Student Sociologist's Handbook*. 3rd ed. Glenview, IL: Scott, Foresman, 1981.

Chalfant, H. Paul. *Sociological Aspects of Poverty: A Bibliography*. Monticello, IL: Vance Bibliographies, 1980.

Fairchild, Henry Pratt, ed. *Dictionary of Sociology and Related Sciences*. Totowa, NJ: Littlefield, 1977.

Harvard University Library. *Sociology: Classification Schedule, Author and Title Listing, Chronological Listing*. 2 vols. Cambridge, MA: Harvard Univ. Press, n.d.

Johnson, Gayle, ed. *Encyclopedia of Sociology*. Guilford, CT: Dushkin, 1974.

Klovdahl, Alden S. *Social Networks: Selected References for Course Design and Research Planning*. Monticello, IL: Vance Bibliographies, 1978.

Mitchell, G. Duncan, ed. *Dictionary of Sociology*. Hawthorne, NY: Aldine Publishing, 1967.

Reuter, Edward B. *Handbook of Sociology*. 1941; rpt. Darby, PA: Darby Books, 1980.

Social Sciences and Humanities Index. New York: H. W. Wilson, 1965–74.

Social Sciences Index. New York: H. W. Wilson, 1974–date.

Sociological Abstracts. New York: Sociological Abstracts, 1952–date.

Turner, John, ed. *Encyclopedia of Social Work*. 2 vols. New York: National Association of Social Workers, 1977.

Journals

American Behavioral Scientist
American Journal of Sociology
American Sociological Review
American Sociologist
British Journal of Sociology
Civilisations
Contemporary Sociology
Current Sociology
Environment and Behavior
Family Planning Perspectives
Family Process
Human Organization
International Journal of Comparative Sociology
International Journal of Contemporary Sociology
International Journal of Family Counseling
Journal for the Theory of Social Behavior
Journal of Applied Social Psychology
Journal Current Social Issues
Journal of Educational Sociology
Journal of Ethnic Studies
Journal of Health and Social Behavior
Journal of Human Resources
Journal of Marriage and the Family
Journal of Political and Military Sociology
Journal of Social Issues
New Society
Race Today
Rural Sociology
Small Group Behavior
Social Education
Social Forces
Social Problems
Social Research
Social Science
Social Science Abstracts
Social Science Review
Society
Sociological Analysis
Sociological Inquiry
Sociological Methods and Research
Sociological Quarterly
Sociologial Review
Sociology
Sociology and Social Research
Sociometry
Theory and Society
Urban Life and Culture

WOMEN'S STUDIES
Books

Backscheider, Paula R., and Felicity A. Nussbaum. *Annotated Bibliography of Twentieth Century Critical Studies of Women and Literature, 1660–1800*. New York: Garland, 1977.

Baker, M. A., et. al. *Women Today: A Multidisciplinary Approach to Women's Studies.* Monterey, CA: Brooks/Cole, 1979.

Bibliography on Women Workers: 1861–1965. 2nd ed. Washington, DC: International Labor Office, 1974.

Ireland, Norma. *Index to Women of the World from Ancient to Modern Times. Biographies and Portraits.* Westwood, MA: Faxon, 1970.

Lerner, Gerda. *Black Women in White America.* New York: Pantheon, 1972.

Oakes, Elizabeth H., and Kathleeen E. Sheldon. *Guide to Social Science Resources in Women's Studies.* Santa Barbara, CA: ABC-Clio, 1978.

Stineman, Esther, and Catherine Loeb. *Women's Studies: A Recommended Core Bibliography.* Littleton, CO: Libraries Unlimited, 1979.

United Nations. *The Status of Women: A Selected Bibliography.*

Wheeler, Helen Rippier. *Womanhood Media: Current Resources About Women.* Metuchen, NJ: Scarecrow, 1972.

Who's Who of American Women. Chicago: A. N. Marquis, 1958–date.

Williamson, Jane, ed. *New Feminist Scholarship: A Guide to Bibliographies.* Westbury, NY: Feminist Press, 1979.

Women's Action Alliance. *Women's Action Almanac. A Complete Resource Guide.* Jane Williamson, et al., eds. New York: Morrow, 1979.

Journals

Collegiate Women's Career Magazine
Chrysalis
Feminist Studies
Frontiers
Moving Out
Ms.
Signs
Womanpower
Woman Activist
Woman's Journal
Women and Literature
Women Studies Abstracts
Women's Studies
Women's World

SPEECH AND DRAMA

Books

Auer, John J. *Introduction to Research in Speech.* 1959; rpt. Westport, CT: Greenwood, 1977.

Chicorel, Marietta, ed. and intro. *Chicorel Bibliography to the Performing Arts.* Vol. 3A. New York: American Library Publishing, 1972.

Connor, John M., and Billie M. Connor. *Ottemiller's Index to Plays in Collections.* 6th ed. Metuchen, NJ: Scarecrow, 1976.

Cooper, Lane, trans. *The Rhetoric of Aristotle.* Englewood Cliffs, NJ: Prentice-Hall, 1960.

Cumulated Dramatic Index, 1909–1949. 2 vols. Boston: G. K. Hall, 1965.

Duker, Sam. *Time-Compressed Speech.* 3 vols. Metuchen, NJ: Scarecrow, 1974.

Gassner, John, and Edward Quinn, eds. *Reader's Encyclopedia of World Drama.* New York: Crowell, 1969.

Greg, W. W. *A Bibliography of the English Printed Drama to the Restoration.* 4 vols. London: Oxford Univ. Press, n.d.

Haberman, Frederick W., and James W. Cleary, comps. *Rhetoric and Public Address: A Bibliography: 1947–1961.* Madison: Univ. of Wisconsin Press, 1964. (Continued annually in *Speech Monographs.*)

Hiler, Hilaire, and Meyer Hiler, comps. *Bibliography of Costume.* 1939; rpt. New York: Arno, 1967.

Index to Full Length Plays. 3 vols. Westwood, MA: Faxon, 1956–1965.

Keller, Dean H. *Index to Plays in Periodicals.* Rev. and expanded ed. Metuchen, NJ: Scarecrow, 1979.

Logasa, Hannah, and Winifred Ver Nooy, comps. *An Index to One-Act Plays, 1900–1924.* Westwood, MA: Faxon, 1924. Supplements, 1932–date.

McCavitt, William E. *Radio and Television: A Selected, Annotated Bibliography.* Metuchen, NJ: Scarecrow, 1978.

Mulgrave, Dorothy, et al. *Bibliography of Speech and Allied Areas, 1950–1960.* Westport, CT: Greenwood, 1972.

New York Public Library. *Catalog of the Theatre and Drama Collections.* Boston: G. K. Hall, 1967. Supplement.

Ptacek, Paul, et al., eds. *Index to Speech, Language, and Hearing: Journal Titles, 1954–78.* San Diego, CA: College Hill, n.d.

The New York Times Theatre Reviews 1920–1974. 10 vols. New York: Arno, 1974.

Smith, Bruce L., and Chitra M. Smith. *International Communication and Political Opinion.* Westport, CT: Greenwood, 1972.

Stratman, Carl J. *Britain's Theatrical Periodicals, 1720–1967: A Bibliography.* 2nd ed. New York: New York Public Library, 1972.

———. *Bibliography of English Printed Tragedy.* Carbondale: Southern Illinois Univ. Press, 1966.

————. *Bibliography of Medieval Drama*. New York: Ungar, 1972.

Summers, Montague. *A Bibliography of the Restoration Drama*. 1934; rpt. New York: Russell & Russell, 1970.

Journals

American Forensic Association Journal
Amusement Business
Audio-Visual Communication Review
Business Screen
Communication
Communication Quarterly
Comparative Drama
Creative Drama
Drama
Drama Review
Dramatics
Education Theatre Journal
Film News
Film Quarterly
Journal of Communication
Modern Drama
New York Guide and Theatre Magazine
New York Theatre Critics Review
Onstage
Performing Arts Journal
Performing Arts Review
Players Magazine
Plays and Players
Quarterly Journal of Speech
Radio and Television News
Speech Monographs
Speech Teacher
Studies in Public Communication
Television Magazine
Television Quarterly
Theater
Theatre Arts
Theatre Arts Monthly
Theatre Quarterly
Theatre Research International
Theatre Survey

Postal Abbreviations

Alabama	AL	Montana	MT
Alaska	AK	Nebraska	NB
Arizona	AZ	Nevada	NV
Arkansas	AR	New Hampshire	NH
California	CA	New Jersey	NJ
Colorado	CO	New Mexico	NM
Connecticut	CT	New York	NY
Delaware	DE	North Carolina	NC
District of Columbia	DC	North Dakota	ND
Florida	FL	Ohio	OH
Georgia	GA	Oklahoma	OK
Guam	GU	Oregon	OR
Hawaii	HI	Pennsylvania	PA
Idaho	ID	Puerto Rico	PR
Illinois	IL	Rhode Island	RI
Indiana	IN	South Carolina	SC
Iowa	IA	South Dakota	SD
Kansas	KS	Tennessee	TN
Kentucky	KY	Texas	TX
Louisiana	LA	Utah	UT
Maine	ME	Vermont	VT
Maryland	MD	Virgin Islands	VI
Massachusetts	MA	Virginia	VA
Michigan	MI	Washington	WA
Minnesota	MN	West Virginia	WV
Mississippi	MS	Wisconsin	WI
Missouri	MO	Wyoming	WY

Index

ACKNOWLEDGMENTS (cont.)

Wilson Company. Reproduced by permission of the publisher. Material from *Humanities Index,* April 1981–March 1982, p. 778. Copyright © 1981, 1982 by The H. W. Wilson Company. Reproduced by permission of the publisher. Excerpt reprinted with permission from "Franklin, Benjamin" in *Encyclopaedia Britannica,* 15th edition, © 1979 by Encyclopaedia Britannica, Inc. Material from *Bibliographic Index,* 1971, Volume 11, pp. 188–189. Copyright © 1971, 1972 by The H. W. Wilson Company. Reproduced by permission of the publisher. Excerpt reprinted from *Subject Guide to Books in Print 1974* by permission of R. R. Bowker Company (A Xerox Publishing Company). Copyright © 1974 by Xerox Corporation. Material from *Essay and General Literature Index,* 1965–1969, Volume 7, p. 498, is reproduced by permission of The H. W. Wilson Company. Material from *Biography Index,* September 1970–August 1973, Volume 9, p. 242. Copyright © 1970, 1971, 1972, 1973 by The H. W. Wilson Company. Reproduced by permission of the publisher. Excerpt from *Comprehensive Dissertation Index,* 1861–1972, Literature Volume 29, p. 509. Reprinted by permission of University Microfilms International. Excerpts from "Franklin's Style: Irony and the Comic" from *Dissertation Abstracts International,* Vol. 28, No. 1A, p. 622. Material from *Readers' Guide to Periodical Literature,* March 1955–February 1957, Volume 20, pp. 935–936, is reproduced by permission of The H. W. Wilson Company. Material from *International Index,* April 1958–March 1960, p. 378, is reproduced by permission of The H. W. Wilson Company. Entry for "Franklin, Benjamin" from *The New York Times Index* 1973, Vol. 1. © 1973 by The New York Times Company. Reprinted by permission. From "File 148: Trade and Industry Index Database, 81–83/April." Reprinted by permission of Information Access Company. From "File 75: Management Contents Database, 74–83/Mar." Copyright © 1983 by Management Contents, Inc. Reprinted by permission of Management Contents Database, 2265 Carlson Drive, Suite 5000, Northbrook, Illinois, 60062, John D. Kuranz, President. Material from *Book Review Digest,* 1970, p. 986. Copyright © 1971 by The H. W. Wilson Company. Reproduced by permission of the publisher. From "The Love Song of J. Alfred Prufrock" in *Collected Poems* 1909–1962 by T. S. Eliot. Copyright 1936 by Harcourt Brace Jovanovich, Inc., copyright © 1963, 1964 by T. S. Eliot. Reprinted by permission of Harcourt Brace Jovanovich, Inc., and Faber and Faber Ltd. Mean Number of Matches by Subjects With and Without Standards (By Trial). From Edwin A. Locke and Judith F. Bryan. Cognitive Aspects of Psychomotor Performance. *Journal of Applied Psychology,* 1966, 50, 289. Copyright 1966 by the American Psychological Association. Reprinted by permission. From Anna H. Live, "Pattern in Language." The Journal of General Education. The Pennsylvania State University Press, University Park, Pa. 18 (July 1966). 94. Chart from Carmen J. Finley, Jack M. Thompson, and Alberta Cognata, "Stability of the California Short Form Test of Mental Maturity: Grades 3, 5, and 7," *California Journal of Educational Research,* 17 (September, 1966), 165. Reprinted by permission of the *Educational Research Quarterly.* Chart from Shoki Nishida and Masaaki Imaizumi. 1966. Toxigenicity of *Clostridium histolyticum.* J. Bacteriol. *91:*481. Edward F. Zigler, "The Unmet Needs of America's Children." *Children Today,* May–June 1976. From "Child Abuse and Violence Against the Family" by Peter C. Kratcoski in *Child Welfare,* September/October 1982. Copyright © 1982 by the Child Welfare League of America, Inc. Reprinted by permission. From "Self-Injurious Behavior in Incest Victims: A Research Note" by Mary de Young in *Child Welfare,* November/December 1982. Copyright © 1982 by the Child Welfare League of America, Inc. Reprinted by permission.

NOTES

NOTES

NOTES

NOTES

NOTES

NOTES